Ministering to Muslims
Islam Undone by the Word of God

Copyright © 2018 by Abel & Solomon
Awakening Edition

All rights reserved.
This book or any portion thereof may not be reproduced or copied in any manner whatsoever without the express written permission of the publisher except for the use of brief quotations, appearing with an acknowledgement of their source and authorship, as allowed by law

Permission is given to freely copy and distribute the TICCET evangelism tool for the purposes of Christian ministry

Paperback ISBN: 978-0-9557140-2-3

List of Contents	2
Preface	4
Introduction	6
Part One; What is Islam? What is Sharia?	10
A Brief History	10
The Five Pillars	12
Sharia Law	14
Human Rights vs Sharia	20
Politics	25
Economics	27
Part Two; Islamic Beliefs	30
Women and Misogyny	32
Slavery and FGM	36
Racism and Xenophobia	40
Tactical Lying	43
Terrorism	46
Jihad and Qatala	51
Part Three; Mohammed's life, an example to follow?	56
Death in the family	57
Pagan education	58
The Illiterate Prophet	59
War stories	61
A child bride	64
A taste for killing	66
Sex-slaves	69
Poison!	72
Part Four; Prophet, true or false?	74
Prophet, true or false?	75
The Satanic Verses	83
Abrogation	86
Fatalism	88
Genocide	92
Part Five; A false testament?	96
Inconsistencies and self-contradictions	97
Impossibilities!	99
Incorrect facts?	100
Failures of logic and reason	105

And more! 110

Part Six; The Bible and Koran compared 113
Historical confusion 114
Revisionism 122
Corrupted Scripture 125
Fight the good fight, or terrorize? 130
No Salvation, no Holy Spirit 134
Personal demons 139

Part Seven; Is Allah the same God? 142
One God, or different deities? 145
There is no god but God, so who is Islam's Allah? 150
The Star and Crescent 155

Part Eight; Islam and the Apocalypse 161
Revelation 13:8 – A World Caliphate? 163
666 - The Mark of the Beast 166
World War III and Satan's Throne 173
Armageddon; the Valley of Decision 181

Part Nine; The Undoing 189
A Time for the Truth 197
The Islamic Revival 206
Peace, Love and Respect 212
Can a tolerant society overcome intolerance? 219
Human Rights and human wrongs 224
Islam Undone 234

Part Ten; Ministering to Muslims 236
Intercession 236
Spreading the Truth 244
In the Community 248
Personal Ministry 254
After Salvation 261
Isaiah 1:17 265
Future Positive 270

Appendix: The TICCET evangelism tool 274

Preface

Jesus said we are to be *"as wise as serpents but as gentle as doves"* (Matthew 10:16). This entails walking with love towards all people whilst always remaining aware of the wiles of our spiritual enemy. And following His example, we are called to; *"destroy the works of the devil"* (1 John 3:8). This is done by various means including, *"demolishing arguments and every pretension that sets itself up against the knowledge of God"* (2 Corinthians 10:5). Quite simply that's what this book is about, setting people free from a false religion built on lies and demonic submission. We just simply need to bring them the truth. As you will read, Muslims follow a religion invented by Satan that keeps its followers in darkness and ignorance about the true nature of God.

Remembering that *"we fight not against flesh and blood, but against the rulers, against the powers, against the world forces of this darkness, against the spiritual forces of wickedness in the heavenly places"* (Ephesians 6:12), we go out to them with love and understanding that they have been seriously misled into believing their religion is the definitive word of God. Until now, even though there have been many criticisms of it, no-one seems to have been able to elucidate the absolute proof that Islam is a falsity. But that proof is now written within the pages of this book for all to see.

"pull down the altar of Baal..." (Judges 6:25)

Bringing down their false religion aligns with a principle that occurs several times in the Old Testament, that when we, the servants of God, arise and destroy the altars of Baal and of other false gods, revival comes. Islam with its deceiving god Allah is such an altar. The fall of Islam in the West will bring with it a huge revival and a great harvest of souls. This book seeks to help equip you to bring in that harvest for Jesus. In order to bring in that harvest of Muslims, we first need to understand what Islam is from a biblical perspective and how it works spiritually. That is why it has been necessary to include so much information about Islamic beliefs, which also constitute false worship, just like the altars of Baal. We must bring them down spiritually and intellectually and then we will see Islam fall physically. Christ in us needs to manifest so we can destroy Satan's handiwork.

"For this purpose the Son of God was manifested, that He might destroy the works of the devil" (1 John 3:8)

We have endeavoured to make this book as easy to read as is possible given the subject matter. It avoids unnecessary discussions of apologetics and other superfluous topics, focussing on the essential information needed to understand the facts. Our focus remains on that which is needed to be able to effectively minister to Muslims and bring them out of the darkness and into the Light of Christ. The number of quotes we have included in this book from the Koran reflect just how much it commands terrorism, how much it denigrates women, and how much it teaches anti-Semitism and xenophobia. When we Christians understand how Islam works we are no longer to be fearful of it, and we will be empowered to take our stand against the deception that it is.

"If God is for us, who can be against us ?" (Romans 8:31)

It does take some wisdom to know how to deal with it. Recently the Lord gave us a message, initially in tongues, which interpreted said; **"There are places where Christians have invited Muslims into their churches to pray with them, but the Muslims have prayed in Arabic without those Christians understanding what was being prayed. The standard Islamic Surah Ikhlaas prayer includes a declaration that *'God has no son',* so these Christian sanctuaries have been invaded and defiled by this without them even realising"**. The Bible is clear on such issues.

"Do not be yoked together with unbelievers. For what do righteousness and wickedness have in common? Or what fellowship can light have with darkness?", "Therefore, 'Come out from them and be separate,' says the Lord, 'Touch no unclean thing, and I will receive you"
(2nd Corinthians 6:14,17)

That is a perfect illustration of why we need to be as wise as serpents. This was by no means the only supernatural input Jesus had into this book. Regularly during its writing, the Holy Spirit would give us a word, even sometimes an Arabic one, leading us to content that God wanted in the text. Quite often webpages would even open up on their own, without anyone even touching the computer, so we could not miss the things He wanted.

"For He shall give His angels charge over you, to keep you in all your ways." (Psalm 91:11)

It is now nearly 15 years since the Lord commissioned this work, since the night He came right into my room, flooding it with so much light and heat, that all I could do was stay face down on the bed as He talked to me and asked so courteously to share the truth I had discovered about the dark side of Islam.

"The light shines in the darkness, and the darkness does not overcome it." (John 1:5)

Introduction

"The LORD made it known to me, and so I understood"
(Jeremiah 11:18)

This work is about truth and lies. The truth coming up against religious lies that have been propagated by the enemy of our souls to keep people from knowing God. In this book, we have tried to give a well-ordered topic by topic analysis of the subject matter. Everything covered has been very diligently researched from Islamic sacred texts and other primary source material. References are given throughout the text so anyone can go to the source material and verify it.

"For I will give you a voice and wisdom, which none of your opponents will be able to withstand or contradict" (Luke 21:15)

Islam, as a set of beliefs and rules, is a fair topic for intellectual debate and consideration. After all the Koran, in verse 4:82, says; *"Will they (the non-Muslims) not then ponder on the Qur'an (Koran)? If it had been from other than Allah they would have found therein much incongruity."* The Koran thus invites us to carefully consider its content and to look for inconsistencies, contradictions and incorrect statements within it. The use of the plural *"will they not ponder"* clearly implies debate and discussion of the issues it raises. Having given that careful consideration we have the right to openly disagree with the Koran and other ideas that are fundamental to Islam. This does not imply criticism of individuals, most Muslims believe in Islam solely because of their family, social or national background. Very few of them have been exposed to open debate about different spiritualities. The vast majority do not even know much of what the Islamic sacred texts actually say. They know even less about other people's belief systems.

"They are darkened in their understanding, alienated from the life of God because of the ignorance that is in them, due to their hardness of heart." (Ephesians 4:18)

Even though we may disagree with what they believe in, it is important to treat all individuals with proper respect and dignity without an aggressive attitude. Hate speech and violent confrontation help no one, whichever side they come from. Even though we have a right to criticize Islam, no one should use that as an excuse to attack individual Muslims, most of whom are good and caring people. The contents of this book are a good cause for intellectual discussion. They are never an excuse for violent incitation, which often is only an expression of frustration. As Christians, we should be able to talk through any topic with others in a dignified, respectful manner. A calm, informed, open dialogue is always the one that best establishes the truth.

"refuse foolish and ignorant speculations, knowing that they produce quarrels" (2 Timothy 2:23)

This book is written for all Christians, regardless of denomination, so that each of us may understand what Islam is from a true Biblical viewpoint. Then armed with that understanding of how it works spiritually, we can know how to intercede and pray for our nations and communities, as well as know how to reach out to effectively evangelize people from a Muslim background. In order to give a true understanding of the subject matter, we have included many quotes from the Koran and other Islamic sacred texts. Do not be fooled by the misinformation that circulates about the religion. Islam's true nature lies in what it commands Muslims to do, in the values it propagates, and in the spiritual forces that are behind it. These things are made very clear in this book by using Islam's own words and, where appropriate, comparing them to what the Bible says. We apologize for anything that you may find upsetting in this work, the subjects of terrorism, race-hatred, misogyny, FGM and sex-slavery are not easy to write about, but we must face up to the truth of what really is happening in our world.

"whatever you loose on earth will be loosed in heaven" (Matthew 18:18)

As Christians, we are all called to take part in the Great Commission, Jesus commanded us in Mark 16:15, *"Go into all the world and proclaim the gospel to all creation"*, and in Matthew 28:19, *"Go therefore and make disciples of all nations"*. Many prophetic voices in the Body of Christ are now talking of a billion-soul harvest about to come to Christ. By far the largest unsaved people group in the world today is the Muslims, numbering 1.8 billion. They even outnumber the population of China. Historically they have proved very resistant to receiving the truth of the Gospel due to reasons you will understand as you read on. It is of crucial importance for us to know how to break down this resistance for us to succeed in our mandate to make disciples from the Muslim nation. Much of this resistance to the Gospel comes, of course, because of Islamic teachings which contradict, distort and devalue what the Bible says. Muslims are also taught that Islam supersedes Christianity and that the Koran replaces the Bible. Several sections of this book highlight these issues and prove unequivocally from the content of their holy books that this is a lie. We are called to spiritually and intellectually free Muslims from the snare of this lie for them to be free to find the truth.

"a time to uproot what is planted... and a time to build up..."
(Ecclesiastes 3:2-3)

It is also important to understand God's timing in all this. The release of this book comes precisely 100 years after the end of 400 years of Ottoman Islamic Caliphate control over Jerusalem, 70 years after Israel's declaration of independence, and 50 years after the return of Jerusalem to Jewish authority. Jerusalem is God's chosen city for the site of His Temple, but the Temple Mount remains for the instant under the authority of a Jordanian Islamic Waqf Trust. This is the only obstacle stopping the building of a new Jewish Temple on the site, the Temple where Jesus will return to Earth and reign from. The rebuilding of the Temple on this site is God's clearly expressed will as explained in the Bible, and we are supposed to pray for His will to; *"be done on Earth as it is in Heaven"*. It is clear therefore we must pray for the Temple Mount compound to come under Jewish control so that the New Temple can be built. Events at the site in July 2017 have shown that Islam with its powerful political and financial influence is pushing hard against this aspect of God's Will being done. However, there is a stunning prediction based on Biblical prophecy, especially from the Book of Daniel, made by author S. Noka in the book **"Physical History Predicted 2017-2053"**, that the rebuilding of the Temple will commence in 2027.

"When the word and the Spirit come together, there will be the biggest move of the Holy Spirit that the nations, and indeed, the world have ever seen. It will mark the beginning of a revival that will eclipse anything that has been witnessed within these shores, even the Wesleyan and Welsh revivals of former years. The outpouring of God's Spirit will flow over from the UK to the mainland of Europe, and from there will begin a missionary move to the ends of the earth."
(Smith-Wigglesworth, 1947)

It is also a time when true Christian revival has broken out in several places on the planet, and notably in London. Exactly 70 years ago, in 1947, evangelist Smith-Wigglesworth prophesied a mighty revival to come forth in the UK and spread out from there around the globe. This great end-times move of God has now begun and will bring many millions of souls into Christ's Kingdom. Already large numbers of Muslims have started to find their way to the truth. Even in Islamic nations like Iran, Egypt, Indonesia, Pakistan and elsewhere there are millions of new converts. Some are even coming without hearing the Gospel, they are visited in the night with dreams and visions by Jesus who asks them to follow Him. As this Revival grows many Muslims will come to be saved and healed, or even come into church meetings out of curiosity. We must be ready to minister to them when they come. And not only that, we must be prepared to take the Gospel out to wherever there are people who need to hear it. In the final Part of this book, there are some guidelines on going out ministering to Muslims as well as a powerful evangelism tool to help you with this.

"My mouth will speak wisdom"
(Psalm 49:3)

So, with this book, we seek to arm you with the truth, with all the necessary information for you to play your part in God's great end-time harvest. Part Ten also gives some tips on intercession and personal ministry, but of course there is no magic formula we can give you for ministering to Muslims, because each person is unique. But if you have read the whole book you will be equipped with spiritual wisdom for whatever the Lord calls you to do. Then just let the Holy Spirit guide you....

"Since we live by the Spirit, by the Spirit let us also be guided" (Galatians 5:25)

"If any of you lacks wisdom, let him ask God" (James 1:5)

And just in case you are a reader who likes to flick through and sample a book before reading it cover to cover, we invite you to start with p149, followed by 58-9, then 139-40, 74-5, 100-1, 168-9, 53-4 and 245-6.

Whichever way you decide to approach reading this book, maybe think about putting some worship music on in the room where you are. Some aspects of Islam are not very nice to read about, but we are obliged to mention them in a comprehensive book like this. To be victorious, we must remain aware of what Satan is plotting. His ways are always unpleasant. The music can help you stay spiritually in a place of peace. Remember that Jesus has already paid the price and won the victory for us. All we need to do is to reach out and bring His salvation to Muslims with love and understanding.

"in order that Satan might not outwit us, we should not be unaware of his schemes" (2nd Corinthians 2:11)

"Never pay back evil with more evil" (Romans 12:17)

"whoever turns a sinner from the error of his way will save his soul from death and cover a multitude of sins" (James 5:20)

"walk in love, just as Christ also loved you and gave Himself up for us, an offering and a sacrifice to God, as a fragrant aroma" (Ephesians 5:2)

NB. Please note that the quotations of scripture used in this book are taken from various popular translations of the Bible and Koran. Some quotes are composites including phrases from more than one version, whilst a few passages have been translated directly from the Hebrew, Greek or Arabic for clearer understanding.

Part One: What is Islam? What is Sharia?

"For whatever is hidden is meant to be disclosed, and whatever is concealed is meant to be brought out into the open" (Mark 4:22)

Because some readers will have little previous understanding of what Islam is, we start the book with the kind of simplistic overview of the faith that you will find in many books on comparative religion. But unlike those books, this present work does not shy away from the controversial issues that affect that faith. Terrorism, FGM, the mistreatment of women, anti-Semitism, and other difficult topics all receive proper attention as we show how they are inextricably rooted in Islamic doctrine. Quoting many verses from the Koran and other sacred books, we uncover the dark side of the religion which many people would like to keep hidden.

"the god of this world has blinded the minds of the unbelievers, to keep them from seeing the light of the Gospel of the Glory of Christ" (2nd Corinthians 4:4)

In this section, we will also start to consider Sharia law, politics and economics which amount to the very literal application of the commands and doctrines found in the Koran and other sacred texts. And as you will learn some Islamic values are totally at odds with ours.

"There are those who turn justice into bitterness and cast righteousness to the ground" (Amos 5:7)

A Brief History

Mohammed, the founder of the religion, was born in 570 AD in the town of Mecca in what is now Saudi Arabia. When he was about forty he said that he had been visited by an angel who had called him as the *"Prophet of Allah"*. From 613 he began publicly preaching revelations that he said were given by the angel Jibril sent to him from God. At first, he only had a few followers and when he started criticizing the local practice of idol worship, he began to make enemies because the Ka'aba shrine in Mecca was at that time the centre for a large annual pagan pilgrimage. However, thanks in part to the wealth and status of his first wife, and the success of their merchant trading, he persevered and began to get more and more interest in his new religion. This in turn became an even greater perceived threat to those with power in Mecca, because the pilgrimage was a great source of income. Eventually they sought to kill Mohammed who had been under the powerful protection of the Quraysh tribe of which his clan, the Banu Hashim, was a part. But in time his clan became isolated from the rest of the tribe and in 622, to escape assassination, he fled Mecca and went to Yathrib.

In his new home, Medina as it is now called, he rose to great influence in the political arena, being given a role of mediator between the different religious communities. After winning some influential local leaders over to his new religion, many of the inhabitants followed suite. But back in Mecca, the authorities seized the property of the Muslims who had gone with Mohammed, causing great economic difficulty for them. So, he and his followers retaliated by attacking the desert caravans of Meccan traders. After several such raids, the people of Mecca began sending troops to protect their caravans. And after more skirmishes Mohammed's men defeated a larger Meccan force in full battle at Badr. After this they began to make a stronghold for themselves at Medina by ridding themselves of local opponents.

Further battles and a siege of Medina followed in which the Muslims stood firm against superior forces. With time, the reputation and power of Mecca began to diminish whilst the numbers of those following Mohammed continued to grow. In 628 Mohammed with a large contingent of followers marched on Mecca during the annual pilgrimage. The authorities there, fearing trouble, negotiated a peace treaty with him to withdraw. The treaty, which had been intended to last ten years, only lasted two and in 630 Mohammed with a force of 10,000 men took Mecca almost unopposed. By the time of his death in 632 he had conquered almost all of the Arabian Peninsula.

After his death and the compilation of the Koran, disputes arose as to who should succeed Mohammed and be Caliph. Two distinct camps arose who are still in dispute today, the Sunnis and the Shias. The latter believe that the succession should continue through the Hashemite family bloodline of his daughter Fatima, whereas the Sunnis believe that Mohammed appointed his companion Abu Bakr to succeed him. The Sunnis also believed that Caliphs should be agreed by a consensus of the whole Muslim community. Matters came to a head in 680 when his grandson Hussein ibn Ali and other family members were killed at Karbala.

Yet, despite the infighting, the Islamic Caliphate was expanding quickly adding Syria in 637, Armenia and Egypt in 639, the areas of Iraq and Iran in 642, Libya in 647, Cyprus 654, Tunisia 670, Morocco 698, Spain 711-718, Pakistan 712, Georgia 736, Afghanistan 751, Sicily 827, Sudan 1315, and Indonesia 1527. Not all of the bloody campaigns of the Muslim armies were successful, several attempts to invade France between 721 and 732 ended in defeat and a slow Christian re-conquest of the Iberian Peninsula that ensued saw Islam being finally defeated and driven out of Spain in 1492. Later incarnations of the Caliphate such as the Ottoman Empire continued to expand, moving into the Balkans and Greece in the 14th and 15th centuries. This expansion came to a final end in 1683 at the siege of Vienna.

The Caliphate was disbanded in 1924 following the defeat of the Ottoman Empire in the First World War. During the 20th and early 21st centuries Islam spread greatly through immigration into many other parts of the world. Since the Second World War many millions of dollars of revenue from the oil industry has been spent by Arabian Gulf States in spreading fundamentalist Islamic beliefs around the world. The rise in aspirations that this brought included the desire for a new Islamic Caliphate. This was declared by the Islamic State in Iraq and Syria in 2014. Many moderate Muslims have tried to distance themselves from this Caliphate because of its barbarity, but the Islamic State itself vehemently claims that its way is true Mohammedan Islam.

Today the majority of Muslims are Sunnis, with about 15% Shias. Saudi Arabia and Iran respectively are the most influential Sunni and Shia nations. The primary disagreement between the two sects is still over the historical succession as Caliph after Mohammed's death. It is worth noting that Jordan is today ruled by a descendant of Mohammed's Hashemite dynasty, Abdullah II. There are currently many tensions in the Muslim world because of the Sunni/Shia divide, most of the regular mosque bombings and other terrorism inside the Muslim world are connected to this because they treat each other as apostates and thus infidels alongside non-Muslims.

Beyond the Sunni/Shia divide there are many different Islamic denominations; Salafist, Wahhabite, Twelver and so on. Their differences do not really concern us here because all Muslims believe that the Koran is the word of God that must be obeyed, that Mohammed is the only prophet whose word and lifestyle should be relied upon for guidance today, and that Islam supersedes, and is superior to, all other religions.

The Five Pillars of Islam

The religion is often considered as comprising of five pillars on which individual faith is built. Islam literally means submission to the Islamic god Allah and comes from the Arabic word *"aslama"*. It does not, as some say, mean peace which in Arabic is a similar but distinct word *"salaam"*.

The first of these pillars is the declaration of faith which asserts that; *"there is only one God, Allah, and Muhammad is His Messenger"*. This confession of faith is key to being a Muslim, it is required of every convert to Islam.

Unlike most other faiths where the revelation of God has been an ongoing process through a number of enlightened persons over an extended period of time, Islam really only depends on the revelation of Mohammed as expressed through the Koran, which he claimed to have received from God, through historically authenticated records of how he lived his life, called *"Hadiths"*, which include his verbatim statements on many issues, and his biographies. The content of these writings will be considered in the subsequent sections of this book. The declaration of faith by a Muslim implies that a person believes the content of the Koran is true and from God, and must be obeyed by them.

The second pillar of the faith is a routine of prayer, with specific prayers said at dawn, at noon, in the afternoon, evening and at night. Prayer is only made after ritual washing of the face, hands, forearms and feet, and prayer is made towards the Ka'aba shrine in the great mosque of Mecca. Repetitive cycles of ritualised actions of standing, kneeling, bowing and prescribed arm movements are carried out in synchronization with pre-determined recited utterances in Arabic. These scripted prayers always include the Faatiha which includes this; *"Guide us to the Straight Way, The Way of those on whom You have bestowed Your Grace, not (the way) of those who earned Your Anger, nor of those who went astray."* This is evidently not prayer such as Christians, Jews and others practice which involves dialogue with God, Islamic prayer is standardized, formalized ritual.

Another pillar of Islam, is all Muslims giving to their mosque, or to charity, some fixed percentage (e.g. 2.5% or 5%) of their income. This money is supposed to be redistributed in the local community, or given to charitable works and distributed in accordance with Sharia rules. In practice, however, most goes to those who run the mosques. This giving is obligatory and is thought of as a purification of a person's wealth.

A further requirement of faith, the fourth pillar, is fasting during the month of Ramadan. This is obligatory for all Muslims, with certain exceptions; young children, breastfeeding mothers, the sick and the elderly. The fast of Ramadan involves abstaining from all food, drink, sex and smoking from dawn to dusk for the whole period.

The final pillar of Islam is the pilgrimage to Mecca in Saudi Arabia which every Muslim should make at least once in their lifetime. As well as retracing events in Mohammed's life, those making the pilgrimage will circle around the Black Stone in the Ka'aba seven times, bowing down before it and even kissing it in veneration, although in the enormous crowds this can be rather difficult.

Whilst adherence to these five practices is fairly universal across all Muslim communities, disagreements exist on the fine points, for example some see bowing down before and kissing the Black Stone as idolatry. It is worth noting too that there are some streams of Islam that have added other pillars, or obligations to the basic five. The duty to undertake *"Jihad"* is one that many Muslims today believe in.

Sharia Law

This is the Islamic legal system which is derived, in order of priority, from a practical application of the content of the Koran and the Hadiths, and to a lesser degree from Islamic jurisprudence. A study in 2013 by the Pew Forum found that most Muslims worldwide want to have Sharia as the legal system of their land, with support exceeding 90% in many Middle Eastern and South Asian countries. In the USA, the figure is 51% (60% among the under 30s) and in Western Europe the figure varies from 29% in the UK to 73% in Austria.

Yet after careful deliberation the European Court of Human Rights has declared; *"Sharia is incompatible with the fundamental principles of democracy"* (Refah Partisi V Turkey, 13th Feb 2003). Interestingly, the Islamic State agrees with this statement and early in 2017 produced a 10-point infographic proving that democracy is truly incompatible with Sharia law. Islamic authorities worldwide all oppose the United Nations **"Universal Declaration of Human Rights"**, because it opposes and disrespects Islamic traditions and customs such as the subservience of women. A rival declaration was made by the Organisation for Islamic Cooperation in 1990 called the **"Cairo Declaration of Human Rights in Islam"** which negates all established Human Rights which do not agree the provisions of Sharia Law. The Cairo Declaration has been criticised for failing to provide freedom of religion, or equal rights for women and also because it leads to discrimination against non-Muslims.

Instead of the freedom of expression guaranteed by Human Rights legislation, the Cairo Declaration Article 22:(a) states *"Everyone shall have the right to express his opinion freely in such manner as would not be contrary to the principles of the Shari'ah."* In other words, all criticism of Sharia and Islam is forbidden. This is not free speech. Author Ann Elizabeth Mayer has written at length about such issues in her book **"Islam and Human Rights"** (Westview Press). According to her;

"many Middle Eastern governments have expressly invoked their cultural particularisms as grounds for their non-compliance with international human rights law."

In recent years, delegates from the Organisation for Islamic Cooperation have infiltrated various United Nations Human Rights committees to hinder any action against Sharia Law and to generally try to stifle all criticism of any aspect of Islam. This is part of a global strategy to bring the whole world under the influence of Sharia. Very recently Saudi Arabia was awarded the chair of one such board. The Executive Director of UN Watch said this about it;

"It is scandalous that the UN chose a country that has beheaded more people this year than ISIS to be head of a key human rights panel...Petro-dollars and politics have trumped human rights....Saudi Arabia has arguably the worst record in the world when it comes to religious freedom and women's rights...This UN appointment is like making a pyromaniac into the town fire chief"

This came only weeks after the country had appointed eight more state executioners to behead those condemned to death by Sharia. It is rather strange that a country that has not signed the United Nations Universal Declaration of Human Rights even be allowed to have a place on such a committee! They are against the human rights values that the UN officially promotes in its Universal Charter.

Also significant is the success bought by millions of petro-dollars being spent on lobbying in the West to open our legal systems to Sharia law, and in particular to sponsor the introduction of laws which aim to take away the right to publicly criticize Islam. Recently, such a motion was under consideration by legislators in the United States, **H.Res.569 - 114th Congress** (2015-2016), which aimed to outlaw *"hateful rhetoric"* against Muslims and Islam. This represented the thin end of the wedge trying to break the First Amendment of the United States Constitution which guarantees absolute freedom of speech. The ultimate aim is to protect Islam from political or intellectual scrutiny which could oppose or even destroy it.

As you read on in this book you should ask yourself, do any of the verses in the Koran constitute hate speech? Ask yourself too why has there been almost no public debate about such an important issue.

In Sharia Law, anyone who leaves Islam, known as apostasy, receives an automatic death sentence in accordance with what Mohammed said,

"Whoever changes his Islamic religion, kill him" (Hadith Bukhari 9/57)

Rejecting Islam is the most serious criminal offence under Sharia. In some countries, it is even quite common for Muslim families to "honour" kill any family member who rejects Islam. Recently, a Muslim shopkeeper who wished his Christian customers; *"Happy Easter"* and called Britain his *"beloved Christian nation"*, was killed by another Muslim.

The case of Afghan Abdul Rahman provides a good example of how Sharia works in practice; he was a Muslim who converted to Christianity and was brought to trial for it in 2006. Denounced by his family, he could not find a lawyer who would represent him after he was found to be in possession of a Bible. Despite the fact that the Constitution of Afghanistan guarantees freedom of religion, it also recognizes the

Hanafi School of Sharia Law which took superiority in the eyes of the Afghan Court. Rahman was described by the prosecution as a *"microbe"* who might infect all Muslim society, and was sentenced to death when he refused to renounce his Christian faith. It was only under much pressure from many Western governments that the country's President intervened and allowed Rahman to leave for Europe. Nonetheless, this sparked a widespread public outcry in the land against the failure to execute the death sentence.

The rest of Sharia criminal law is broken down into a variety of categories, these correspond to crimes with specific punishments prescribed in the Koran; stealing, drinking alcohol, illegal sexual activity and religious deviance which have punishments ranging from flogging for drinking alcohol, or amputation of the hand for theft, through to stoning to death for adultery. The Hadiths, sometimes called *"Sahihs"*, which include sayings of Mohammed, are also referred to delineate punishments, for example Sahih Muslim 17/4192;

"Verily Allah has ordained a way for them (the women who commit fornication): (When) a married man (commits adultery) with a married woman, and an unmarried male with an unmarried woman, then in case of married (persons) there is (a punishment) of one hundred lashes and then stoning (to death). And in case of unmarried persons, (the punishment) is one hundred lashes and exile for one year"

There is not really anything in Sharia equivalent to our Western concept of rape, and Sharia courts regularly treat any accusation of rape as a confession of adultery or illegal sex, often imprisoning the victim unless they marry their rapist. The BBC Arabic Service film **"Pregnant and in Chains"** follows the real-life stories of five unmarried pregnant women in the United Arab Emirates where unmarried mothers are forced to give birth in chains so that they do not run away from the prosecution they face under Sharia Law for *"Unlawful Sex"*, known as Zina. They could not flee because female domestic servants in Dubai are not even allowed to leave the country to go home without the permission of their employers.

Murder and bodily injury is normally dealt with on an eye for eye, tooth for a tooth retaliatory basis even though the Koran also says it is better to seek compensation.

"And We ordained for them therein a life for a life, an eye for an eye, a nose for a nose, an ear for an ear, a tooth for a tooth, and (like for like) for wounds is legal retribution..." (5:45)

"O, you who have believed, prescribed for you is legal retribution for those murdered - the free for the free, the slave for the slave, and the female for the female" (2:178)

In Sharia Muslims are given a higher status than unbelievers; -

"No Muslim should be killed for killing a Kaffir (a non-Muslim)"
(Sahih Bukhari 9/50)

Where no punishment is given by the Koran, as for example with homosexuality, principles found in the Hadiths are employed such as stoning to death or being thrown off a high place, see for example, **The Book of Punishments**, Hadith Abu Dawud 38/4447-4448; -

"kill the one who does it, and the one to whom it is done... an unmarried man seized committing sodomy shall be stoned to death"

The penalty for blasphemy under Sharia Law, like leaving Islam, is death, even mildly criticizing Islam carries severe penalties such as that given to Saudi blogger Raif Badawi, 1,000 lashes, 50 each Friday after prayers, plus 10 years in prison and a fine of one million Riyals. Violent punishments, including beheading, normally take place after the main Friday prayers as they are an expression of the religion. Failing to attend Friday prayers is also an offence under Sharia.

Recent cases in countries as diverse as Sudan and Pakistan have shown that even just publicly saying that one does not believe in Allah is enough to prove one guilty of blasphemy. And as we have seen in the news, acknowledging that you are a Christian can land you in trouble with Sharia, as was the case with Asia Bibi. (See "Blasphemy: A Memoir: Sentenced to Death over a Cup of Water", Bibi & Tollet, Chicago Review Press) According to Human Rights Watch such cases are far from rare.

Lawyers and Judges are obliged to follow Koranic prescriptions; Surah 5:45;

"And whoever does not judge according to what Allah has sent down, then they are unjust"

There is also a whole body of law concerning marriage and divorce. Muslim women may only marry Muslim men whereas Muslim men are free to marry whoever they like and may take non-Muslims as sex slaves. Islamic marriage contracts may be for life but some Islamic countries have temporary marriage contracts as a means of avoiding the rules on what they call "illegal" sex. Some moderates disagree with these as they resemble prostitution and they usually involve the payment of a fee to the women for their participation. Their justification under Sharia law is found in Hadith Sahih Bukhari 7/62/130 where one of Mohammed's fighters recalled;

"We used to participate in the holy battles led by Allah's Apostle and we had nothing (no wives) with us. So we said, 'Shall we get ourselves castrated?' He forbade us that and then allowed us to marry women with a temporary contract."

Sahih Muslim 8/3246 confirms this;

"There came to us the proclaimer of Allah's Messenger and said: Allah's Messenger has granted you permission to benefit yourselves, to contract temporary marriage with women"

Some scholars believe verse 4:24 of the Koran gives permission for temporary marriages in which the woman is paid for her participation;

"those of whom you seek pleasure, give them compensation"

Girls as young as six can be married under Sharia in accordance with Bukhari 7:62:65;

"Aisha, the Prophet married her when she was six years old and he consummated his marriage when she was nine"

Ayatollah Khomeini, writing in the marriage section of Tahrir al Wasilah (Issue 12) confirmed the age of sexual maturity and the consummation of marriages for girls in Islam is the age of nine. Recently politicians in Pakistan were forced to scrap a law banning child marriages because the Sharia law enforcers in the land declared it un-Islamic. One has to ask who is ruling there. It is also recorded that according to Mohammed, a woman's or girl's silence is sufficient to be deemed as the permission to a marriage, so forced or arranged marriages exist in many Muslim countries.

"Should the women be asked for their consent to their marriage? Her silence means her consent." (Sahih Bukhari 9/85/79)

Divorce rights are unequal between the sexes, a man being able to simply renounce and end a marriage by saying; *"I divorce you",* three times over a given period of time.

The wife has no right of defence and no say in the matter whatsoever. A woman however can only divorce a man in a limited number of circumstances and may risk having to lose her children, repay her dowry and could lose her entitlement to a share of the family assets as they usually remain with the husband. Generally speaking, a woman's share of any inheritance or property is only one-half that of a man. There are also rules for divorcing wives who have yet to reach puberty in accordance with verse 65:4 of the Koran.

Whilst child brides, temporary marriages, polygamy and sex-slavery are permissible under Sharia, yet unimaginable as being legal in the West, open displays of affection such as we are used to seeing in public in our free liberal society are in practice punished in some Muslim countries. During the last 12 months, the following "crimes" have met with punishment in the Sharia law countries;

- married couples holding hands in public,
- a husband helping his wife carry heavy shopping through a sex-segregated supermarket checkout,
- two poet friends, one male and one female, sentenced to 10 years in prison and 99 lashes for shaking hands in public, labelled as the crime of "sexual relationship short of adultery",
- and even in moderate Indonesia, a young person being "too friendly" with someone of the opposite sex, a "crime" which was punished with such brutal lashings to the point where urgent hospitalization was required to safeguard her life.

So, with open public tenderness outlawed, but with paedophilia and sex-slavery allowed, and FGM even prescribed under it, Sharia law is clearly incompatible with Western values. It leaves little room for compassionate jurisprudence or reasoned judgement.

Whilst most of the world's legal systems are open to development as society changes and have seen the abolition of slavery, an end to imprisonment for debt, the emancipation of women, and are moving towards a general end to capital punishment, Sharia law cannot evolve. And being firmly based on the Koran and Hadiths, it will always remain rooted in Mohammed's 7th Century values.

In the West, we have developed to the extent where we reject sets of religious rules which everyone must abide by, instead we try to teach our citizens tolerance and how to discern for themselves between right and wrong. Sharia only teaches fear and submission.

Other areas of Sharia law covering the obligatory ritual (halal) killing of animals for consumption, dress codes about the hijab and other compulsory women's clothing, as well as economic and political regulation. Some of these measures, for example, that a woman's face must be fully covered except for the eyes are completely opposite to our laws in the West where for security reasons it can be forbidden for anyone to have their face covered so as to make them unrecognizable.

The Hijab is now illegal in public in countries like France, Belgium, Austria and much of Germany.

Human Rights vs Sharia

Here is a direct comparison between the UN Universal Declaration of Human Rights and relevant provisions of Sharia Law, Article by Article.

1. **Article One declares that all human beings are free and equal**, but Sharia recognizes and condones slavery, for example, (Koran 2:221) *"A slave...is better than a free unbeliever..."* and it also denies equality as in verse (Koran 4:34) which says; *"men are in charge of women..."*. Ibn Kathir's commentary on the Koran explains; *"Men are superior to women, and a man is better than a woman"*.

2. **The Second Article states that there should be no discrimination against anyone on grounds of status**, but Sharia discriminates on many bases, religion, gender, sexual preferences; for example gay men are subject to a death penalty pursuant to the rule (Abu Dawud 38:4447-8) *"kill the one who does it, and the one to whom it is done"*, and under Sharia, charities must donate to fund jihad and must not help non-Muslims *"It is obligatory to distribute... to those fighting for Allah"* , *"It is not permissible to give charity to a non-Muslim"* (Umdat al Salik; Reliance of the Traveller H8.7,17,24).

3. **The right to life, liberty and security** is also negated by provisions of Sharia, private personal issues such as adultery are subject to a death sentence pursuant to the rule; *"Allah has ordained... stoning (to death)"* (Sahih Muslim 17/4192). The Sharia crimes of leaving Islam and blasphemy, which include criticizing the religion, the Prophet, or Allah, also give rise to the punishment of death, again contrary to the right to life and liberty.

4. We have already noted that the rule **there should be no slavery** is broken by Sharia, recent reports say that about 4% of the population of Mauritania are in slavery, a system held in place by Sharia. (source CNN; "Turning point for slavery's last stronghold") Sex-slavery is permissible in Sharia. (Koran 33:50) *"We have made lawful to thee... those (slaves) whom your right hand possesses"* & (4:24) *"Married women are forbidden to you save those captives whom your right hand possesses"*

5. **The forbidding of torture, cruel or degrading treatment** is also ignored, the exceeding cruelty of FGM is a prescribed part of Sharia and its rapid growth in the West is due solely to Islamic immigration. From many Islamic nations, including "moderate" Indonesia, there are many press reports of individuals being cruelly lashed, or even stoned to death for adultery and extramarital sex. Wives are allowed to be beaten and scourged (Koran 38:44); *"take in your hand a stick and beat her with it"*. Even petty thieves' hands can be cut off; *"the thief, male and female, amputate their hands"*. (Koran 5:38)

6. **Everyone has a right to recognition as a person at law**, but Sharia can reduce a woman to being mere property of a man as a sex slave (see Koran 33:50, 4:24, 23:6, 4:3 *"those whom your right hand possesses"*). In strict Sharia countries, a woman may not leave her home without the permission of her male guardian.

7. **This Article says all are equal before the law**, but in Sharia, (Sahih Bukhari 9/50) says that; *"no Muslim should be killed for killing a non-Muslim"*, as a qualification to (Koran 5:45), *"a life for a life"*. Thus, Muslims have greater legal protection under Sharia than non-Muslims. Under Sharia, a woman's witness testimony is only worth half that of a man, (see Koran 2:282).

8. **This Article says that everyone should have the right to an effective remedy for all Human Rights violations they suffer**, but as we have seen Sharia doesn't recognize most human rights! For example, a woman's right to security under **Article 3** is rendered void by rules (Koran 4:34, Abu Dawud 11/2142) which permit a man to beat a woman, *"A man will not be asked as to why he beat his wife"*.

9. **There should be no arbitrary arrest or exile**, but under Sharia law all that is required for punishment is a *"fatwa"*, a declaration made without a trial, by a Mufti, an unelected and non-accountable Islamic cleric.

10. **The right to a fair trial in front of an impartial court**, as required by Article 10, is absent under Sharia. A Sharia court being a religious body composed of Muslim clerics, cannot possibly be impartial in matters of apostasy, leaving Islam, converting to another faith, blasphemy, etc.

11. **The right to presumption of innocence and punishment only according to law** is compromised in Sharia, and it is clear that many Sharia punishments are made with a presumption of guilt, and with no fair trial, contrary to the UN Declaration of Human Rights which sets the standard for international law.

12. **Privacy of one's life, home and correspondence are guaranteed by Article 12**, but Sharia law takes private acts and publicly punishes people for them, including homosexuality, adultery, extramarital sex, drinking alcohol and any private statements expressing disagreement with Islam.

13. **The right to free movement** is not respected in Sharia; many areas of Saudi Arabia are closed to non-Muslims, and workers in Gulf States like Dubai are not allowed to leave the country without the written permission of their employers, this includes unmarried pregnant foreign women, even those who have been raped, trying to get home to avoid being prosecuted for unlawful sex. (source BBC "Pregnant and in Chains")

14. **Article 14 grants the right to seek asylum from persecution**, but Sharia does not recognize any right to leave Islamic countries to escape prosecution and severe punishment for blasphemy, apostasy and other un-Islamic thought or expression. There are a number of high profile cases in Saudi Arabia (Raif Badawi), Pakistan (Asia Bibi) and elsewhere where individuals are incarcerated for such crimes of conscience and not allowed to seek asylum abroad.

15. **The right to nationality** is not greatly affected, but in Morocco, there are thousands of people who were born to single mothers, from rape or extra-marital affairs, whose births were not registered because their mothers feared prosecution for illegal sex. Unregistered, they have no right to education, health-care, social security, voting, or to obtain documents for travel. (source; Euronews "Morocco's Stateless Children" / UNICEF) Some Sharia countries like the Maldives do not allow non-Muslims full citizenship, granting them only an inferior *"Dhimmi"* status.

16. **The right to marry, by consent, with both spouses having equal rights at law during the marriage and upon divorce** is violated by Sharia. Muslim men may have up to four wives, thus violating equality and Muslim women are forbidden to marry any non-Muslim. For a woman, *"her silence means her consent"* (SB9/85/79) under Sharia, and in practice many marriages in mosques are carried out with only the man present. Divorce rights are unequal, a man only has to say; *"I divorce you"*, three times; whereas it is very difficult for a woman to divorce her husband under Sharia. Non-Muslim wives are usually refused access to children in Sharia divorce pronouncements.

17. **The right to own property** is likewise biased in Sharia, with property in married couples belonging only to the husband. Upon divorce, the wife can be left with nothing. Women are only allowed half of what a male receives of any family inheritance, *"the male will have the share of two females"* (K4:11-12,176).

18. **Freedom of thought, conscience and religion and the right to manifest it publicly or to change it**, accorded by Article 18 of the UN Declaration, is at total odds with Sharia which allows no contrary position to Islam to be publicly expressed. *"None has the right to be worshipped except Allah"* (SB59/643). There is no freedom of religion in Sharia law countries, members of other religions are harassed, persecuted and prosecuted for any manifestation of other beliefs. Anyone wanting to leave Islam gets an automatic death sentence; *"Whoever changes his Islamic religion, kill him"* (Sahih Bukhari 9/84/57).

19. **The freedom of opinion and expression** is similarly severely limited under Sharia, there is no freedom whatsoever to express any viewpoint which opposes Islam. In Sharia law countries, the media, including social

media, is all highly censored. (Koran 8:39 & 2:193) *"Make war on them until idolatry (every non-Islamic idea) ends..."*

20. **The right to peaceful assembly** is also greatly restricted, there is no right to have churches, Sunday schools, gospel choirs, yoga classes, film clubs or even the W.I. under strict Sharia.

21. **Everybody has a right to take part in politics**, but Sharia forbids Muslims to submit to the governance of non-Muslims. The Koran 76:24 says, *"obey not...any...disbeliever"*, so non-Muslims are forbidden to hold public office. The truest form of Islamic government is the Caliphate, a religious autocracy working through a Sharia legal system. In Iran and elsewhere, we have seen how undemocratically appointed Mullahs and Muftis oversee democratically elected institutions limiting their power. The *"fatwas"* made by them stand as law. The elected legislature has no power to overrule these. And in practice, the segregation of the sexes under Sharia means women cannot hold public office in any real form.

22. **The right to social security & education** has some scope under Sharia systems but the Zakat charity rules say; *"never be a helper to a non-Muslim"* (Koran 28:86). Sharia restricts school curricula to studies which do not contradict Islamic teachings; for a discussion of this subject please see Parts Four, Five and Six of this book.

23. **The universal right to work, to a fair wage, equal pay and trade union membership** is disrespected in Sharia, there is no equality for women in Islam. Muslim women are expected to stay at home (Koran 33:32-33) *"Wives... stay in your houses"*. This greatly hinders economic growth in many countries, the US Agency for International Development has said, *"for a society that does not integrate women into its economy, the long-run consequences are likely to be severe"*.

24. **With respect to the right to rest and leisure, and to a limit on the number of hours worked**, Sharia does make some provision for this, especially to allow time for prayer. Many Muslim majority countries have a "Morals Police" who are responsible for enforcement of Sharia dress codes, sex-segregation rules, and other Islamic values. Vast numbers of books are forbidden including the Bible, the Torah, and all other works on any kind of un-Islamic religion or philosophy. Most western literature, films and music are forbidden. Sharia is diametrically opposed to our Western concepts of freedom of belief and expression. The choice of leisure activities is severely restricted under Sharia.

25. **Article 25 guarantees the right to a certain standard of living, to maternity rights and to equality for illegitimate children.** Statistically Islamic nations are much poorer than those in the West, and cannot match western standards of living except where they have valuable natural resources like oil. Verse 2:275 of the Koran says, *"Allah permitteth*

trade and forbiddeth usury...", so in Islam the lending of money for gain is illegal. This effectively outlaws all investment banking, mortgages, personal loans and most types of insurance and assurance.

26. **The right to an education which should promote tolerance and respect, and be subject to parental choice** fails under Sharia. Sharia schools are primarily Koranic and the Koran contains many verses which promote anti-Semitism, violence against women and terrorism. The Koran teaches; *"Take not Jews and Christians as friends...they are folk that have no understanding...most are evil...apes and swine,"* (Koran 5:51-60) *"those women from whom you fear disobedience...beat them"* (Koran 4:34) and *"Instill terror into the hearts of the non-Muslims...fight them until all religion is for Allah"* (Koran 8:12,39).

27. **Cultural life, arts and sciences including intellectual property** rights are covered in this Article. Sharia forbids all culture that is un-Islamic and has no copyright protection laws. Much of the science in the Koran has been proved wrong, for example, the earth is not flat but the Koran says (79:30) *"The Earth...he made it flat",* also a foetus does not form bones first and then grow flesh onto the bones, disproving Koran verse 23:14 *"the bones are formed and then clothed with flesh",* or concerning astral physics *"the sun prostrates itself under the throne until it gets permission to rise again"* (Koran 18:86, SB4/54/421) and so on. Because Sharia forbids anything which puts Islam's sacred book in a bad light, even the teaching of science has to be heavily censored. Most films, art and music from non-Islamic cultures are banned under Sharia Law.

28. **Everyone's entitlement to a social and international order guaranteeing respect of Human Rights** is seriously eroded by Sharia, which is the literal legal application of the content of the Koran and the other sacred Islamic writings. The Koran's hundred plus commands to undertake physical jihad; *"instil terror into the hearts of the non-Muslims..."* (Koran 8:12), *"Make war until... all religion is that of Allah"* (Koran 8:39), create a duty under Sharia to spread Islam by violence which is in total opposition to Human Rights culture. All of the classic manuals of Sharia make it clear that *"war against non-Muslims"* is *"obligatory for every Muslim".* (Source; "Umdat al Salik; Reliance of the Traveller" Al Azhar University authorized translation which carries this definition; (o9.0) *"Jihad: Jihad means to war against non-Muslims, and is etymologically derived from the word mujahada, signifying warfare to establish the religion."*)

29. **This Article acknowledges that we have duties to the community ensuring a positive environment for the personal development of all.** Nations are forbidden to limit these Human Rights in any way. But recently politicians in Pakistan were forced to abandon laws protecting under-age girls from child marriages when they were declared un-Islamic by the Council of Islamic Ideology, and were thus unenforceable

in the country's Sharia Court system. Sharia, by imposing a particular world-view, restricts people's choices and limits most of the basic rights and freedoms asserted by the UN Declaration.

30. **Nothing in the Declaration allows countries to destroy the rights and freedoms it describes**, yet many of the Muslim countries who originally signed up to it have violated its safeguards; look at the current total lack of religious freedom in Iran, the killing of civilians by government forces in Syria, and also, at the current ongoing suspension of Human Rights in Turkey where tens of thousands have been detained without trial by the pro-Sharia Islamist government.

As you have read, every Article of the UN Universal Declaration of Human Rights is in some way opposed by provisions of Sharia. Because of the basic incompatibility of Sharia and Human Rights, some Islamic countries like Saudi Arabia have always refused to sign up to the UN Universal Declaration of Human Rights. The 56 Muslim nations of the Organization for Islamic Co-operation, even though some are signatories to the UN charter, have made an alternative agreement, known as the Cairo Declaration which states, *"all rights and freedoms... are subject to Islamic Sharia"*, and *"there shall be no crime or punishment except as provided for in the Sharia"*. This thereby invalidates most of the rights and protections of the UN Declaration, for example, it maintains the stoning to death of adulterers as well as the death penalty for blasphemy and apostasy. Sharia cannot evolve with the times. Being solely based on Prophet Mohammed's words and example, Islam is firmly entrenched in its 7th Century roots. With its Sharia laws threatening to kill anyone who wants to leave it, criticize it, or even simply disagree with it, and banning all books, web content, TV & films that might express any differing viewpoint to it; Islam is clearly the religion of submission to intimidation and indoctrination.

Politics

Sharia forbids Muslims to submit to the governance of non-Muslims.

76:24   *"obey not...any...disbeliever"*

The truest Islamic form of government is the Caliphate, a religious autocracy working through a Sharia legal system with a religious, morals-policing force to enforce the rules. In Islam, there can be no separation between state and religion. Some more liberal Muslim countries have tried to embrace democracy but the two cultures have difficulty co-existing.

Where there is Islamic majority rule in a democracy, history shows that the Muslim majority will usually endeavour to introduce Sharia law to rule over the whole population by one means or another. Watch Turkey as an ongoing contemporary example of how Islam destroys democratic freedoms. Statistically speaking, with Sharia law comes intolerance. Research has shown that the application of Sharia law has led to a disproportionate number of Muslim countries, twenty-one in all, registering the worst ratings in the world for persecution of their citizens. Under strict Sharia law people of other religious viewpoints must pay a special tax even to have a right to live. (as per Koran 9:29)

In Iran and elsewhere, we have seen how undemocratically appointed Mullahs oversee democratically elected institutions limiting their power. Absolute power remains with the clerics who are answerable to no-one but Allah. As noted, those known as Muftis have the power to issue religious edicts or *"fatwas"* which stand as law. The elected legislature has no power to overrule these. In Pakistan, a law passed by Parliament criminalizing wife-beating was declared un-Islamic by the Council of Islamic Ideology and so is unenforceable in the Sharia Court system.

The principle of Koran verse 2:217 *"Fitnah (civil unrest) is worse than killing"* means that Islamic leaders have the right under Sharia Law to kill all political dissenters. What also makes Sharia different from other political systems is that it favours Muslims over all others, and indeed under strict Sharia law the obligations of religious observance, and Jihad, are enforceable.

Non-Muslims are not allowed to inherit property that was once a Muslim's. So, Sharia can become a system for the religious equivalent of ethnic cleansing, where non-Muslim minorities are subtly persecuted and driven out. (For the rules on no Muslim inheritance for non-Muslims; see Bukhari 8/80/756) Many commentators believe this is why the older Muslim nations tend not to have any real religious minorities, as is the case in much of the Middle East and North Africa. We can today see examples of how Christianity in the Middle East is being eradicated. As you will read later in this book, history shows that there have been many pogroms and genocides against other faiths in Muslim countries.

In the West as part of a push towards multiculturalism there have been moves to allow for Sharia law to be used as a means for arbitration in settling disputes between Muslims. In the United Kingdom, such an experiment was ongoing but legislators have now turned against the idea because in practice it has brought forth legal judgements that do not align in any way with the democratically established laws of the land, especially in the area of equality between the sexes, divorce and inheritance.

4:11 *"Allah directs you in regard of your children's (inheritance), to the male a portion equal to that of two females... These are settled portions ordained by Allah"*

Doesn't this clearly discriminate against women and thus infringe Western rules on sex discrimination? The book **"Women and Sharia Law"** by Elham Malea catalogues the lack of justice shown towards women in Sharia Courts in the UK in blatant contradiction to the country's official laws. Indeed, it seems that the UK will soon outlaw such Sharia Courts in order to re-establish the rule of democratically established law in the land.

Sharia also covers education, with enforced rote learning of the Koran being normal practice in most Islamic nations. Subjects such as philosophy are banned, critics say this is akin to brainwashing. Many Muslim majority countries also have a *"Morals Police"* who are responsible for enforcement of strict dress codes for women, rules on marriage and sex, and other Islamic values.

24:31 *"And tell the believing women to lower their gaze (from looking at forbidden things), and protect their private parts (from illegal sexual acts, etc.) and not to show off their adornment except only that which is apparent (like palms of hands or one eye or both eyes for necessity to see the way, or outer dress like veil, gloves, head-covering, apron, etc.), and to draw their veils all over Juyubihinna (i.e. their bodies, faces, necks and bosoms, etc.) and not to reveal their adornment except to their husbands, their fathers, their husband's fathers, their sons, their husband's sons, their brothers or their brother's sons, or their sister's sons, or their (Muslim) women (i.e. their sisters in Islam), or the (female) slaves whom their right hands possess, or old male servants who lack vigour, or small children who have no sense of the shame of sex..."*

Recently the morals police in Iran cleared shops of clothing featuring US and UK flags in their design as they were deemed un-Islamic. As noted vast numbers of books are forbidden including the Bible, the Torah, and any expression of any kind of un-Islamic religion or philosophy. Nearly all western literature (even many academic books), feature films and pop music are banned. Sharia is diametrically opposed to our Western concepts of freedom of speech, belief and expression.

Economics

Verse 2:275 of the Koran says; *"Allah permitteth trade and forbiddeth usury..."*, so in Islam the lending of money for gain is illegal. This outlaws all investment banking, mortgages, personal loans and most types of insurance and assurance. It is very hard to imagine what life would be like in the developed world without these things. For the ordinary Muslim, very often they do try to avoid taking out loans. Because of this one sees many half-built houses in Muslim countries, where families build the ground floor shell first and then as they can afford it save up for the next batch of building materials to add to the home. So-called *"Islamic banking"* has eased the conscience of some on borrowing, but many still see it as a way of calling the lender's profit "fees and commission" instead of calling it "interest".

Mohammed also said; *"Every innovation leads astray"* (Abu Dawud 4607, Tirmidhee 2676) But in practice, of course most Muslim nations have found it impossible to function in the modern world without modern technology. Even the most ardent jihadis seem unable to forgo their smartphones, laptops, 4x4s and other fruits of the tree of capitalism. Needs must and none of us want to live in the dark ages, do we?

Other factors, too, have led to a lack of economic development in the Muslim world. The US Agency for International Development said this;

"for a society that does not integrate women into its economy, the long-run consequences are likely to be severe."

The Koran says (33:33);   *"(wives) stay in your houses..."*

Another negative factor is the fatalism and passivity of the *"Inch' Allah"* (Allah willing) attitude that is found in Islam. The basic idea is that nothing happens except that Allah wills it; *"By no means can aught befall us save what Allah has destined for us..."* (9:51). This means that people are fearful of new ventures in case Allah doesn't like them.

"Whatever of good befalleth thee, it is from Allah, and whatever of ill befalleth thee it is from thyself." (4:79)

If one believes that Allah's pre-ordained decrees nullify one's own life choices, then what is the point of doing anything? If you think Allah would just prosper you when you do nothing, or that Allah will ruin you irrelevant of whether you work hard at something or not, then where's the incentive to work at making anything succeed?

This is very different from the Protestant work ethic with which the countries of the West became rich;

"All hard work brings profit"
(Book of Proverbs 14:23),

"Remember the LORD (Yahweh) your God, for it is he who gives you the ability to produce wealth, and so confirms his covenant,"
(Deuteronomy 8:18)

The Koran of course does promise Muslims reward for some activities;

4:74   *"Whoso fighteth in the way of Allah, on him shall We bestow a vast reward."*,

9:29   *"Fight the unbelievers (that includes Jews and Christians and all other faiths) ...until they pay financial tribute having been subjected".*

This Koran verse calls for a special tax (historically 50%) to be levied on all non-Muslims in return for not being attacked, like a protection racket. Would that really be God's plan for the global economy?

Islamic Charity, called *"Zakat",* is regulated by Sharia Law, with providing funds for waging jihad and spreading Islam taking precedence over all other forms of charity funding. Islamic charities are obliged by Sharia Law to support Jihad. All the recognized commentaries on the Koran, which are the fundamental sources of Sharia Law, agree on this, giving a median figure of one-eighth of Zakat income as a minimum to be put to this cause.

Millions of Dollars of Gulf States oil revenue have accordingly been invested in building and running mosques, in the West as well as in Muslim countries, staffing them with fundamentalist preachers and teachers.

The type of charity which we in the West are more used to, helping the poor, the destitute and the needy does exist in Sharia but in accordance with the Koran;

28:86   *"never be a helper to the unbelievers",*

assistance to non-Muslims is forbidden absolutely. It is a far cry from our Western charity ethic of helping anyone and everyone in need.

In reality, Islamic charities operating in the West have had to compromise on these values or clandestinely function outside of national laws.

Evidently, Islamic values are at odds with ours.

Part Two - Islamic Beliefs

"See to it that no one takes you captive by philosophy and empty deceit, according to human tradition, according to the elemental spirits of the world, and not according to Christ" (Colossians 2:8)

Nearly all the core beliefs in Islam derive from the Koran, which is a compilation of the revelations which Mohammed claimed he received from the angel Jibril (allegedly archangel Gabriel), from his biographies known as *"Sirats"*, and from the Hadiths, the records of his sayings and deeds. The Koran is seen as being the authoritative Word of God, perfect and infallible, which must be obeyed in all circumstances. Whilst individual Muslims may believe all sorts of different things, their sacred texts are clear on what they, as Muslims, should believe.

The content of the Koran includes statements about Mohammed's god "Allah"; how powerful and how merciful he is, and about the benefits of believing in him. There is also a certain amount of legal content which forms the backbone of the Sharia Law. It also contains a lot of doom, destruction and hellfire predicted for those who do not believe in Allah and do not submit to Islam. This is religion based on fear; it brings no enlightenment, it does not teach spiritual growth or personal development, but in fact it teaches false science and untrue history.

The content of the Koran is very varied, ranging from the noble; -

41:34 *"The good deed and the evil deed are not alike. Repel the evil deed with one which is better, then lo ! he between whom and thee there was enmity (will become) as though he was a bosom friend"*

to the inexplicable; -

2:138 *"Colour from Allah, and who is better than Allah at colouring? We are His worshippers"*

Whilst much of the content of the Koran and other sacred texts is fairly straightforward religion, there are a number of topics in Islam which members of other faiths, agnostics and atheists find controversial. The following sections of the book will look at these, where we shall look in depth at specific areas of Islamic doctrine; misogyny and the inequality of women, sex-slavery, FGM, anti-Semitism and xenophobia, terrorism, jihad and tactical lying, which all in turn will come under the spotlight.

A recent documentary made in Denmark had TV crews openly going into a major mosque and interviewing Muslims there about their beliefs. The same production team then sent in undercover reporters with hidden cameras and found that the very same people in the very same mosque were saying things in private very different to those which they expressed publicly. This double standard of communication is sadly, very widespread in Islam, it is even formal Islamic doctrine to conceal one's true agenda to gain advantage over non-Muslims. This tactic has led to great confusion, for example with many Muslims publicly saying that the Islamic State is un-Islamic in what it does, a statement which is untrue. The Islamic State is truly Islamic in its nature and its doctrines are based on the Koran and Mohammed's original Islam. The Koran as you will see, contains a great many commands to attack non-Muslims, who are called *"Kuffir"* - infidels, unbelievers; to terrorize them until they submit to Islam and its ways. This is how Islam spread throughout the centuries until the modern era.

Today immigration is its major means of propagation and this has brought its doctrines into conflict with the core values of our Judeo-Christian society. Muslims are well aware that we reject most Islamic values which is why so often some of them will lie about what they believe. We have had scores of conversations with different Muslims who deny there are any incitements to violence and terrorism in the Koran. They deny it vehemently until one starts quoting such verses from the Koran, it really is such a predictable pattern. The next thing they tell us is that we do not know how to interpret the Koran, and so we talk about jihad which they say is an inner struggle. So, then we have to point out that the word *"Qatala"*, which is used more frequently in the Koran than the word Jihad, literally means to kill or slaughter. This stupid charade of pretence is used so often to try to deflect non-Muslims from the truth of what Islam really is, that you know there is really a cover up going on. In fact, a 2017 study by the Professor of Islamic Theology at the University of Vienna, commissioned by the Austrian Ministry for Foreign Affairs, found that many Islamists have an extensive understanding of Islam. It is the moderates who misunderstand its true nature.

We realise that for most moderate Muslims it can be their sheer and total embarrassment about what their religion teaches that causes them to try to hide the truth. Their discomfort with what the Koran says proves they are ready to leave Islam, a great harvest of souls of Muslim origin beckons. We just have to guide them through the process of getting free.

As for the Islamic beliefs themselves, it is clear many are incompatible with our values in the West. We believe that women are socially equal to men, they are no less intelligent, spiritual or honest, they are not a man's property and that no man has a right to beat them, seize them for sex-slavery or submit them to FGM. Indeed, wisdom teaches us that mistreating women brings them trauma, the untreated victims later become mothers with psychological difficulties who raise troubled children. These children then grow up into abusive adults. This repeating cycle is damaging for society. Reason goes against all the doctrines of demons taught by Islam like beating women, FGM, terrorism, xenophobia and deliberate lying. Anti-Semitism and other xenophobia, we regard as hate speech and the mass migration of many Muslims into the West has brought with it vicious attacks against Jews of a type seldom seen since the rise of fascism in the 1930's. Jews have been forced to leave their homes in areas where there are many Muslims and move to safer areas, thousands have even decided to leave Europe and relocate to Israel. We need to face reality and say that the evil prescriptions of the Koran and Hadiths are acted on by some Muslims, and even if this is a minority say 20% of them, we have a major problem affecting hundreds of thousands who have been taught to hate. Please don't for one minute think we are exaggerating or sensationalizing the issue. It is very real. Our motive here is solely to see an end brought to such evil. We must be very clear about this; the only hate speech you will find in this book is where we quote some of the Islamic sacred texts and other sources.

Women and Misogyny

The treatment of women in Islam has been much criticized in the West. Looking at the verses in the Koran about them it is easy to see the roots of this.

2:222 *"Menstruation is an illness..."*

The female part of the human reproductive system and its cycles are one of life's miracles: Whether one believes in God's intelligent design of creation, or in evolution, menstruation is a natural part of a woman's cycle. Would God really call it an illness?

5:6 *"(when preparing for prayer) if ye have had contact with a woman... then go to clean...your face and hands"*

This verse is one of the roots of segregation of the sexes in Islam, women are seen as impure, evil and unclean. Are women unclean and less spiritual than men? Well what about Kathryn Kuhlman, Aimee Semple Mcpherson and a whole host of other true Christian women of God? Does God think women are unclean, didn't He make them?

The Bible and Torah say (Genesis 1:27); -

"In the image of God, He created them male and female"

Women are made in the likeness of God.

For Mohammed, the opposite is true;

"Woman comes and goes in the form of a devil" (Sahih Muslim 8/3240)

In the Sahih Muslim 4:1296, Mohammed said that the majority of the inhabitants of hell are female. But surely God is not a misogynist, is He?

16:58-59   *"the birth of a female...the evil of that..."*

In the Koran, Allah seems to be. Sahih Bukhari 6/301 gives further revelation;

"Isn't it true that a woman can neither pray nor fast during her menses?'... He (Muhammad) said, 'This is the deficiency in her religion"

Islam says women are inferior;

4:34   *"men are in charge of women because Allah made one of them to excel over the other..."*

As noted, Ibn Kathir's commentary on the Koran explains it like this,

"Men are superior to women, and a man is better than a woman"

Given equality of opportunity who do better at school, boys or girls? National GCSE examination results in the UK show that two-thirds of the top grades went to girls.

Yet in Islam women are worth less;

4:11   *"Allah directs you in regard of your children's (inheritance), to the male a portion equal to that of two females... These are settled portions ordained by Allah"*

Violence against them is encouraged, and women must obey men in all things. Does the Koran promote domestic violence? Yes, it does!

4:34 (continued)   *"...As for those (women) from whom you fear disobedience.... beat them !"*

Some translations say to "***scourge***", to whip them.

"The Prophet said, 'A man will not be asked as to why he beat his wife" (Abu Dawud 11/2142)

It covers it up too, Sharia Courts have often been reported as quoting this Hadith to protect abusive men.

It is an unquestionable right in Islam for a man to beat his wife and Sharia Courts uphold it. Mohammed's wife Aisha said publicly to him regarding the status of women (Sahih Muslim 4/1039);

"You have made us equal to the dogs and the asses".

Just recently, a leading Imam in France is reported as saying;

"No matter how much good you bestow upon a woman, she will refuse it. Her selfishness drives her to refuse it... this holds true for all women, this is the nature of women."

The Koran even repeats some of these ideas to emphasize them;

2:228 *"men are a degree above women..."*

4:176 *"Unto the male is the equivalent of two shares of the female."*

Is Islam compatible with Human Rights which guarantee equality for women? Clearly not. As already noted, the European Court of Human Rights, the world's leading authority on the subject say Islam is incompatible with democracy. Obviously, what the Koran teaches so violates the principles of the United Nations Declaration of Human Rights that the Muslim nations had to make a rival charter to whitewash over the bigotry of Sharia.

Islam and Sharia have no room for gender equality, and other equal rights, freedom of expression and many other things which are now widespread in the West.

2:282 *"(in law)... call two witnesses from among your men... if two men be not at hand, then a man and two women"*

Do women tell more lies than men? Are women statistically less honest? Google it, most surveys find the opposite. A conversation of Mohammed's is recorded in which he said,

"Is not the evidence of two women equal to the witness of one man? This is the deficiency in her intelligence." (Sahih Bukhari 6/301)

Mohammed also said;

"O womenfolk...you lack common sense, you fail in religion and rob the wisdom of the wise... your lack of common sense can be determined from the fact that the evidence of two women is equal to one man. That is a proof." (Sahih Muslim 1/142)

Now this is what academics call a circular argument, using one's own conclusion as a logical justification of itself. In recent years two girls Nicole Barr in the UK and Neha Ramu from India have scored 162 in IQ tests showing a higher intelligence than even Albert Einstein and Stephen Hawking. There is the proof that women are by nature no less intelligent than men.

There are still places where they do not allow women to drive, and some Islamic countries women are not legally allowed to go out of their home without the permission of a male and without a male guardian accompanying them. In Saudi Arabia, a woman was stopped whilst driving herself to the Emergency Room at hospital because there was no man around to help her, the policemen who stopped her escorted her to hospital and then arrested her once she had been treated.

Indeed, in Saudi Arabia following their first ever elections involving women, the female politicians elected have been forced to sit in a room separate from the men and watch the debates on screen, they may only speak by intercom when given permission. A Dutch academic recently reporting of the implementation of Sharia law in the UK legal system found what she described as the *"captivity"* of the women subject to it. In many Sharia law countries women are required to be completely covered from head to foot with only their eyes showing, even their hands must be covered. In Iran, the fine for "bad hijab" is 9 million Rials.

Surah 24:31 *"And tell the believing women to reduce (some) of their vision and guard their private parts and not expose their adornment except that which (necessarily) appears thereof and to wrap (a portion of) their headcovers over their chests and not expose their adornment..."*

The historical origin of the covering up of women like this was to stop them being stolen by other men. It is a sign of them being a man's property. It is worth noting that the Islamic requirement of women being covered from head to foot with a burka does not lead to less sexual harassment. On the contrary, women in cities like Cairo and Tehran report very high levels of unwelcome attention from men.

Psychologically, entirely covering a woman in uniform black shapeless robes says she has no personality, no individuality, no right to express herself openly, with no rights in herself whatsoever. She is nothing more than a possession, no more than a sex object which brings temptation to men if even her hands or ankles are uncovered. In Islam, the main reason women are segregated from men is because they are seen as being an unclean evil temptation. Indeed, the Burka and Hijab are the ultimate statement of women as owned objects whose primary function is the sexual gratification of men.

Slavery and FGM

Slavery of both men and women still exists in the Islamic world. Mohammed had slaves himself and the Hadiths tell of this;

"There came a slave and pledged allegiance to Allah's Apostle on migration; he (the Holy Prophet) did not know that he was a slave. Then there came his master and demanded him back, whereupon Allah's Apostle said: Sell him to me. And he bought him for two black slaves, and he did not afterwards take allegiance from anyone until he had asked him whether he was a slave (or a free man)"
(Sahih Muslim 10/3901)

Following Mohammed's example Sharia Law allows slavery.

"Mohammed had many male and female slaves. He used to buy and sell them, but he purchased more slaves than he sold, especially after God empowered him by His message... His purchases of slaves were more than he sold. He was used to renting out and hiring many slaves, but he hired more slaves than he rented out."
(Ibn Qayyim al-Jawziyya, Zad al-Ma'ad, Part 1, p. 160)

The slave trade was an important part of the economy of Islam even before the Western colonial powers began using slave labour in their empires. Despite the abolition of slavery in the West, slavery continues to be widespread in many parts of the Islamic world. According to a report by E. Benjamin Skinner in TIME magazine, there are in Pakistan, *'millions of forced labourers in 'private prisons' across the country'.* (**Pakistan's Forgotten Plight: Modern Day Slavery**, published October 27, 2009) Another report in the Telegraph in 2009 estimated there to be at least half a million slaves in Mauritania alone. (Nick Meo - **Half a million African slaves are at the heart of Mauritania's presidential election** - Telegraph, July 12, 2009) Senegalese anthropologist Tidiane N'Diaye, author of the book **"The Veiled Genocide"** (Gallimard), estimates that there are currently 46 million people in slavery across the Islamic world, 71% of them women and girls. Clearly the problem is widespread, but because of the Islamic State it is the sex slavery of women that has been the focus of Western attention. The Koran demotes women to the status of slaves or items of personal property;

2:221 *"A slave...is better than an unbelieving woman"*

When wives are just possessions, a man may have more than one;

4:3 *"marry of the women, who seem good to you, 2,3 or 4..."*

Polygamy is legal in Sharia law. In the West, some Muslims have an official wife under civil law and other wives who they have "married" in a mosque. Certain provisions of Sharia treat women as chattels, just a man's property;

4:20   *"If ye wish to exchange one wife for another..."*

Hadith Ibn Ishaq 593 says that according to Mohammed;

"Women are plentiful, and you can easily change one for another"

Mohammed's farewell sermon included this on women;

"Allah permits you to shut them in separate rooms and to beat them....for they are (like) domestic animals with you and do not possess anything for themselves." (Al Tabari 9/1754 p113)

Under strict Sharia Law women are mere possessions of men with their legal status and identity determined through their husband, father, owner or other male guardian. In addition to having their wives, men are allowed to keep other women captive as sex-slaves.

33:50   *"We have made lawful to thee (for sex), thy wives...and those (slaves) whom your right hand possesses"*

4:24   *"Married women are forbidden to you save those captives whom your right hand possesses"*

These are amongst the Koran verses that the Islamic State often quote to justify their enslavement of non-Muslim women and even young girls as sex-slaves. They even deny it is rape to take a non-Muslim captive and force sex upon them. The issue was openly addressed in the May 2015, Issue 9, of their Dabiq magazine, in an article entitled **"Slave-Girls or Prostitutes"**, where they say they are;

"reviving a prophetic Sunnah (Islamic practice), which both the Arab and non-Arab enemies of Allah had buried. By Allah we brought it back by the edge of the sword, we did not do so through pacifism, negotiations, democracy or elections. We established it accordance to the prophetic way, with blood-red swords, not with fingers for voting or tweeting."

They justify this as being wholly Islamic quoting Koran verses; -

23:5-6   *"They who guard their private parts, except from their wives, and from those which their right hand possesses (slaves), are blameless (free from sin)"*

24:32 *"Marry...your female slaves..."*

4:3 *"Marry women of your choice, Two or three or four... or (a captive) that your right hands possess, that will be more suitable"*

2:221 *"indeed a slave woman...is better than a (free) Mushrikah (non-Muslim/unbeliever)"*

In their Dabiq magazine, Issue 9 they also quote numerous Hadiths;

"Approaching any married woman is fornication, except for a woman who has been enslaved' (Al-Hakim narrated it and said, 'It is an authentic Hadith according to the criteria of Al-Bukhari and Muslim')" The Sirat is witness to our Prophet's raiding of the Kuffir. He would kill their men and enslave their women and children.... The scholars of Sirat mentioned that the Prophet took... slave-girls as concubines... followers who treaded the path of the Prophet...we almost cannot find a companion who didn't practice "saby" (sex-slavery)"

Studying this article carefully leaves one in no doubt that the Islamic State is truly Islamic, conforming itself to what the Koran and Hadiths say, and thus staying faithful to Mohammed's true Islam which itself also demonstrated such male tyranny over women and girls. The Islamic State even produced a booklet of Islamic guidance for dealing with sex-slaves, **"Questions and Answers on Taking Captives and Slaves"**, which clarifies their status and how they should be treated.

According to the Caliphate (Dabiq, Issue 9, Questions 2 & 6) sex-slavery is permissible in Islam for anyone who is;

"unbelieving [a Non-Muslim]... captured and brought into the abode of Islam..., after the imam distributes them"

"It is permissible to buy, sell, or give as a gift, female captives and slaves, for they are merely property, which can be disposed of"

A leading professor, Saud Saleh, at the prestigious Al-Azhar University in Cairo, Egypt is reported to have said that Allah allows Muslim men to rape non-Muslim women to humiliate them whilst also confirming their right to take unbelievers as sex slaves. A leading Muslim in the UK said he thought young Muslims were joining the Islamic State "for the women", in other words to have sex-slaves. After being captured the women and girls are sold at slave auctions where they are stripped naked for the buyers. Credible witness reports from girls who have escaped the Islamic State confirm not only this, but also the fact that they were later traded on several times from jihadi to jihadi.

Girls as young as 6 have been taken and sold according to NGO charity reports, with girls under nine fetching the highest prices. These reports confirm that today some sex-slaves captured by the Islamic State are being sold to rich men in other Muslim countries like Saudi Arabia and Turkey. This sex slavery is nothing new in Islam, The Islamic warriors who invaded Spain in 711AD were promised *"ravishingly beautiful"* women as booty, and the women's slave market in Tunis only effectively closed in 1880, after continuously trading for over a thousand years since the days of the Fatimid Caliphate, even throughout the so called *"Golden Age"* of Islam. It was the French colonial powers who closed it down.

But it did not start there, Sahih Muslim recounts a conversation with Mohammed (3/432);

"...we said, 'Oh! Allah's messenger, we have female captives, and we are concerned about their prices, what is your opinion about coitus interruptus?' The Prophet said, 'Do you really do that? It is better for you not to, any soul that Allah has destined to exist shall surely come to live."

Do you understand what they are saying there? They do not want to lose money on a sex-slave by getting her pregnant and not being able to re-sell her. And as we have seen, Mohammed kept and traded sex slaves too. In today's Islamic State women are taken captive as and held as sex-slaves being sold on from one man to another. Could it be that the Islamic State might be a lot like Mohammed's original Islam?

Female Genital Mutilation (female circumcision) is a prescribed part of Sharia Law being part of the *"fitrah"*, basic Muslim hygiene, and thus is *"khatna"*, a religious obligation - (see Bukhari 7/72/779 and Muslim 2/495). Mohammed himself is reported as saying;

"Circumcision is a law for men and a preservation of honour for women" (see Sahih Ahmad 5/75; Abu Dawud, Adab 167).

According to John of Damascus (676-749) in "**The Fount of Knowledge**", FGM was the norm for Muslim women in his day. The Eighth Century classic manual of Islamic Sacred Sharia Law, "**Reliance of the Traveller**" by Ahmad ibn Naqib al-Misri says;

"Circumcision is obligatory (for every male and female) by cutting off the piece of skin on the glans of the penis of the male, but circumcision of the female is by cutting out the clitoris (this is called Hufaad)". (translation by Kellers, paragraph e4.3)

It has just come to light that the Islamic State issued a fatwa in 2015 ordering that all new-born girls had to be subject to this Hufaad.

As well as the beliefs which are rooted directly in what the Koran and other sacred texts say, Islamic society also has secondary belief systems which underlay diverse practices like sewing up the vagina (especially after temporary marriages and for the selling on of sex-slaves), right through to marabouting (Islamic witchcraft). Whilst these practices are not part of the main cannon of Islam, they are fairly particular to Islamic culture.

Racism and Xenophobia

The Koran also contains much racist, anti-Semitic and xenophobic content (you will find a further selection starting on p213);

2:96 *"you will find them (the Jews) the greediest of mankind"*

2:90 *"evil is that for which they sell their souls"*

3:78 *"they lie about God"*

3:110 *"If only the people of the book (the Jews and the Christians) had faith...but most of them are perverted transgressors"*

4:51 *"They believe in idols and false deities"*

4:161 *"their taking of usury...their devouring of people's wealth by false pretences."*

5:13 *"You will not cease to discover treachery in all but a few of them"*

5:41 *"Jews...will listen to any lie."*

5:45 *"...are unjust wrong-doers"*

5:51 *"Take not Jews and Christians as friends"*

5:53 *"they...have become losers"*

5:58 *"They are a folk that understand not."*

5:59 *"...most are evil-livers,"*

5:60 *"...apes and swine."*

5:62 *"You see many of them vying in sin and transgression and devouring illicit gain. Verily evil is what they do."*

5:63 *"rabbis and priests...evil is their handiwork"*

5:64 *"We have cast among them enmity and hatred. Often they light a fire of war, their effort is for corruption"*

5:82 *"You will find the most vehement of mankind, in hostility to those who believe, to be the Jews."*

7:138 *"Israel...a people...given up to idols"*

9:29 *"Fight against such of those who have been given the Scripture (Jews and Christians) but do not believe in Allah...until they pay tribute and are brought low."*

9:30 *"How perverse they are,"*

9:31 *"they have taken as lords besides God, their rabbis and monks."*

9:34 *"rabbis and monks wantonly devour the wealth of mankind and prevent people from the way."*

62:5 *"those who are entrusted with the Law of Moses, yet not applying it are like asses carrying books."*

"the hour of resurrection will not be established unless you fight the Jews and kill them...until the Jews would hide...and even a stone or tree would say 'Muslim, there is a Jew here, come and kill him."
(Bukhari 4/52/177, also quoted in Sahih Muslim 49/6985)

Isn't some of this hate speech? Look again at Surah 9:29 above, look at this last quote again. Isn't all this hate speech? An incitement to violence? Could this be why a survey undertaken by ICM in 2015 found that British Muslims are three times more likely to have anti-Semitic opinions than the general population.

How come we get so upset about people reading **"Mein Kampf"** yet quite happily allow all the anti-Semitic, racist and xenophobic incitements in the Islamic sacred books to be propagated even in our schools and universities, not to mention the bookshops on every high street, as well as by all the mosques and Islamic associations?

There are other Hadiths in Bukhari's volumes that give examples of Mohammed's own behaviour towards Jews, including the ritual beheading of 600 men in a single day (some sources say it might have been 900) and the enslavement of women and children. Eventually he drove all of the Jews out of the Medina area where he was based at the time. (see Bukhari 4/2813, 5/4117-25, 5/4368-73 and Ibn Ishaq p466, p693) Some historians have estimated that altogether he exterminated about 24,000 Jews during his lifetime.

And once again the call of hatred against the Jews and Christians (and other non-Muslims) is not just historical, recent statements include the following; -

"Read history and you will understand that the Jews of yesterday are the evil fathers of the Jews today, who are of evil offspring, infidels, distorters of other's words, calf-worshippers, prophet-murderers, prophecy deniers, the scum of the human race whom Allah cursed and turned into apes and pigs." (Imam at the Grand Mosque in Mecca 2002)

"Jews rule the world by proxy, they get others to fight and die for them. They invented socialism, communism, human rights and democracy so that persecuting them would appear wrong..." (The Prime Minister of a "moderate" Muslim country 2003)

"Their Bible has no light and no teachings. The Bible today is just a bunch of notes that were written down by people who lie about God, His prophets and His Bible...Those who do these things...are descendants of Satan...they fabricated a Jewish history book full of promises to Abraham, Isaac and Jacob that He would give them the land of Palestine. The Jews are the Jews. There never was among them a supporter of peace. They are all liars; true criminals, terrorists, therefore it is necessary to slaughter and murder them...according to the Words of Allah...it is forbidden to have mercy on them, any place you encounter them, kill them and kill the Americans likewise. Have no mercy, murder them everywhere." (Palestinian TV, Nov 3rd 1998, Oct 13th 2000)

In the standard Muslim Faatiha prayer, Muslims make negative mention of *"those who earned your anger"* and *"those who went astray"*. A search of Koran commentaries will reveal the former group to be *"Jews"* and *"Zionists"*, whilst the latter, to quote al-islam.org, are *"Christians, who... believed in the Father, the Son, and the Holy Ghost instead of... the worship of Allah"*.

Are Muslims focussing negativity against Jews and Christians each and every time they pray? Yes, they are.

Tactical Lying

Deliberate lying, known in Islam as *"Taqiyya"*, and concealing the truth, known as *"Kithman"*, are important principles in the Islam. Essentially Taqiyya is tactical lying to promote or protect Islam. In Hadith Ahmad 6/549, it is recorded that Mohammed said;

"Lying is wrong except the lie of a man to his wife, to lie to an enemy, or a lie to settle trouble between people."

The Koran clearly designates all non-Muslims as enemies so lying to them is sadly normal, even encouraged.

4:101   *"the unbelievers are ever unto you open enemies"*

The author Sami Makarem in his recent book **"Dissimulation in Islam"** (Ibrahim translation p7) concluded;

"Taqiyya is of fundamental importance to Islam. Practically every sect agrees to it and practices it. We can go so far as to say that the practice of Taqiyya is mainstream in Islam, and that those few sects not practising it diverge from the mainstream...Taqiyya is very prevalent in Islamic politics, especially in the modern era."

A good example of how tactical lying is employed is illustrated by the public claims of the Council for American Islamic Relations (CAIR) to have never been involved with the Muslim Brotherhood or to have supported any terrorist activity or organisation. However, the US Court of Appeals fifth section found *"ample evidence to the contrary"* linking it to the Izz al-Din al-Qasem Brigades. Even the wider question as to whether Islam is really *"the religion of peace"* is subject to this kind of deception.

Another example of tactical lying is found in the English translation of the classic Islamic Sharia law book; **"The Reliance of the Traveller"**, where it talks about female circumcision (FGM). In the original Arabic it says; -

"Circumcision is obligatory (for every male and female) by cutting off the piece of skin on the glans of the penis of the male, but circumcision of the female is by cutting out the clitoris (this is called Hufaad)" (Original version, translation by Kellers)

but the recent translation made available in the West reads;

"Circumcision is obligatory (O: for both men and women). For men it consists of removing the prepuce from the penis, and for women, removing the prepuce (Arabic 'Bazr') of the clitoris (not the clitoris itself, as some mistakenly assert)" (1997 Revised Edition)

However, most scholars agree that the Arabic word *"Bazr"* means the clitoris, as Kecia Ali in her book Sexual Ethics in Islam (Oneworld Publications) points out. The intent to deceive is very evident here.

Indeed, the Reliance of the Traveller itself says that in some circumstances tactical lying is obligatory;

"When it is possible to achieve an aim by lying but not by telling the truth, it is permissible to lie if attaining the goal is permissible, and lying is obligatory if the goal is obligatory." (Para r8.2)

As Jihad is an obligatory sacred duty under Sharia Law then endeavouring to make Jihad succeed by employing tactical lying is obligatory too. The Boston marathon bombers denied following any terror group just weeks before planting Al-Qaeda designed bombs.

Websites such as answering-islam.org, thereligionofpeace.com, jihadwatch.org and shariawatch.org.uk have reported many similar instances of Taqiyya and Kithman.

"Tawriya" and *"Muruna"* are similar deceptions, the former involves the deliberate use of statements with double meanings to give misleading impressions whilst Muruna, which translates as flexibility, allows a Muslim to hide his objective; this may involve a would-be terrorist adopting western style of dress, even by wearing a Christian cross, or lying about being a Muslim to get a job with security clearance. On another level, it could involve not telling a person the full truth about Islam in order to get them to convert to it. Calling it the religion of peace is Muruna. Another related deception is Hudna, making a truce or agreement that is expected to be broken, they are all further examples of tactical lying. They are by no means rare.

So, whenever anyone points out that the Koran contains verses that seem like incitations to violence (see the following chapter for a list of some), western Imams tell us authoritatively that these verses are only to be interpreted allegorically or poetically.

In truth, there are a few allegorical passages in the Koran and these are self-evident, like;

2:223 *"Your women are like tilth for you to go to when and however you will."*

But what does the Koran itself say about how it is to be interpreted?

69:41 *"It (the Koran) is not poet's speech"*

44:58 *"Verily We have made this (Koran) easy in thy tongue, in order that simple people may give heed..."*

54:17 *"And We have indeed made the Koran simple to understand."*

That's quite clear, so let's look at how Mohammed himself interpreted verses from the Koran, taking the example of verse

9:5 *"kill the unbelievers wherever you find them".*

So how did the author of the Koran interpret it himself; literally, or metaphorically? Mohammed took the Koran very literally;

"I decided to order a man to lead prayer and then take a flame and burn all those who had not left their houses for the prayer, burning them alive inside their homes." (Sahih Bukhari 11/626)

Under Sharia, attending Islamic prayers in obligatory and says children should be beaten if they don't want to go;

"Command a boy to pray when he reaches the age of seven years. When he becomes ten years old, then beat him for prayer"
(Sahih Abu Dawud 2/494)

Besides, Sharia Law is the conclusive proof that the Koran is to be taken to the letter, it is based on interpreting the Koran as literally as it can be. Sharia Law is a fundamental part of all Islamic culture, so any insinuation that the Koran is to be taken allegorically is tactical lying.

Moreover, a 2013 study by Professor Koopmans from the Berlin Social Sciences Centre found that 75% of the Muslims in his international study believed there is only one possible interpretation of the Koran, obviously that has to be the literal one.

And what about all the genocides in history committed in the name of Islam? We'll look at those in a later section of this book. Weren't they literal obedience to the commands in the Koran to kill non-Muslims?

Philosophically it is clear that if tactical lying is ever used by anyone, then they themselves must actually be aware that what they are trying to cover up is wrong, otherwise they would not need to lie or hide the truth.

Those who say they know the Koran, but still pretend that Islam is the "Religion of Peace", must know deep down inside of them that all these exhortations to violence are wrong. Remember that the San Bernardino gunman is on record as having said; *"Islam is a religion of peace"*, not long before going on violent jihad. By implication the tactical lying is a tacit acknowledgement that the violent content of the Islamic faith is morally wrong. When you know you're in the right, you don't need to lie, and you don't need to be violent to force others to agree with you.

As St Paul said; *"For we cannot do anything against the truth, but only for the truth."* (2 Corinthians 13:8)

Terrorism

Recent news reports about the former head of Islamic State operations in Iraq say that he used to read the Koran with suicide bombers just before they went out on mission. It sounds like it strengthens the resolve of terrorists, so what does the Koran truly say about this barbarism? In fact, it contains more than one hundred and twenty verses that command holy war and violence against non-Muslims. Here's a selection of some of these verses which illustrate plainly just how central the call to terrorism is in Islam.

2:190	*"Fight for the cause of Allah..."*
2:191	*"Slay the unbelievers wherever you find them"*
2:216	*"Warfare is obligatory for you, even if you dislike it."*
2:244	*"Fight for the cause of Allah..."*
3:151	*"We shall cast terror into the hearts of those who do not believe (in Islam)"*
4:76	*"Those who believe fight for the cause of Allah."*
4:95	*"Allah has granted a higher rank to those who fight with their wealth over those who sit at home."*
4:101	*"The non-Muslims are an open enemy to you..."*
4:89, 4:91	*"then take them and kill them wherever ye find them"*

4:104	"Relent not in pursuit of the enemy."
5:33	"...enemies of Allah...will be killed or crucified...or have their hands and feet cut off"
7:4	"How many a town have we destroyed...our terror came upon them"
8:1	"The spoils of war belong to Allah and His messenger..."
8:12	"instil terror into the hearts of the non-Muslims...then smite their necks..."
8:39	"Make war until... all religion is that of Allah"
8:41	"...ye take the spoils of war...if ye believe in Allah"
8:60	"Make ready all thou canst of force..."
8:65	"O Prophet exhort the believers to battle...because the non-Muslims are a people without intelligence"
8:67	"It is not... to have captives...till slaughter is made in the land."
8:74	"Those who believed and left their homes behind to fight for the cause of Allah...these are true believers."
9:5	"Kill the unbelievers wherever ye find them, take them, besiege them and lie in ambush for them everywhere."
9:14	"Fight them, Allah will punish them at your hands"
9:29	"Fight the non-Muslims...until they pay a (monetary) tribute with surrender"
9:41	"Go forth, heavily or lightly armed..."
9:73	"Make war on the non-Muslims..."
9:111	"...believers.... shall fight for the cause of Allah and so kill and be killed..."

9:123   *"O ye who believe, fight those unbelievers who are near to you..."*

25:14   *"...pray for many destructions..."*

25:52   *"Do not listen to non-Muslims, but fight forcefully against them"*

33:60, 61   *"We verily shall urge thee on against them... Accursed, they will be seized wherever found and slain with a (fierce) slaughter"*

47:4   *"When you meet the non-Muslims, smite their necks...and those who die fighting for the cause of Allah, He will never let their deeds be lost"*

48:20   *"Allah promises you much booty you will capture..."*

48:29   *"Those who follow Mohammed are merciless with disbelievers..."*

60:4   *"...having renounced you non-Muslims, enmity and hatred is between us forever...until ye believe in Allah"*

61:10-11   *"O ye who believe. Shall I show you a covenant that will save you from a painful doom? Ye should believe in Allah and His messenger and should fight for the cause of Allah with all your wealth and with the lives of your people. This is best for you if you knew it"*

5:101   *"Ask not questions about that which has been made plain..."*

4:47   *"The commands of Allah must be carried out!"*

9:20   *"Those who believe, have left their homes and used their wealth to fight for the cause...are of much greater worth... These...achieve Allah's salvation"*

48:16   *"Ye will be called...to fight...if ye turn away...He will punish you with a painful doom"*

69:41   *"It (the Koran) is not poet's speech."*

3:132, 4:59, 8:20   *"Obey Allah..."*

Wherever it says unbelievers or disbelievers that includes you and me, indeed all non-Muslims, and even other Muslims who don't believe the same type of Islam. So, it seems as if the Islamic State is right about the Koran being the rationale for their reign of terror, including their recent attacks in Paris. Isn't that a copy of the Koran there in the hand of the suspected ringleader in those photos? Wasn't it said of the Imam who was part of the Barcelona terror group that he knew the Koran better than anyone else? Would those massacres have taken place if the Koran didn't contain such violent commands?

And it is not just the Islamic State, the Muslim Brotherhood logo includes, under the Koran and crossed swords symbols, the phrase *"Make Ready"*, which refers to verse 8:60;

"Make ready all you have of force... to terrorize the enemies of Allah (the infidels/non-Muslims) ..."

Even the regular obligatory five times a day Du'aa-e-Qunoot prayer ends with every Muslim declaring;

"torment is going to overtake the infidels".

Islam is a religion of war!

Of late we have seen numerous "lone-wolf" terror attacks where the attackers are not really connected to larger Islamist groups. The San Bernardino killers weren't real members of the Islamic State. There is increasingly more and more terror now being perpetrated in the name of Islam by Muslims inspired by, rather than belonging to, the Islamic State, Al Qaeda, and other Islamist brands. That inspiration ultimately comes from the Koran.

Terror takes other forms too. In certain UK jails, Muslims were running *"jizya"* protection rackets forcing non-Muslim prisoners to pay a financial tribute tax in order to not be beaten up. And negative Islamic attitudes towards non-Muslim women are apparent in the large number of rapes and sexual assaults carried out by Muslim immigrants in the West. In the UK thousands of young girls have been targetted by Muslim "grooming gangs".

In Cologne, Germany, a vast apparently organised gang of as many as 1,000 Middle Eastern and North African Muslims went raping, sexually assaulting, and stealing from, non-Muslim women coming home from New Year's Eve celebrations. Over 500 women were attacked by them in one night. This too is Islamic terror because it comes from an Islamic mindset, one which does not respect women, especially non-Muslims. These attacks were similar to those carried out on women without hijabs in Tahrir Square, Cairo during the Arab Spring demonstrations.

Imam Shahid Medhi in Copenhagen, said this on the issue;

"Women are not entitled to respect when they walk around without a Hijab. They are to blame for it when they are attacked..."

Is he saying to Muslim men that it is OK to rape non-Muslim women just because they don't wear a burka? The local Salafist Imam in Cologne said the attacks had been the fault of the women because they had been *"wearing perfume"*. Isn't this a prime example of tactical lying, blaming the victims for being attacked. A recent article in a Swedish newspaper the Daily Caller reported;

"But under Sharia, this rape culture also impacts upon Swedish women as they are 'infidels' and, as such, are... according to Allah's teachings... sanctioned targets for rape by Muslim men. Such an Islamic belief system has born witness to a drastic increase in rapes in Sweden... more than a thousand-fold... since first opening its doors to Muslim immigration.
A 1996 Swedish National Council for Crime Prevention report bears this out. It noted that Muslim immigrants from North Africa were 23 times more likely to commit rape than Swedish men. It is no wonder why today Sweden is deemed the rape capital of the Western world."

Worse still the media and Police forces seem to have been caught covering it all of this up for "political" reasons. A false report saying that all was well appeared on the local authority website in Cologne the morning following the attacks. It took five days for the truth to leak out and then reports of other similar attacks in other German cities came to light as well. At the time of writing most of the attackers so far traced are Syrian and North African migrants and there is, apparently, evidence the attacks were planned in advance.

And the goal of all this, to provoke fear and thereby gain power by appeasement; -

8:12   *"instil terror into the hearts of the unbelievers"*

2:193   *"Wage (mental & physical) war on them (the non-Muslims) until there is no more idolatry and all religion is for Allah. When they desist let there be no hostility"*

Local authorities in Germany and Austria have issued guidelines for women advising them not to go out alone, or to wear clothes that loosely cover the whole body. But this is equivalent to creeping Sharia, established unconstitutionally, enforced by rape and sexual harassment. Sex crimes are terrorism just as much as killing and maiming. The Islamic State uses rape as a systematic weapon against Yazidi and Christian communities in Iraq. United Nations Resolution 1820 (2008) recognized sexual violence as a weapon, and that the perpetrators can be punished, noting that; *"rape is a kind of slow murder"*.

It is recorded that Mohammed said;

"I have been ordered by Allah to strive against the people until they testify that none has the right to be worshipped but Allah" (Bukhari 1/24)

The aim is to establish a worldwide dominion of Islam, a world Caliphate with nothing but Islamic religious law and values. Recent terror attacks in Paris, Berlin, London, Manchester, Nice and elsewhere have targeted our way of life; football games, music and dancing, cafes and restaurants. Islam doesn't like our social freedoms. Islam seeks to destroy everything un-Islamic.

Clearly Islam could only be a peaceful religion if everyone in the world was subjugated to it. That is impossible. Yet sadly, and most ironically, the reality is that the bulk of victims of Islamic terrorism are Muslims themselves in Islamic nations. But what is truly bizarre is the Islamic notion that a martyr can be someone who attacks innocent people. This is horribly twisted. A true martyr is not someone who is armed. The dictionary definition is; *"a person who willingly suffers death rather than renounce his or her religion, is put to death or endures great suffering on behalf of any belief, principle, or cause"*.

In no way do suicide bombers qualify as true martyrs.

Jihad and Qatala

"Jihad" is the duty imposed by Sharia Law derived from all of these terrorist verses in the Koran and Hadiths. Jihad literally means to fight, strive, or struggle. According to Mohammed it is a physical thing;

"[the] act which elevates the position of a man in Paradise to a grade one hundred (higher)... Jihad in the way of Allah! Jihad in the way of Allah!" (Sahih Muslim 20/4645)

"Allah desires killing them (non-Muslims/unbelievers) to manifest the religion" (Ishaq; Life of Muhammad, trans Hisham, p484)

As jihad is obligatory for all Muslims under Sharia Law, it is obviously not an inner mental struggle but an outward active one. It is truly striving for Islam to rule over everything religiously, politically, physically, by persuasion, force or trickery, by fair means or foul. It is thus both an individual and communal duty to spread Islam by whatever means possible, including genocide, and impose on the world a Caliphate with an Islamic government and Sharia legal system. Evidently Jihad includes waging psychological warfare against the unbelievers to create duress.

Islamic historian/philosopher Ibn Khaldun (1332-1406) who greatly influenced the Ottoman Caliphate said this; -

"In the Muslim community, the holy war is a religious duty, because of the universalism of the Muslim mission and the obligation to convert everybody to Islam either by persuasion or by force... The other religious groups did not have a universal mission, and the holy war was not a religious duty for them, save only for purposes of defense... Islam is under obligation to gain power over other nations." (The Muqudimmah, Trans F Rosenthal, Pantheon Books, 1958, volume 1, p473)

Islamic scholars and leaders throughout the centuries have echoed the call to physical Jihad. Many Muslims when speaking to non-Muslims pretend that it is just a form of internal struggle, but that sadly is tactical lying. Look at the way in Turkey that the one minute's silence to pay respect to the dead in the recent Paris attacks was interrupted with mass chants of "Allahu-Akbar". Sadly, we see a very large number of Muslims who applaud Islamic terrorism. Regularly Twitter is awash with messages of support for the latest successful terrorists.

The Dictionary of Islam by renowned scholar T P Hughes (1838-1911) explains Jihad like this;

"A religious war with those who are unbelievers in the mission of Muhammad. It is an incumbent religious duty, established in the Qur'an and in the Traditions as a divine institution, and enjoined specially for the purpose of advancing Islam."

Ayatollah Khomeini was probably the most influential Muslim cleric in the last hundred years, he expressed it like this;

"Islam makes it incumbent on all adult males, provided they are not disabled or incapacitated, to prepare themselves for the conquest of other countries so that the writ of Islam is obeyed in every country of the world. But those who study Islamic Holy War will understand why Islam

wants to conquer the whole world. Islam says 'kill all the unbelievers... kill them, put them to the sword and scatter them. Whatever good there is exists thanks to the sword and in the shadow of the sword. People cannot be made to be obedient except by the sword.' The sword is the key to paradise which can be opened only for holy warriors.... There are hundreds of other Koranic verses and Hadiths urging Muslims to make war and fight."* (From the Little Green Book, Khomeini 1979)

So how did this most influential of Muslim clerics interpret the Koran, as a way of peace, or as a way of war? Abu Bakr al-Baghdadi, Caliph of the Islamic State, with a doctorate in Islamic Studies agrees that true Jihad is a way of war. A recent video released by the Islamic State shows its members reciting the Koran prior to beheading captives

47:4 *"So, when you meet (in fighting Jihad in Allah's Cause), those who disbelieve, smite at their necks (behead them) till when you have killed and wounded many of them, binding a bond firmly (on them, i.e. taking them as captives) ... Thus [you] are ordered by Allah to continue in carrying out Jihad against the disbelievers till they embrace Islam..."*

Mohammed himself did the same on a big scale to the Jews from Banu Qurayza;

"The messenger of God went out into the marketplace of Medina and had trenches dug in it; then he sent for them and had them beheaded in those trenches. They were brought out to him in groups... They numbered 600 or 700, the largest estimate says they were between 800 and 900." (Al-Tabari, Vol 8, the Victory of Islam p35-36)

This proves that Mohammed himself acted on the Koran verses in a literal manner. The word jihad in various forms occurs about 34 times in the Koran, and has three general meanings; to fight Holy War *"Jihad"* (yajahid) which is by far the most common meaning, more rarely it is used to mean inner struggle *"Ijtihad"* (yajtahid) and duress *"Yajhad"*, but far more important is the word *"Qatala"* (verb)/ *"Qital"* (noun) which is the most revealing of the true meaning of the Koran.

Qatala/Qital in various forms is used about 170 times and means literally to kill, slaughter or fight militarily. In reality, the discourse about jihad as being an inner struggle is a tactical lie to divert attention away from the clear message to kill, to slay and to wage war throughout the text.

Next time anyone tells you jihad is an inner struggle ask them what Qatala is. It means to literally kill as in verse 9:5.

9:5 *"slay the non-Muslims wherever ye find them..."*

Is this literal nature of the incitements to violence in the Koran why we see so many new converts to Islam getting involved in Islamist terrorism? It seems obviously so. It is also the reason why there is almost no theological debate by moderate Muslims against so-called extremists?

Islamists like the Islamic State and Al Qaeda are quite willing to quote verses from the Koran and other holy books which give religious justification to their atrocities. So-called moderates say they disagree with them but there is no public debate from them about whether what the Islamists say is valid or not. Surely if they think the Islamists wrong couldn't they quote some Koran verses or something? But no, all they can do is keep on saying "Islam is religion of peace" and not much more.

In fact, the moderate Imams who, when asked about terrorism and genocides pretend that the Koran should be interpreted allegorically, give the game away when asked about Sharia Law where they apply the literal meaning of the Koran to the letter. The truth is that the Islamists are right; true Islam is violent. Over 95% of all terrorism in the world is Islamic. There are some nice peaceable verses in the Koran but they were abrogated, rendered invalid, as we will explain in a later chapter on that subject. Take a look at what Mohammed's life was really like too, if you're not sure what true Islam looks like.

Using the Koran to try to debate Islamists into a peace-loving mindset cannot work! That's why the moderates don't try. Hoping that Islam might somehow evolve into something peaceful will not work either because each new generation of Muslims can discover all the Koran's terrorist verses for themselves. As the book itself, and Mohammed's personal example, both say that it should be taken literally, then Islamic terror will perpetuate itself as long as the Koran is believed to be the word of god. The highest authority in Islam, it is the product of 7th Century barbarianism and cannot change or be updated.

Besides, moderate Islam is really only a by-product of Muslims' exposure to Christianity, Buddhism, Humanism and our free Western lifestyle. It does not come from the Koran and Hadiths. According to Muslim-born author Nonie Darwish, whose books include "Cruel and Usual Punishment: The terrifying global implications of Islamic law" (Nelson);

"American public-school kids have become the victims of Islamic propaganda and misinformation that paints Islam in sharp contrast to how Islam is actually being taught today in 54 Muslim countries. While Muslim kids in the Islamic world are being taught to value martyrdom, violent jihad, killing Jews, despising non-Muslims and bringing the world under the control of Sharia, we in the West are spoon-feeding American kids a politically correct unrealistic image of Islamic teachings."

And just to clarify matters, here's the dictionary definition of an Islamist;

"an Islamist is someone who believes in Islamism, which is the belief that Islam should govern religion, law and all other aspects of life"

The Koran, the Hadiths and Sharia Law say that Islam should govern these things. For example, the Koran says;

8:39/2:193   *"Make war on them (non-Muslims) until idolatry (every non-Islamic idea) ends and Allah's religion reigns supreme."*

Allah's religion reigning supreme would mean Islam ruling over every aspect of life everywhere in the world. Patently, the Koran calls for Muslims to fight to establish a world governed by Sharia law, an Islamic Caliphate. Thus, if someone believes in the first Pillar of Islam, that the Koran is the Word of God and must be obeyed, then they must therefore by definition be an Islamist. That's a lot of people.

The shocking truth is that the true meaning of the word Islamist has been hijacked to divert attention away from the real roots of Islamic terrorism, anti-Semitism and the degradation of women. We had all been led to believe that these things come from some kind of un-Islamic influence affecting certain fringe Muslim groups, whereas in fact they come from the core texts of the faith. Moderates who have made a confession of faith and sometimes go to pray at the mosque have no idea what the true nature of Islam is, they have never bothered to look into it, they do not know what the Islamic sacred texts really say.

The Koran commands Muslims to undertake jihad, to struggle using violence, deception, or any means available to them to establish Islamic domination, to subjugate the whole world to its ways.

What kind of person could have come up with such murderous prescriptions?

Mohammed was no ordinary man.

In the next section, we will look at his life-story.

Part Three – Mohammed's life, an example to follow ?

"Let no one deceive you in any way, for it will not come until the rebellion occurs and the man of lawlessness (the son of destruction) is revealed." (2 Thessalonians 2:3)

Mohammed's life story is important, not only for historical reasons but because his deeds and sayings recorded in the Hadiths and biographies provide the second highest authority in Islam after the Koran. True Muslims are supposed to emulate the Prophet's lifestyle. But for us, it is important to get to grips with what kind of person he really was. For us, anyone who kept and traded sex-slaves, carried out mass beheadings of his opponents, burned people alive in their homes for not attending prayers, and the like, was someone who lacked humanity. Mohammed's contempt for women and his taste for killing prove he is no godly man by our standards. We apologise if any of the content of this section shocks you, but it is important that the whole truth is told.

It is interesting that the Islamic State, who have most fully lived out a true Mohammedan lifestyle, are branded un-Islamic by moderate Muslims who themselves only have a limited knowledge of their prophet's true life. The dichotomy between today's moderate Muslims and Mohammed's true Islam is proof that millions and millions of Muslims are ready to abandon their religion. All they need is the right encouragement and guidance. From a Christian perspective, the understanding that Islam is a demonic religion helps us fit Mohammed's life story into a proper perspective. We must be sympathetic to Muslims who have been taught that Islam is the only true way and help them see that right from the start of his life he was groomed to talk with demons. The death spirit over his family is also easy for us to spot but would seem like a string of coincidences for anyone without spiritual understanding.

With the death of his first wife and being forced to flee his home in Mecca, Mohammed's life changed and instead of being a largely ignored self-proclaimed prophet, he became a religious warlord. The peaceful messages which he preached at first in Mecca were now replaced with open incitements to war. Mohammed's initial religion of peace now was transformed into a totalitarian war machine. Jews and Christians who were once seen as allies now were depicted as enemies to his growing religion. Genocides followed as he fell into alignment with Satan's plan to dominate the world. With time, the peaceful verses of Mohammed's early revelations were abrogated by calls to arms. We even have evidence in the Hadiths of how some of the dark verses in the Koran were really inspired. As Christians, we have an immediate gut feeling that these things are not right. In later sections of this book we will look at whether Mohammed fits the bill as the False Prophet of the Book of Revelation. Certainly, he fits the description for the Son of Destruction.

Death in the Family

Mohammed was born in the Banu Hashim tribe, Hashim in Arabic means breaker, crusher or destroyer, and Banu means "sons of" so he was a "son of the destroyer". Yes! even his family name proves he was the son of destruction.

Before he was born, his father, Abd Allah bin Al-Muttalib, died and he grew up under the guardianship of his grandfather who was the custodian of the sacred site of the Ka'aba at Mecca, at that time a major centre of pagan idol worship and pilgrimage.

His family were not poor and at a few months old, as was the custom locally, he was sent to grow up outside of the city of Mecca in the care of a wet nurse named Halima.

Receiving no formal education, Mohammed never learnt to read or write, although he did gain a good command of the Arabic tongue. It is recorded by Ibn Ishaq (**"The Life of Muhammad"**, p71-72) that Halima thought that Mohammed was demon possessed and recounted him having seizures and bizarre spiritual manifestations.

At about the age of five or six he went with his mother Aminah on a visit to his father's grave, where tragically she fell ill and shortly afterwards died.

Halima subsequently took young Mohammed back to Mecca where he was then raised and taught by his grandfather at the Ka'aba sanctuary, which in those days housed 360 idols as well as a living snake in the Zamzam well that was also worshipped as a deity.

But within a couple of years, death struck again, with the grandfather, before dying, putting Mohammed into the care of his uncle Abu Talib who then took him in as a member of his family where he remained until old enough to start working.

All of this death and separation in his early years must have been very distressing for young Mohammed and may have had serious consequences on his psychological development.

It is certain that there was a spirit of death hanging over his life, not only did he suffer so much loss early on, but he also later lost six out of his seven children very young, with only his daughter Fatima surviving him.

Pagan Education

Evidently Mohammed was quite intelligent and showed early signs of spiritual sensitivity. We understand from the Book of Halabieh (1/175) that his mother Aminah subjected Mohammed, whilst quite young, to a demonic Spiritism initiation ceremony where he was established as a medium so that the "jinn" (demons) could speak through him.

Certainly, he would have spent much time with his grandfather, Al-Muttalib, at the pagan Ka'aba shrine in Mecca which is where Grand Mosque now stands. There, Mohammed would have become very familiar with the rituals and all the ways of the pagan faith his family practised. We know that the grandfather worshipped the moon god *"Al-ilah"* (known as *"Nanna"*, or *"Sin"*, in other cultures and depicted by a crescent moon symbol) at the shrine, and that his father, as a child, was dedicated to this god as his forename Abd'allah means *"faithful of Al-ilah"*.

Remember that at this time, the young Mohammed had not yet received the revelation to worship only one god. That came, when he was much older, at around forty years old. Indeed, as a youngster his grandfather probably groomed him to be a future guardian of the sanctuary, which was the high place of pagan idolatry in the whole region. He would have seen the naked perambulation around the Black Stone during the big annual pilgrimage and other acts of worship to the idols at the site, but some rituals such as temple prostitution he would not have understood until he was older. (see Bukhari 2/164 and Halabieh 1/15)

We also know that the Black Stone was worshipped and addressed as a goddess called Akbar in those times from Ibn Ishaq's **"The Life of Muhammad"** (trans Guillaume OUP). Even after the time with his grandfather, when he lived with his uncle Abu Talib, it was again in a highly charged demonic atmosphere (see Ibn Hisham 1/147).

By all accounts Mohammed was very superstitious as a result of this upbringing, he believed in magic, the evil eye, spells, omens, and was even afraid of strong winds and eclipses. The Sahihs Muslim and Bukhari both contain many accounts of these beliefs, (see Bukhari 1/144-158, 2/144 &167, 4/110-111, 400, 490, 7/636, 644, 649-650, 660 and Muslim 1/458 & 3/5424-5427). For example, he is recorded as having said; *"If anyone of you sees (in a dream) something he dislikes, when he gets up he should blow thrice on his left side and seek refuge with Allah from its evil for then it will not harm him"* (Bukhari 7/643).

Evidently Mohammed stayed very much connected to the pagan sanctuary. He was greatly respected there and later in life, when he was about thirty-five he was called upon to reset the Black Stone back in place after the sanctuary had been devastated by a flood and the Ka'aba shrine rebuilt. This was no small thing, so Mohammed must have been very well thought of in pagan circles. He always viewed this place as being the focus of worship and even today all Muslims must face the direction of this pre-Islamic idol when they pray. Hadiths show that late in his life in 629 AD Mohammed made the pilgrimage to the Ka'aba in Mecca, and sacrificing cows there, even though it was then still a pagan shrine and sanctuary with the 360 pagan idols and a living snake being worshipped there (see Bukhari 1/6/293). The annual pilgrimage to Mecca still includes the circling around the Black Stone idol, bowing down and bowing before it, touching and even kissing it.

When Mohammed came to marry, his first wife was from a family of occult spiritual leaders and had been left a widow by a clairvoyant who worked with demons. She kept an idol of the goddess *al-Uzza* (see Ibn Hanbal; **"Musnad"**, Vol 4, p222). Throughout his life, he continued to have demonic visitations whilst praying;

"The delegate of Jinns (demons) of (the city of) Nasibin came to me, and how nice those Jinns (demons) were" (Sahih Bukhari 5/58/200)

"Last night a big demon (afreet) from the Jinns came to me". (Sahih Bukhari 1/8/450)

"They (the demons) asked him (the Holy Prophet) about their provision and he said: 'Every bone on which the name of Allah is recited is your provision..." (Sahih Muslim 4/0903)

It is clear that Mohammed would communicate with them; Yes, Mohammed talked with demons.

The Illiterate Prophet

At the age of twelve Mohammed began to accompany his uncle in caravans on the trade routes to Syria and elsewhere, at first helping drive the camels, but later taking a role in the trading. He began to gain a reputation for trustworthiness and it was this that led to him meeting his first wife Khadijah whom, although much older than him, he soon fell in love with. It seems that, apart from the early loss of six out of seven children, they had a very good marriage.

It was around the age of forty that Mohammed began to experience powerful spiritual visitations. These for the most part frightened him and at first, he did not share about them publicly. He recounted later having a wide range of unpleasant experiences whilst he believed he was receiving revelation from the Angel Jibril (allegedly Gabriel). He never claimed to have direct revelation from God in the way that Jesus or Moses or many of the other Jewish Prophets received.

Mohammed used to have seizures, delusions and would often foam at the mouth during his spiritual encounters leading some around him to believe he was demon possessed. Mohammed himself even thought he was going mad and contemplated suicide; he is recounted as saying

"O Khadijah, I see light and hear sounds and fear I am mad,"
("Kitab al-Tabaqat al-Kabir" by Ibn Sa'd trans S. Moinal Haq p225).

She was a great strength for him at that time. With encouragement from his wife, Mohammed began to talk publicly about his "angelic" visitations, but with little impact, gaining only small following of converts. Whilst preaching a generally monotheistic doctrine, he also delivered Koran verses saying that it was honourable to worship three popular local Mecca goddesses, a move which for a while seems to have increased his popularity.

However, he later abrogated these verses, saying Satan had inspired them, thereafter returning to a strict monotheism. This angered the authorities who gained much financially from the idol worshipping pilgrims who used to visit the city and so Mohammed's, albeit at that time, peaceful preaching became less and less welcome there.

It seems that Mohammed was quite fussy about going to the toilet, **"The Book of Purification"** (Abu Dawud) has much about it,

"One day I was in the company of the Apostle of Allah. He wanted to urinate. Then he came to a soft ground at the foot of a wall and urinated. He then said: If any of you wants to urinate, he should look for a place (like this) for his urination"
(Abu Dawud 1/0005)

"Your Prophet teaches you everything, even about excrement... Yes. He has forbidden us to face the qiblah at the time of easing or urinating, and cleansing with right hand, and cleansing with less than three stones, or cleansing with dung or bone"
(Abu Dawud 1/0007)

"I heard the Apostle of Allah say: When two persons go together for relieving themselves uncovering their private parts and talking together, Allah, the Great and Majestic, becomes wrathful at this"
(Abu Dawud 1/0015)

Most of us would laugh at this but to Muslims this is a very holy book.

It seems as if he didn't like explaining or debating his revelations. In Maududi's book "**The Meaning of the Koran**" (vol III, p76-77), it is noted; -

"The Holy Prophet himself forbade people to ask questions...so do not try to probe into such things".

Bukhari also tells of his dislike for anyone who questions him; -

(1/91)   *"The Prophet got angry and his cheeks and his face became red"*

(2/555, 3/591)   *"Allah has hated you...[for] asking too many questions"*

The Koran's Allah asks people to blindly follow him without asking questions; -

5:102   *"Some people before you did ask such questions, and on that account lost their faith."*

The Meccans did not like this attitude.

In 620 Khadijah died leaving Mohammed, already unpopular in his home town, now grieving for the one person whom he had truly loved. With his uncle and protector Abu Talib having died not long before, Mohammed left Mecca, within two years taking up residence in Medina.

War Stories

The move to Medina is the starting point of the Islamic calendar, and the real starting point of Mohammed's life as a statesman. He was given a role as a mediator between the different tribal communities in the area (at the time known as Yathrib). Tensions existed between the local Arabs and the rich Jewish tribes who controlled much of the land and business in Arabia. Jews were particularly despised for their money lending with high interest to other groups, something which many Arabs blamed for their becoming poor.

One of the first things Mohammed did there was to draft a local constitution, a set of rules, to allow for peaceful coexistence between the different ethnic and cultural groups. Not long after this he began building the first ever mosque there.

Through this constitution, he managed to forge alliances which would help him in his own personal battles against those who had opposed him in Mecca, he now had the assurance that others in Medina would defend against any attempt to attack him there.

Within a year of coming to Medina, open hostilities began between Mohammed's followers and Meccan traders on the caravan routes. These appear to have been reprisals for the confiscation of property belonging to Mohammed and his followers by the Meccans. Before long these first Muslims began raiding the caravans of the Meccan people. Tabari's detailed history of that time tells (vol 7 p10);

"In the month of Ramadan, seven months after the Hijrah (the migration to Medina), Muhammad entrusted a white war banner to Hamzah with the command of thirty Emigrants (who had followed Muhammad to Medina). Their aim was to intercept a Qurayash caravan."

The Qurayash, the dominant tribe in Mecca, were powerful and rich but trickery helped the Muslim attackers succeed. In this first successful caravan raid at Nakhla, the Muslims attacked during the "Holy Month" of the pagan pilgrimage when fighting is normally forbidden, shaving their heads to disguise themselves as pilgrims and thus taking their victims by surprise.

This banditry against the Meccans continued and increased to become the most important source of income for Mohammed and his growing band of Muslim followers. The raids on the Qurayash caravans escalated to all-out war at the battle of Badr later in 624. Further battles followed and Mohammed, who on arriving at Medina had preached peace with Jews and other non-Muslims; and had even temporarily allowed for the direction of prayer to be made towards Jerusalem, now turned against the local Jewish tribes in the area and renounced all concessions.

The **Jewish Encyclopedia** tells of this;

"When the prophet first went to Medina he was inclined to be friendly toward the Jews. They were included in the treaty between him and the inhabitants of Medina. He also made certain concessions to them on the ground of religion, and adopted their Qiblah (direction of prayer)... Jerusalem... in the hope of winning them to his cause. They, however, ridiculed him, and delighted in drawing him into arguments to expose his ignorance; so that his conciliatory attitude was soon changed to enmity"
("Medina", Jewish Encyclopedia [1906], Jacobs & Montgomery)

His personality seemed to have changed, no longer being the gifted merchant and messenger of a merciful god, he now became a religious warlord. Koran verses from this period moved away from earlier themes of tolerance and respect towards other faiths and now abrogated them to allow permission to attack the Meccans (22:39-40), to command the killing of those who did not believe in his new religion, and giving details on how to divide the spoils of war.

Many reliable contemporary accounts remain of what life was like then; -

"We fought against the Fazara and Abu Bakr was the commander over us. He had been appointed by the Messenger of Allah. When we were only at an hour's distance from the water of the enemy, Abu Bakr ordered us to attack. We made a halt during the last part of the night to rest and then we attacked from all sides and reached their watering-place where a battle was fought. Some of the enemies were killed and some were taken prisoners. I saw a group of persons that consisted of women and children. I was afraid lest they should reach the mountain before me, so I shot an arrow between them and the mountain. When they saw the arrow, they stopped. So I brought them, driving them along. Among them was a woman from Banu Fazara. She was wearing a leather coat. With her was her daughter who was one of the prettiest girls in Arabia. I drove them along until I brought them to Abu Bakr who bestowed that girl upon me as a prize. So we arrived in Medina. I had not yet disrobed her when the Messenger of Allah met me in the street and said: Give me that girl, O Salama. I said: Messenger of Allah, she has fascinated me. I had not yet disrobed her. When on the next day, the Messenger of Allah again met me in the street, he said: O Salama, give me that girl, may God bless your father. I said: She is for you, Messenger of Allah! By Allah. I have not yet disrobed her. The Messenger of Allah sent her to the people of Mecca, and surrendered her as ransom for a number of Muslims who had been kept as prisoners at Mecca."
(Sahih Muslim 19/4345)

Mohammed would stop at nothing to get his way. Sometime later, when he was seeking to take Mecca and make it Muslim, he used the tactic of "Hudna" to make a treaty which he would go on to break the terms of, saying that Allah had forbidden him to obey the treaty. Conveniently Allah gave Mohammed a new Koran verse for the occasion;

9:3   *"And an announcement from Allah and His Messenger, to the people... that Allah and His Messenger dissolve (treaty) obligations with the Pagans"*

So accordingly, Mohammed refused to give back some captured women whom the Meccans had asked to be returned to them under the treaty.

This was followed by the killing of a Muslim at the hand of the Meccans which also infringed the terms of the treaty. Even though the Meccans wanted to keep the truce Mohammed used this second breach as a pretext to invade. So, with ten thousand armed Muslims he marched on Mecca and took it without any real resistance.

Mohammed was clearly a very clever manipulator of people, Hadith Bukhari 4/52/268 records that; *"Allah's Apostle said, 'War is deceit".*

A child bride

Mohammed took further wives after the death of his beloved Khadijah. The one we know most about is Aisha, who, in her own words, married;

"when I was six and we consummated the marriage when I was nine. I still used to play with dolls..." (Sa'ad translated by Bewley 8:24, also confirmed by Sahih Muslim 8/3310 and Tabari vol 39 p171).

Abu Dawud 2116 clarifies with the child bride confessing;
"He had intercourse with me when I was nine years old."

Mohammed already in his fifties had erotic dreams about her even before she was six;

"Allah's Apostle said to me, 'You were shown to me twice (in my dream) before I married you. I saw an angel carrying you in a silken piece of cloth, and I said to him, 'Uncover (her),' and behold, it was you. I said (to myself), 'If this is from Allah, then it must happen".

Indeed, the marriage might have been consummated earlier, had it not been for the poor distressed girl falling sick and losing her hair straight after the marriage. The consummation only took place after she had recovered and her hair had grown back.

"The Prophet engaged me when I was a girl of six. Then I got ill and my hair fell down. Later on my hair grew (again) and my mother, Um Ruman, came to me while I was playing in a swing with some of my girlfriends. She called me, and I went to her, not knowing what she wanted to do to me. She caught me by the hand and made me stand at the door of the house. I was breathless then, and when my breathing became alright, she took some water and rubbed my face and head with it. Then she took me into the house. There in the house I saw some Ansari women who said, 'Best wishes and Allah's Blessing and a good luck.' Then she entrusted me to them and they prepared me (for the marriage). Unexpectedly Allah's Apostle came to me in the forenoon and my mother handed me over to him, and at that time I was a girl of nine years of age" (Bukhari 5/58/234).

Bukhari's Hadith 1/6/298 describes how Mohammed would take a bath with the little girl and fondle her; -

"The Prophet and I used to take a bath from a single pot while we were Junub. During the menses, he used to order me to put on an Izar (dress worn below the waist) and used to fondle me. While in Itikaf, he used to bring his head near me and I would wash it while I used to be in my periods".

Aisha also admitted that Mohammed would beat her (recorded in Sahih Muslim 4/2127). She was housed alone in a small 5m x 4m hut made of unbaked mud bricks with palm leaves as a roof situated in the Rawdah Mubarak, in what is now the Green Dome mosque in Medina where Mohammed is since buried. This marriage became a model for child marriages which is enshrined in Sharia Law as we see enacted today in parts of the Muslim world.

The United Nations and medical charities report that in Muslim countries some children die from these child marriages because their bodies are not yet ready for sex or childbearing. Mohammed even went so far to include in the Koran a verse (65:4) that gives instructions for divorcing pre-pubescent girls. He is even recorded in Bukhari 7/62/172 as openly recommending child marriage in asking a companion why hadn't he taken a child bride for himself

"who could have played with you and you with her?"

Mohammed took a growing number of other wives too, conveniently Allah gave Mohammed a Koran verse (33:50) allowing him to have as many wives as he pleased despite the fact a previous verse had limited a man to four only. Indeed, the new verse even allowed for the Prophet to "marry" to a woman without the payment of the bride price to her which seals the Ketubah (marriage contract). This is one of many instances where critics accuse Mohammed of simply making up Koran verses to suit himself. Historians believe he may have had up to eleven wives at the same time.

"The Prophet used to go round (have sexual relations with) all his wives in one night, and he had nine wives"
(Bukhari 7/62/6)

"The Holy Prophet had the sexual power of 30 men"
(Bukhari 1/189)

Another Koran verse which conveniently came down from Allah suited Mohammed's personal justification concerning his marriage to another woman, Zaynab, who had been his adopted son's wife beforehand.

33:37 *'And (remember) when you (Muhammad) said to him (Zaid, adopted son) on whom Allah has bestowed Grace (by guiding him to Islam) and you (O Muhammad) have done favour (by manumitting him); 'Keep your wife to yourself, and fear Allah.' But you did hide in yourself (i.e. what Allah has already made known to you that He will give her to you in marriage) that which Allah will make manifest, you did fear the people (i.e., Muhammad married the divorced wife of his manumitted slave) whereas Allah had a better right that you should* fear Him. So when Zaid had accomplished his desire from her (i.e. divorced her), We gave her to you in marriage, so that (in future) there may be no difficulty to the believers in respect of (the marriage of) the wives of their adopted sons when the latter have no desire to keep them (i.e. they have divorced them). And Allah's Command must be fulfilled."

Allah also readily gave Mohammed Koran verses that helped him keep his wives in order, 66:5 reads;

"Maybe, if he (Muhammad) divorce you, Allah will give him in your place wives better than you, submissive, faithful, obedient, penitent, adorers..."

Is this really the stuff of a holy book?

A taste for killing

As well as attacking the Meccan caravans, Mohammed also turned against the Jews in the Medina area. When they refused to convert to Islam he tried to drive them away and when they refused to leave he attacked them. Local Jewish leaders were killed and all-out hostility broke out. In 627 Mohammed even claimed that the angel Jibril appeared, head covered in dust, and told him to attack the Jews at Banu Qurayza where he besieged them for twenty-five days. (Bukhari 56/29).

We have already read one account of the aftermath of this siege, here's Ibn Ishaq's version (Guillaume translation p464);

"Then they (the Jews) surrendered, and the apostle confined them in Medina...the apostle went out to the market of Medina and dug trenches in it. Then he sent for them and struck off their heads in those trenches as they were brought out in batches...There were 600 or 700 in all, though some put the figure as high as 800 or 900."

Al-Tabari adds this (8/38); -

"The Messenger of Allah commanded that all of the Jewish men and boys who had reached puberty should be beheaded. Then the Prophet divided the wealth, wives, and children of the Banu Qurayza Jews among the Muslims."

Sounds like a scene from the latest Islamic State video, where do you think they get most of their inspiration from?

Those who fought alongside Mohammed shared the spoils with him;

"We set out along with the Prophet during the year of the battle of Hunain, and when we faced the enemy, the Muslims with the exception of the Prophet and some of his companions retreated before the enemy. I saw one of the pagans overpowering one of the Muslims, so I struck the pagan from behind his neck causing his armour to be cut off. The pagan headed towards me and pressed me so forcibly that I felt as if I was dying. Then death took him over and he released me. Afterwards I followed 'Umar and said to him, 'What is wrong with the people?' He said, 'It is the Order of Allah.' Then the Muslims returned (to the battle after the flight) and after overcoming the enemy the Prophet sat and said, 'Whoever had killed an Infidel and has an evidence to this issue, will have the Salb (i.e. the belonging of the deceased e.g. clothes, arms, horse, etc.).' I stood up and said, 'Who will be my witness?' and then sat down. Then the Prophet repeated his question. Then the Prophet said the same (for the third time). I got up and said, 'Who will be my witness?' and then sat down. The Prophet asked his former question again. So I got up. The Prophet said, 'What is the matter, O Abu Qatada?' So I narrated the whole story; A man said, 'Abu Qatada has spoken the truth, and the Salb of the deceased is with me, so please compensate Abu Qatada on my behalf.' Abu Bakr said, 'No! By Allah, it will never happen that the Prophet will leave a Lion of Allah who fights for the Sake of Allah and His Apostle and give his spoils to you.' The Prophet said, 'Abu Bakr has spoken the truth. Give it (the spoils) back to him (O man)!' So he gave it to me and I bought a garden in the land of Banu Salama with it (i.e. the spoils) and that was the first property I got after embracing Islam" (Bukhari 5/59/610)

A statement quoted by Al-Tabari (9/69) reveals Mohammed's feelings about fighting; *"Killing unbelievers is a small matter for us..."*

He was a proponent of torture; -

"The Prophet gave orders concerning Kinanah to Zubayr, saying, 'Torture him until you extract what he has.' So Zubayr kindled a fire on Kinanah's chest, twirling it with his firestick until Kinanah was near death. Then the Messenger gave him to Maslamah, who beheaded him." (Ibn Ishaq 515, Al-Tabari 8/122)

Some stories show the pleasure Mohammed's followers felt;

"he seized about four hundred men from the Jews who had been allies of the Aus against Khazraj and ordered that they should be beheaded. Accordingly, Khazraj cut off their heads with great satisfaction." (Sirat Rasul Allah, Ishaq trans Guillaume; Ibn Hisham's Notes no. 580)

Doesn't it sound just like the Islamic State?

Mohammed and his army were not always victorious;

"Abu Waqqas pelted the apostle that day and broke his right lower incisor and wounded his lower lip, and al Zuhri wounded him in the forehead and Ibn Qamia wounded his cheekbone. Two rings from his helmet were forced into his cheek and the apostle fell into a hole which Abu Amir had made so the Muslims might fall in unawares. Ali took hold of the apostle's hand and Ubaydullah lifted him till he stood upright. Malik bin Sinan sucked the blood from the apostle's face then he swallowed it....al Jarrah pulled out one of the rings from the apostle's face and his front tooth fell out. He pulled out another ring and the other incisor fell out" (Sirat Rasul Allah, Ishaq trans Guillaume; Ibn Hisham's Notes no. 598)

Re-reading Bukhari 11/626 illustrates his attitude on faith issues;

"I decided to order a man to lead prayer and then to take a flame to burn all those who had not left their houses for prayer, burning them alive inside their homes."

This isn't even a military situation, this is a question of religion; it seems only a certain type of man could do such a thing, and straight after prayers? They certainly weren't praying to God! Al Tabari 9/61 records Mohammed saying to his followers;

"Go to this mosque whose owners are unjust and burn it !"

So they did as they were told and burnt it down with people still inside. (Koran verses 9:108-110 refer to this incident.) Another episode tells the story of a man seeking absolution;

"A man came to Muhammad saying he had illegal sex with a woman, Muhammad asked him; 'What do you want from what you have said?' The man said; 'I want you to purify me.' So Muhammad gave orders that he be stoned to death." (Abu Dawud 38/4414)

When someone at the scene questioned this as being a bit harsh, Mohammed gave orders that they be forced to eat from the carcass of a dead donkey that was nearby. Mohammed evidently also believed in the religious equivalent of ethnic cleansing, numerous sources recount him saying;

"I will expel the Jews and Christians from the Arabian Peninsula and will not leave anyone but Muslims." (Sahih Muslim 19/4366)

Groups such as the Islamic State and Boko Haram are today following his example trying to eradicate all other ideologies from their regions.

Sex-slaves

Mohammed had several sex-slaves as well as his wives, Al-Tabari's history (39/194) talks of Mariyah, a gift to him from a fellow Muslim; -

"he had intercourse with her by virtue of her being his property."

She had been given to him by the King of Egypt; -

"the ruler of Egypt sent a rich present of a thousand measures of gold, twenty robes of fine cloth, a mule, a she-ass and, as the crown of the gift, two Coptic Christian slave girls... sisters, Mariyah and Sirin, and both were beautiful, but Mariyah was exceptionally so, the Prophet marvelled at her beauty". (Sirajuddin, **Muhammad: His Life Based on the Earliest Sources**, 71/p277-278)

Because she was a slave we don't even know her age but it is recorded that Mariyah gave birth to Mohammed's son Ibrahim who died at the age of two. Another sex-slave was a 15-year-old girl Mohammed himself had captured during warfare and enslaved;

"Allah granted Rayhana of the Qurayza to Muhammad as booty" (Tabari 9/137).

"Then the Apostle divided the property, wives and children...the Apostle had chosen one of the women for himself...she remained with him until he died, in his power" (Ishaq/Guillaume p466).

Again, we don't know much more about her except that when she was captured she preferred to remain a slave rather than convert to Islam. Mohammed had many sex-slaves during the course of his life, some of them even converted to Islam and became wives, whilst others like Rayhana refused to accept his faith. The keeping of women as captives was not a moral issue in early Islam.

We have previously covered the discussion involving Mohammed about trying to preserve the resale value of sex slaves by not getting them pregnant; -

"(Al-Khudri) sitting with Allah's Apostle asked, 'O Allah's Apostle! We get female captives as our share of booty, and we are interested in their prices, what is your opinion about coitus interruptus?' The Prophet said, 'Do you really do that?" (Sahih Bukhari 3/34/432)

"Muhairiz said 'I entered the mosque and saw Abu Sa'id Al Khudri. I sat with him and asked about withdrawing the penis (while having intercourse). Abu Sa'id said 'We went out with the Apostle of Allah on

the expedition to Banu Al-Mustaliq and took some Arab women captive and we desired the women for we were suffering from the absence of our wives and we wanted ransom, so we intended to withdraw the penis (while having intercourse with the slave women)'. But we asked ourselves 'can we draw the penis when the Apostle of Allah is among us before asking him about it?' So we asked him about it. He said 'it does not matter if you do not do it, for every soul that is to be born up to the Day of Resurrection will be born"* (Abu Dawud 2/12/2167)

Is this spirituality or carnality? There are other similar records; Sahih Muslim 2/8/3432 and Abu Dawud 2/12/2150 explain;

"The apostle of Allah sent a military expedition to Awtas on the occasion of the battle of Hunain. They met their enemy and fought with them, they defeated them and took them captive. Some of the companions of the apostle of Allah were reluctant to have intercourse with them as their husbands were unbelievers. So Allah, the Exalted sent down the Quranic verse (4:24); 'And all married women are forbidden unto you save those (captives) whom your right hands possess'. That is to say the slaves are lawful (for sex) when they have completed the waiting period (completed their menstrual cycle)."

Reports coming from inside the Islamic State and Boko Haram show that what is happening there today is very little different from Mohammed's original Islamic war machine. This very Koran verse (4:24) is quoted, in its correct context, as the Sharia justification for the brutal raping and trading of Yazidi and Christian women and girls by today's jihadis.
And it seems that Mohammed did not like the idea of letting a female slave go free;

"Maimuna bint Al-Harith told that she manumitted a slave-girl without taking the permission of the Prophet. On the day when it was her turn to be with the Prophet, she said, 'Do you know, O Allah's Apostle, that I have manumitted my slave-girl?' He said, 'Have you really?' She replied in the affirmative. He said, 'You would have got more reward if you had given her to one of your maternal uncles" (Sahih Bukhari 3/47/765)

Mohammed's biographer Al-Tabari and the Hadiths recount the fate of more captured farm wives, whom the Muslims traded amongst themselves as sex slaves;

"Dihya came and said, 'O Allah's Prophet! Give me a slave girl from the captives.' The Prophet said, 'Go and take any slave girl" (Muslim 1/8/367)

"the Apostle traded for Safiyah by giving Dihyah her two cousins (and five others). The women of Khaybar were distributed among the Muslims." (Muslim 1/8/117)

'a beautiful girl (Safiyah) and Allah's Messenger got her in exchange of seven heads, and then entrusted her to Umm Sulaim so that she might embellish her and prepare her for him" (Muslim 8/3328)

This same Safiyah, according to Tabari, was just seventeen at the time, and the two cousins were only nine and ten. (Tabari 39 p185)

But later one of her fellow captives from Khaybar would eventually get their revenge on Mohammed. Ibn Ishaq 593 tells of another similar story;

"From the captives of Hunayn, Allah's Messenger gave (his son-in-law) Ali a slave girl called Baytab and he gave (future Caliph) Uthman a slave girl called Zaynab and (future Caliph) Umar another."

"And during the expedition of Hunayn, Allah's messenger enslaved from Hawazin until the amount of slaves reached six thousand" (At-Tabaqat al-Khubra - Ibn Sa'd).

With all this violence going on against women in early Islam and continuing in Islam today, one has to ask the question; what were Mohammed's own feelings about women?

There is some evidence in other writings of the direct expression of his misogyny towards women; Sahih Bukhari (7/62/33) says that in his opinion he had never experienced *"any affliction worse"* than women.

Sahih Muslim 8/3466 quotes him as saying;

"Woman is like a rib, when you attempt to straighten it, it will break. And if you leave her alone, crookedness will remain in her."

Tuffula, Amhad Zaky, **Al-mar'ah wal Islam, Dar al-Kitab al-Lubani**, (first edition, Beirut 1995, p180) records the saying;

"The woman is a toy..."

Had women become to him just objects for his own self-gratification?

Clearly the Prophet's attitude was that the women were just property to be used or possibly traded; -

"Then the apostle sent Sa-d b. Zayd al-Ansari, brother of Abdu'l-Ashal with some of the captive women of Banu Qurayza to Najd and he sold them for horses and weapons." (Ibn Ishaq 693)

Poison!

Not surprisingly Mohammed's violent lifestyle finally caught up with him.

After years of trickery and deceit, from attacking Meccan caravans in the pagan Holy months when fighting was forbidden, through to broken peace treaties like the Hudaybiyya truce, and leaving a heritage of thousands killed, dispossessed or raped, it was finally a woman who killed him.

After a campaign of driving out and slaughtering Jews from the Arabian Peninsula, including the mass expulsion from Bani An-Nadir and the genocide at Banu Qurayza, Mohammed died at the hands of a Jewess (Ibn Ishaq 436-464, Tabari 8/34).

It happened after he and his followers had attacked the Jewish settlement at Khaybar, publicly beheading one of the leaders and taking the wife, Safiyah, as a sex-slave after he bartered her for seven others slaves with one of his followers.

There at Khaybar, a fellow captive named Zaynab, who, in revenge for what Mohammed had done to her people, plotted to prepare him a meal which she would poison, saying to herself; -

"if he was a true prophet he would not be tricked, but if he merely was a king he would eat and die". (Ibn Sa'd 251-252)

So she went ahead with her plan;

"When the messenger of Allah rested from his labour, Zaynab bt. al-Harith, the wife of Sallam b. Mishkam (whom Muhammad had killed), served him a roast sheep. She had asked what part of the sheep the messenger of Allah liked best and was told that it was the foreleg. So she loaded that part with poison..."
(Tabari, Volume 8, p123-124)

He took the poisoned meat and it was a long slow and painful demise lasting over three years

"he suffered much pain" (Ibn Ishaq/Hisham 1006)

"I never saw anyone suffer more pain than the Messenger of Allah," (Sunan Ibn Majah 1622)

Eventually Mohammed died from the poisoning, being well aware that this was the cause, saying thereafter;

"I did not cease to feel the effect of the poisoned morsel"
(Sahih Bukhari 3/47/786)

"The Prophet in his ailment in which he died, used to say, 'Oh Aisha! I still feel the pain caused by the food I ate at Khaibar, and at this time, I feel as if my aorta is being cut from that poison"
(Bukhari 5/59/713)

"Aisha said, 'When the Prophet became sick and his condition became serious, he requested his wives to allow him to be treated in my house, and they allowed him. He came out leaning on two men while his feet were dragging on the ground."
(Sahih al-Bukhari 2588)

Mohammed's last words are recorded in Sahih Bukhari 1/8/427; -

"May Allah curse the Jews and Christians..."

Mohammed returned to his Allah, who, by this statement, is very evidently not the same as the God of the Jews and Christians.

Part Four - Prophet, true or false?

"Dear friends, do not believe everyone who claims to speak by the Spirit. You must test them to see if the spirit they have comes from God. For there are many false prophets in the world" (1 John 4:1)

Traditionally Islamic scholars have put forth a number of supposed "truths" that they say prove the Koran is from God. Detractors have also put forward reasons why it can't be of divine inspiration. For ease of understanding the arguments can be collated into several broad categories; -
- **the fact that Mohammed had the seal of a prophet**
- **the fact he was illiterate**
- **the visitations he experienced when receiving the Koran**
- **the fact it provides guidance**
- **the accuracy of the content**
- **the fact that it is perfect and infallible**

Let's have a look at all of these.

No Christian would be at all impressed by these alleged proofs put forward to give credibility to the claim that Mohammed was a prophet of God. Given his pagan background and education, it is clear his spiritual encounters were demonic in nature. We will expose more of the demonic in the religion in a later section, but for now let's just keep in mind what Jesus said in Matthew Chapter 7, verses 15-16; -

"Beware of false prophets who come to you in sheep's clothing but inwardly they are ravaging wolves. You will recognize them by their fruit..."

A consistent fruit of Islam is genocide, it started in Mohammed's time and it is still continuing. It is a matter of much sadness that several of the genocides we mention in this book are on-going; Syria, Iraq, Nigeria, Afghanistan. Even though our political leaders are claiming the higher moral ground by acknowledging the 1915 Armenian genocide, they have largely failed to take any concrete action concerning the atrocities taking place in the world on their watch. Even the West's Christian community has failed our brothers and sisters in Christ who live in lands where there is persecution today, which it must be said are mostly Islamic countries.

We feel obliged to tell you about a story that came to us via some missionary friends of friends in Iraq at the time the Islamic State emerged. We got fairly detailed and reliable reports of children being tortured and mutilated in front of their parents by ISIS jihadis trying to force the parents to convert to Islam. We passed the information and contact details through to a Christian News agency who we knew of that specialise in breaking news stories, in the hope that the story would get around, so fellow Christians could pray into the issue and put pressure on our politicians to do something. Tragically they didn't want to know about this kind of thing and to be honest we have had several Christian ministries who have asked us very politely not to contact them again about such things. So, the story went untold for months and months whilst the situation deteriorated for the Christians in Iraq, many were killed and the women and girls taken into sex-slavery. Finally, the mainstream press in the UK were bold enough to break the story but still our governments hesitated whilst thousands more Christians were affected. Even now our governments in the West are still not affording proper protection to Christians fleeing Islamic persecution. We must push them to do it. We are the Body of Christ, we must be concerned about and fight for the parts of OUR body who are under threat. We don't want a Bride of Christ who has had bits of her amputated because the rest of the body wouldn't protect her. Church, we need to stop hiding from the truth, we ought to stand up, be fearless and courageous and then we will bring in the billion-soul harvest the Lord has promised us. It is time to stand up against the murderous ways of Islamism and defeat it.

Prophet, true or false?

Whether a person believes or not that the Koran is the Word of God depends greatly on whether they believe that Mohammed was a true prophet of God, a false one or not even a prophet at all. Muslims have put forward certain justifications for their belief that he was a true prophet. These include having the seal of a prophet, which disappointingly turns out to be a big hairy lump on his back. (Sahih Muslim 4/5790, Bukhari 1/189, 4/741)

"I saw the seal on his back as if it were a pigeon's egg"

"I stood behind him and saw the seal of Prophethood between his shoulders, and it was like the 'Zir-al-Hijla' (means the button of a small tent, but some said; 'egg of a partridge.' etc.)"

For most readers, this will not convince at all, surely the true seal of the prophet is their ability to accurately prophesy future events, and nothing else. The Jewish prophet Isaiah, with God's inspiration, accurately predicted many future events. For example, about 150 years before King Cyrus of Persia lived, this prophet foretold his name and his decree which would lead to the rebuilding the Temple in Jerusalem. (Isaiah 44:28) The stone cylinder on which the decree is written can be seen in the British Museum in London.

Having some kind of physical mark on the body has no effect on one's intellectual or spiritual capabilities. Isn't that just superstition to think otherwise? Many of Mohammed's contemporaries did not believe he was a prophet because he performed no miracles, the Koran verses 17:90-93 and 13:7 admit it; -

"Those who disbelieve say 'If only some portent were sent down upon him from his Lord ! He is only a warner".

There is even a Koran verse that says he is no more than this;

25:56 *"And We have sent thee (O Muhammad) only as a bearer of good tidings and a warner."*

This contradicts other verses such as 7:157 which call Mohammed a prophet. The Koran contains many self-contradictions, which we will carefully consider in Part Five of this book.

The second alleged proof given of his prophethood is the fact he was illiterate; Verse 7:157 says

"the Prophet who can neither read nor write, who they find mentioned in the Torah and the Gospels..."

Again, this only impresses Muslims, indeed critics of the Koran say that Mohammed's inability to read or write is the reason why there are so many errors in it. Certainly Jesus, Moses, Daniel, Joseph and other earlier prophets were all very well educated and well read. In fact, Jesus was an AAA student, at the age of 12 he astounded people with his wisdom;

"they found him (Jesus) in the temple courts, sitting among the teachers, listening to them and asking them questions. Everyone who heard him was amazed at his understanding and his answers"
(Gospel of Luke 2:46-47)

Unlike the Jewish and Christian prophets who have seen God, Mohammed never claimed to have had a direct encounter with God.

"not that anyone has seen the Father except he who is from God"
(Gospel of John 6:46)

"the thing that He sees The Father is doing... these also The Son does like him" (Gospel of John 5:19)

"the Lord used to speak to Moses face to face, as a man speaks to his friend" (Exodus 33:11)

Following on from what is said in Koran verse 7:157, Muslims claim that the verses Deuteronomy 18:15 and John 14:16 foretell of Mohammed. However, this is not true, the whole passage in the Torah where Moses addresses the Israelites starting from Deuteronomy chapter 18 verse 15 is clear;

"The Lord your God will raise up for you a Prophet like me from your midst, from your brethren. Him you shall hear, according to all you desired of the Lord your God in Horeb in the day of the assembly, saying, 'Let me not hear again the voice of the Lord my God, nor let me see this great fire anymore, lest I die'. And the Lord said to me, 'What they have spoken is good. I will raise up for them a Prophet like you from among their brethren, and will put My words in His mouth, and He shall speak to them all that I command Him."

This passage must be speaking of a Jewish prophet because the use of the word brethren. But Mohammed was an Ishmaelite, an Arab, not a Jew. Besides Jesus had already fulfilled this prophecy given by Moses hundreds of years before Mohammed was born.

"But this is how God fulfilled what He had foretold through all the prophets, saying... Jesus...as he promised long ago through his holy prophets... The Lord your God will raise up for you a prophet like me from among your own people." (Book of Acts 3:18-22)

When Jesus was born, angels told many people about it, even shepherds out watching over their sheep. (See the quote from Gospel of Luke 2:8-14 later in this chapter.) Wise men even came from other lands bringing expensive gifts having seen the signs of His coming in the stars;

"wise men from the East came to Jerusalem, saying, 'Where is He who has been born King of the Jews ? For we have seen His star in the East and have come to worship Him." (Gospel of Matthew 2:1-2)

Mohammed's birth was not accompanied by such signs. The other verse which Muslims often point to, in the Gospel of John, reads,

"And I will pray to the Father, and He shall give you another Comforter, that He may abide with you forever". (John 14:16)

The key word in this passage is "forever", Mohammed was not eternal, so the verse is not talking about him, it is talking about the coming of the Holy Spirit who is eternal and is now with mankind forever. That passage in the Gospel of John does say clearly who the Comforter is;

"But the Comforter, who is the Holy Spirit, whom the Father will send in my name, he shall teach you all things." (John 14:26)

The coming of the Holy Spirit was fulfilled on the day of Pentecost centuries before Mohammed lived. It is described in the Book of Acts;

"When the day of Pentecost came, they were all together in one place. Suddenly a sound like the blowing of a violent wind came from heaven and filled the whole house where they were sitting. They saw what seemed to be tongues of fire that separated and came to rest on each of them. All of them were filled with the Holy Spirit and began to speak in other tongues as the Spirit enabled them." (Book of Acts 2:1-5)

Islam has no equivalent of the Holy Spirit of God coming to live inside you and guiding you. A further verse in the Koran says that Jesus even predicted Mohammed by name 61:6

"when Jesus the son of Mary said, 'O children of Israel, indeed I am the messenger of Allah to you confirming what came before me of the Torah and bringing good tidings of a messenger to come, whose name is Ahmad".

There is no record of this statement anywhere in the Torah, the Gospels, or elsewhere outside of Islam. Its style is totally unlike Jesus speech which is recorded extensively in the Gospels. Certainly, He never used the word *"Allah",* and His intimacy with God was such that He used the term *"Abba"* (Father) much of the time. Jesus is never found referring to Himself as *"the Messenger"* because He is much more than that. The Gospels only use this word either for angels or when talking of John the Baptist. Mohammed did refer to himself as the messenger.

Islam says that Jesus was only a prophet but the Bible says He is the only begotten Son of God.

"For God so loved the world, that he gave his only begotten Son, that whosoever believeth in Him should not perish, but have everlasting life." (Gospel of John 3:16)

The Koran does not even confirm the Gospels on this fundamental core issue. The standard Islamic Surah-Ikhlaas prayer denies that God begot anyone and thus denies Jesus is Christ, Messiah, Son of God. Jesus did not confirm the whole Torah but instead overruled the law of retaliation

"an eye for an eye, a tooth for a tooth..." (Exodus 21:24, Leviticus 24:20)

replacing it with the stronger principle;

"You have heard that it was said, 'an eye for an eye, a tooth for a tooth'... but if anyone slaps you on the right cheek, turn to them the other cheek also." (Gospel of Matthew 5:38-39)

Jesus also gives differing opinions from the Torah on several other issues in the Sermon on the Mount, as transcribed in the Gospel of Matthew Chapter 5. The issue of whether the Koran confirms the Torah and Gospels is considered further in Part Six of this book.

Muslim scholars have also cited other verses besides these in the Bible as also predicting Mohammed, but none of these claims stand the test of close scrutiny. Habakkuk 3:3 is an example, which strictly speaking is not in the Torah, nor in the Gospels, as it is in the Books of the Jewish Prophets, the Ketuvim. The verse reads;

*"God came from Teman, the Holy One from Mount Paran
His glory covered the heavens, and his praise filled the earth."*

This verse is obviously talking about God and not any man. Because it talks about Paran, which some Muslims say is Mecca, they say it is about Mohammed. This is crazy! Not even Mohammed claimed he was God! Anyhow critics say that Biblical Paran is the area around Wadi Paran in the Negev desert, and Mount Paran is now known as Jebel Rum on the Jordanian side of the border with Israel and definitely not Mecca.

The claims that Mohammed was predicted by earlier prophets are there to try to give credibility to the idea he was called by God. After all Jesus' life had been predicted in significant detail by Jewish prophets in the Old Testament; Isaiah 7:14, 9:6, Micah 5:2, Zechariah 9:9, Psalm 22:18 and many, many other verses besides, accurately foretell of His coming.

But the Torah and the Gospels do warn of the coming of false prophets;

"The prophets prophesy lies in My name. I sent them not...they prophesy unto you a false vision." (Jeremiah 14:14)

"If what a prophet proclaims in the Name of the Lord does not take place or come true, that is a word the Lord has not spoken."
(Deuteronomy 18:22)

"For such men are false apostles, deceitful workmen, disguising themselves...even Satan disguises himself as an angel of light. So it is no surprise if his servants, also, disguise themselves as servants of righteousness..." (2 Corinthians 11:13-15)

Another supposed proof that the Koran is from God is evidenced by what Mohammed experienced whilst receiving the revelation of its verses. According to historians Tabari and Ibn Ishaq, Mohammed first received inspiration for the Koran in a cave named Hira in the mountain Jabal-an-Nar which is close to Mecca. In his own words, he recalled;

"when I was midway on the mountain I heard a voice from heaven saying 'O Muhammad, you are the Apostle of Allah and I am Gabriel..."
(Tabari "The Life of Muhammad", 2/207)

Ibn Ishaq (trans Guillaume) recounts that the Prophet said he was squeezed so tight that he thought he would die during the encounter. These unpleasant feelings persisted as he received later revelations, he also reported having headaches and hearing sounds like bees buzzing or bells ringing in his ears as detailed in Sahih Muslim 4/28/5765-5767.

In fact, Mohammed himself was concerned he was demon possessed as a result, especially as he thought; *"the bell is an instrument of Satan"* (Sahih Muslim 3/22 /5279). Certainly, Mohammed used to have delusions, imagining things that were not actually happening. His child bride tells of these in Bukhari 7/71/660 and Sahih Muslim 26/5428; -

"A'isha reported that a Jew... cast a spell upon Allah's Messenger with the result that he felt that he had been doing something whereas in fact he had not been doing that"

He would also have fits or seizures with foaming at the mouth;

"He became distressed, foaming at the mouth and closing his eyes. At times he snorted like a young camel."
(Ahmad b. Hanbal I, 34, 464, vi.163)

Could these manifestations be demonic? They seem a far cry from the heavenly encounters of the prophets in the Bible, as in the Gospel of Luke; -

"And an angel of the Lord appeared to him, standing to the right of the altar of incense. Zacharias was troubled when he saw the angel, and fear gripped him. But the angel said to him, 'Do not be afraid, Zacharias, for your petition has been heard, and your wife Elizabeth will bear you a son, and you will give him the name John. You will have joy and gladness, and many will rejoice at his birth. For he will be great in the sight of the Lord; and he will drink no wine or liquor, and he will be filled with the Holy Spirit while yet in his mother's womb. And he will turn many of the sons of Israel back to the Lord their God. It is he who will go as a forerunner before Him in the spirit and power of Elijah, to turn the hearts of the fathers back to the children, and the disobedient to the attitude of the righteous, so as to make ready a people prepared for the Lord.' Zacharias said to the angel,

'How will I know this for certain? For I am an old man and my wife is advanced in years.' The angel answered and said to him, 'I am Gabriel, who stands in the presence of God, and I have been sent to speak to

you and to bring you this good news. And behold, you shall be silent and unable to speak until the day when these things take place, because you did not believe my words, which will be fulfilled in their proper time." (Gospel of Luke 1:11-20)

"Now in the sixth month the angel Gabriel was sent from God to a city in Galilee called Nazareth, to a virgin engaged to a man whose name was Joseph, of the descendants of David; and the virgin's name was Mary. And coming in, he said to her, 'Greetings, favoured one! The Lord is with you.' But she was very perplexed at this statement, and kept pondering what kind of salutation this was. The angel said to her, 'Do not be afraid, Mary; for you have found favour with God. And behold, you will conceive in your womb and bear a son, and you shall name Him Jesus. He will be great and will be called the Son of the Most High; and the Lord God will give Him the throne of His father David; and He will reign over the house of Jacob forever, and His kingdom will have no end.' Mary said to the angel, 'How can this be, since I am a virgin?' The angel answered and said to her, 'The Holy Spirit will come upon you, and the power of the Most High will overshadow you; and for that reason the holy Child shall be called the Son of God. And behold, even your relative Elizabeth has also conceived a son in her old age; and she who was called barren is now in her sixth month. For nothing will be impossible with God.' And Mary said, 'Behold, the bondslave of the Lord; may it be done to me according to your word.' And the angel departed from her." (Gospel of Luke; 1:26-38)

"And there were in the same country shepherds abiding in the field, keeping watch over their flock by night. And, lo, the angel of the Lord came upon them, and the glory of the Lord shone round about them: and they were sore afraid. And the angel said unto them, 'Fear not: for, behold, I bring you good tidings of great joy, which shall be to all people. For unto you is born this day in the city of David a Saviour, which is Christ the Lord. And this shall be a sign unto you; Ye shall find the babe wrapped in swaddling clothes, lying in a manger' And suddenly there was with the angel a multitude of the heavenly host praising God, and saying; 'Glory to God in the highest, and on earth peace, goodwill toward all men" (Gospel of Luke 2:8-14)

On each occasion, the angel Gabriel says, **"do not be afraid"**, or **"fear not"**. These experiences appear uplifting, even joyful, not at all painful. Mohammed did not have this kind of positive heavenly encounter with angels. Nor did he have direct encounters with God, like Jesus, Moses, Isaiah, Ezekiel or other Jewish prophets had. There are several examples in the Bible of these prophets encountering God face to face.

"In the year that King Uzziah died I saw the Lord sitting upon a throne, high and lifted up; and the train of his robe filled the temple" (Isaiah 6:1)

Mohammed never seems to have had this level of encounter, he only saw *"angels"* accompanied by troubling signs. One time he said Jibril appeared to him in the visible form of his companion Diyha (Bukhari 6/61/503). Demonologists agree that God's angels, having their own identity, may appear as human but never come in the form of another angel or person. Fallen angels and demons, however, have been known to usurp the identities of others.

As we know from the Book of Revelation (13:4), a third of the angels fell with Satan. Could Mohammed's angels have been fallen ones or even Satan himself who deceived him? Satan is a liar; -

"he is a liar and father of lies" (Gospel of John 8:44)

and appears like an angel; -

"Even Satan disguises himself as an angel of light"
(St Paul's second letter to the Corinthians 11:14)

Surely the seal of a true prophet is to give only very specific prophetic predictions which come true, like Isaiah who accurately predicted many future events.

Some 2,500 years ago Isaiah wrote this (Isaiah 31:4-5);

"This is what the LORD says to me: 'As a lion growls, or a young lion over its prey; and though a whole band of shepherds is called together against it, it is not frightened by their shouts or disturbed by their clamour, so the LORD Almighty will come down to do battle on Mount Zion and on its heights. Like hovering birds, so the LORD of Hosts will protect Jerusalem; by protecting it, He will rescue it, by sparing it, He will deliver it."

On 8th December 1917, this prophecy was fulfilled, when the British led by General Allenby, symbolized by the lion, together with the ANZAC forces, the young lion, successfully took Jerusalem from the Ottoman Caliphate. They did so by filling the skies over the city with aircraft and dropping leaflets calling for the surrender of the Turkish forces (called bands of shepherds in the prophecy as they often wore sheepskin body warmers in the winter months). The Turks surrendered the next morning and Jerusalem was spared from any siege which could have been very destructive.

The book *"As Birds Flying"* by Andrew Adams looks at this story in some depth and notes fulfilment of several Biblical prophecies at the same time with Daniel 12:12 foretelling the year and Haggai 2:18-20 predicting the day;

"Consider now from this day and upward, from the four and twentieth day of the ninth month, even from the day that the foundation of the Lord's temple was laid, consider it.

Is the seed yet in the barn ? yea, as yet the vine, and the fig tree, and the pomegranate, and the olive tree, hath not brought forth: from this day will I bless you..."

The Turkish forces surrendered on the 24th day of the Hebrew month Kislev (their ninth month). After the capture of Jerusalem, a massive replanting of fruit and olive trees began. The taking of Jerusalem by the British and their subsequent total victory over the Caliphate opened the way for the establishment of the State of Israel which now governs the area.

In a later section, we will consider the decisive battle of Megiddo that followed on from this amazing fulfilment of ancient prophecy. Another startlingly true prophecy is found in Chapter 9 of the Book of Daniel verse 25, it predicts to the day the triumphal entry of Jesus the true Messiah into Jerusalem.

True prophets give true prophecy.

The Satanic Verses

In any event, Mohammed later, after having previously maintained that every word in the Koran had been given to him by God, admitted that he had been tricked into including Satanically inspired verses. This is confirmed by both Ibn Ishaq 165-167 and Tabari 107-112;

"Then Gabriel came down to the Apostle and said, 'What have you done Muhammad ? You have told these people that which I did not bring to you from God and you have said what He did not say to you..."

"informing him that ...Satan had interjected something into his desires."

So instead of the verses 53:19-21 that you will find in today's Koran, the original had the following text; -

"Have ye thought upon Al-Lat and Al-'Uzzá and Manāt, the third, the other? These are the exalted gharāniq (fig. goddesses), whose intercession is hoped for"
(Ibn Ishaq trans Guillaume; **"The Life of Mohammed"**, p165-7)

Here the Koran was recommending making prayer and supplication through three pagan goddesses. This is paganism.

A detailed analysis of this episode given by Tabari (Vol 1, p108-112), concludes that Mohammed's will was the vehicle by which the ungodly material got into the Koran. In other words, does this mean that Satan caused him to make up things that were not from God?

"I (Muhammad) have fabricated things against God and have imputed to Him words which He has not spoken" (recounted by Al-Tabari 6:111)

Philosophically, the consequences of this are dire. If any statement, previously held up by Mohammed as being from God, is later by his own admission proven not to be from God, but from Satan, then it begs the question whether other parts of the Koran might be from Satan also. If Mohammed could not discern the true source of the Satanic verses at the time of receiving them, then by direct implication there is no guarantee that other parts of the Koran are not from that same source. Critics point out, using this logic, that the whole of the Koran could have come from Satan too, and that the alleged visitations by Angel Gabriel (Jibril) could be just an invented fiction. Mohammed countered this criticism by declaring that the words of all previous prophetic messengers of God, including Jesus, were as equally tainted as his and conveniently brought forth a verse for the Koran to that effect (22:52).

There is some evidence as to how Mohammed received certain verses in the Koran. Take another look at this one concerning sex slaves; -

"The Apostle of Allah sent a military expedition to Awtas on the occasion of the battle of Hunayn. They met their enemy and fought with them. They defeated them and took them captives. Some of the Companions of the Apostle of Allah were reluctant to have intercourse with the female captives in the presence of their husbands who were unbelievers. So Allah, the Exalted, sent down the Qur'anic verse: (4:24) 'And all married women (are forbidden) unto you save those (captives) whom your right hands possesses..."
(Abu Dawud 2/2150 p.577, and also in Sahih Muslim 8/3432)

What does this say to you about how the Koran was inspired, and who really is speaking through it? Was Mohammed just making up verses to suit the circumstances? Absolutely!

Before leaving the question of Mohammed's prophethood, it is revealing to consider the story of one of his scribes named Ibn Sahr. Never having learned how to read or write, Mohammed had to employ scribes to put his speech into written form. Ibn Sahr was one of about 40 such employees, and we learn from Al Baidawi's commentary on the Koran **"Tanzil wa Asrar al-Ta'wil"** (6:93), that when Mohammed was receiving and speaking out the revelation of verses 23:12-13, Ibn Sahr declared;

"So blessed be Allah, the fairest of creators !"

Hearing this, Mohammed told him to write that down too and it became part of the Koran. Ibn Sahr began to doubt Mohammed's prophetic abilities openly saying; *"I receive the revelation as much as he does".* In Al-Sira by al-Iraqi, he is noted as having said, *"I used to direct Muhammad wherever I willed..."* and would even change what Mohammed had said. Ibn Sahr believed that the prophet was just making up Koran verses as he went along, and eventually he became so disillusioned that he left Islam. Mohammed later had him killed.

Ibn Sahr was not the only one to doubt Mohammed's prophetic abilities, another un-named scribe decided to denounce the Mohammedan faith and return to the religion of his earlier years, Christianity. He is recorded as saying; *"Muhammad knows nothing but what I have written for him".* One day he was found dead and people openly said; *"This is the doing of Muhammad and his companions."* They buried the man but the next morning found his body lying out of the grave, so they reburied him only to find the same thing the next morning. They buried him four times, the last time very deeply, but each time his body was found out of the grave in the morning. The people concluded; *"this was not done by human beings",* and had to leave the body out of the ground. (recorded in Sahih Bukhari 3421 & Sahih Muslim 2781) Was the spirit of this dead man trying to tell us something from beyond the grave?

Is the Koran all from God? One verse says

5:45   *"And We ordained... a life for a life, an eye for an eye... a tooth for a tooth... for wounds as legal retribution"*

Yet over 2,000 years before Mohammed received this, it already existed in Hammurabi's Law Code;
#196 *"If a man destroy the eye of another man, they shall destroy his eye",*
#197 *"If one breaks a man's bone, they shall break his bone"...*
#200 *"If a patrician has knocked out the tooth of a man that is his equal, his tooth shall be knocked out."*
This Law of Retaliation was given to Hammurabi, a Babylonian King, by his pagan gods *Anu, Bel, Ea* and *Marduk.* Clearly, Mohammed is simply repeating the already existing laws of pagan gods and not bringing fresh revelation from above. This also explains why Jesus, who truly spoke from God's authority, countermanded the equivalent rules of retaliatory retribution from the Torah, Book of Exodus 21:24; *"an eye for an eye, a tooth for a tooth..."* (see the Gospel of Matthew 5:38-9).

Ironically the Koran says; -

2:23-24 *"And if you (Jews, Christians and other unbelievers) are in doubt about what We have sent down through Our servant (Muhammad), then produce a Surah like it......But if you do not - and you will never be able to - then fear the Fire...prepared for the disbelievers."*

Don't you think Exodus 21:24 and Hammurabi's laws, given to him by his pagan gods, look very much like the law of retaliation found in the Koran? The wording may be a bit different but the meanings are the same. The use of pre-existing material in the Koran might be confirmed by the recent discovery of the world's oldest copy of the Koran in a collection belonging to the University of Birmingham (UK). This has led to some controversy because carbon dating has shown that some of the pages might date from as early as 568 AD, thereby placing them before the time Mohammed was even born. This is well before the start of Islam, dating from a time when the term Allah was used for the head of a pre-Islamic pagan polytheist pantheon. Until now it had been assumed that the Koran was put together about 650 AD.

Only God knows!

Abrogation

Rather than being eternal and unchanging like the words of the Torah and Bible, the words of the Koran were subject to updating, or abrogating, by the Prophet. Existing verses could be replaced or overruled, the mechanism of abrogation is summed up in verses; -

16:31 *"When We substitute one revelation for another..."*

13:39 *"Allah doth blot out or confirm what He pleaseth, with Him is the mother of the book."*

2:106 *"We do not abrogate a verse or cause it to be forgotten except that We bring forth (one) better..."*

So, in other words when a new verse arrived that was in contradiction with an earlier revelation, the earlier verse was blotted out or forgotten. For many Jews and Christians this would constitute proof that the Koran is not from an eternal all-wise, all-knowing God, but just from a man who could not see prophetically into the future. In practice abrogation creates a great difficulty in understanding the Koran because its verses are not in the chronological order of their revelation.

Strangely the chapters are mostly arranged by the number of verses which each contains, with the longest first. This complicates academic study. However, there are records of the order in which the verses were received, so, for example, we know that Chapter 2 was revealed before Chapter 8.

Thus verse 2:256 *"Let there be no compulsion in religion",*

which meant that everyone be free to practice their own religion, was abrogated by a later verse;

8:39 *"Make war until...all religion is for Allah."*

Is this then the reason why there are no churches in a major country like Saudi Arabia, and why the Islamic State, Boko Haram and other Islamists destroy all places of worship that are un-Islamic? Critics of Islam who have studied the chronology of the chapters say that Mohammed seemed to make up verses when he needed them. Allah despite having said that Muslims may have up to four wives made an exception for Mohammed so he could have; -

33:50 *"...any believing woman who gives herself to the Prophet if the Prophet wishes to marry her, (this is) only for you (Mohammed), excluding the (other) believers."*

One rule for the Prophet and another for everyone else. Did Mohammed just make this up for himself? Sounds just like a sect! Then later on, when Mohammed was evidently having problems keeping all of his wives in order, and it seems he may have had up to 19 altogether, Allah gave him this, a verse just for his wives; -

66:5 *"It may be if he (Mohammed) divorced you that his Lord will give him instead of you, wives better than you...obedient to Allah, submissive, faithful, obedient, penitent, adorers... previously married and virgins."*

A Hadith explains how Allah revealed this verse; -

"Umar narrated what Mohammed had said; 'The wives of the Prophet out of their jealousy, backed each other against the Prophet, so I said to them, 'It may be, if he divorced you all, that Allah will give him, instead of you wives better than you.' So this Verse was revealed."
(Sahih Bukhari 6/60/438)

Where's the divine inspiration in that? Was the Koran written by God or by a man?

It is worth noting that the penultimate chapter of the Koran in terms of chronological revelation, Surah 9 also known as "The Ultimatum", is one of the most violent in its incitations and so abrogates all of the earlier given, more peaceable content (which because it has been abrogated does not feature much in this book).

This chapter includes the following commands;

9:5	*"Slay the unbelievers wherever you find them..."*,
9:14	*"Fight them..."*,
9:29	*"Fight the unbelievers..."*,
9:73	*"Make war on the unbelievers..."*, and
9:123	*"O ye who believe, fight those unbelievers who are near to you."*

The chronologically last received Chapter, 110, has only three verses which do not abrogate any of the violent content of Chapter 9.

Now if God is eternal, wise and all-knowing, would He have to change his Word with temporary changing circumstances on the earth? Would God, who made mankind, want to see humanity destroying itself over religion?

In the Torah, Book of Numbers 23:19 it says

"God is not human, that he should lie, not a human being, that he should change his mind".

In Psalm 89:34 God says

"I will not violate my covenant or alter what my lips have uttered".

Abrogation goes against this eternal principle. Therefore, the Koran is not from an everlasting, all-knowing God.

Fatalism

Islamic culture is well known for its fatalistic *"Inch' Allah"* (Allah willing) attitude towards life.

9:51	*"Naught befalleth us save that which Allah has decreed for us"*

13:11 *"if Allah willeth misfortune for a folk there is none that can repel it"*

Allah is seen as being in control of everything so one's free will is seen as being of little importance or even use.

"Verily Allah has fixed the very portion of adultery which a man will indulge in, and which he of necessity must commit..."
(Sahih Muslim 33/6421)

There are many verses that clearly tell you that it is Allah's choice whether you live well or go astray. It's all Allah's fault ! ; -

10:100 *"It is not for any soul to believe save by the permission of Allah."*

13:27 *"Lo, Allah sendeth whom He will astray..."*

7:178 *"he whom Allah sendeth astray - they indeed are losers"*

14:27 *"Allah sendeth the wrongdoers astray..."*

39:36, 39:23, 40:33 *"he whom Allah sendeth astray..."*

6:125 *"whomsoever it is His will to send astray...."*

30:29 *"Who is able to guide him whom Allah hath sent astray?"*

16:9 *"And had He willed He would have led you all aright"*

61:5 *"Allah sent their hearts astray"*

9:127 *"Allah turneth away their hearts..."*

17:97 *"...as for him who He sendeth astray..."*

4:88 *"Would you guide him whom Allah has led into error? For whomever Allah leads into error, for him you will never find a way.*

7:155   *"My Lord (Allah)... Thou sendest whom Thou wilt astray"*

40:74   *"Thus Allah leads the disbelievers into error"*

7:186   *"Whomever Allah leads into error...He leaves them blundering in their blindness"*

2:17,18   *"Allah takes away their light and leaves them in darkness, where they cannot see, deaf, dumb and blind"*

45:23   *"Allah sendest him astray purposely and sealeth up his hearing and setting on his sight a covering..."*

47:23-24   *"...they whom Allah curseth so that He deafeneth them and maketh blind their eyes. Will they not meditate on the Koran?"*

17:46, 6:25   *"We place upon their hearts veils lest they should understand, and in their ears a deafness..."*

2:6-7   *"disbelievers...Allah hath sealed their hearing and their hearts and blinded their eyes...Theirs will be an awful doom"*

Is it possible to properly meditate on something if you are blind and deaf? How can you get to know what it is if you're blinded and made deaf and so can't read it or have anyone recount it to you? And it seems Allah won't offer forgiveness either; -

4:48   *"Lo, Allah forgiveth not..."*

4:116   *"Allah pardoneth not"*

47:34, 4:137   *"Allah will never pardon..."*

4:168   *"Allah will never forgive them..."*

9:80, 60:3-6   *"Allah will not forgive them..."*

What does Allah have in store for those who He leads astray and does not forgive for being led astray?

72:15-17   *"The fires of hell will be fuelled with the bodies of idolaters and unbelievers. They will experience an ever greater torment."*

74:31   *"Allah has appointed angels to tend the fire and has prepared stumbling blocks for those who disbelieve. He sends whom He wills astray"*

78:21-30   *"Those who deny the revelations given to Muhammad will burn forever in hell."*

83:10-17   *"Those who reject Allah's revelations will burn in hell"*

66:9   *"disbelievers...hell will be their home"*

58:8   *"disobedience...hell will suffice them"*

2:39   *"Those who disbelieve and deny our revelations... the fire, they will abide therein."*

2:167   *"They will never get out of the fire."*

2:221   *"Those who marry unbelievers will burn in the fire"*

3:91   *"Those who disbelieve...theirs will be a painful doom"*

If Allah has caused people to go astray, won't forgive them, and then sends them to hell because of it, is that fair? Surely their straying is all Allah's fault! There are hundreds of verses like these which constitute much of the Koran. One leading website has compiled a list of what they claim are 769 such unjust proclamations in the Koran alone without even considering all those in the other sacred Islamic works.

With all this fatalism, is there a failure here to understand the philosophy of free will? If it is Allah that causes people to go astray, and they are powerless to stop him because he is in control of everything that happens, then aren't those people innocent and only Allah guilty of their sin?

The God of the Bible gives right guidance;

"He guides the humble in what is right"
(Psalm 25:9)

Genocide

Most of us have met some lovely Muslim people at some time in our lives, just ordinary folks trying to live a good moral life. Nearly all of them will misguidedly tell you that the Koran supersedes both the Bible and the Torah, and that Islam is now the only true religion. A great many don't really know what the Koran says and could only quote a few simple verses, although most are very quick to point the finger at anything that might appear immoral to them.

At the other end of the scale we have the Islamic State and Boko Haram who happily quote the Koran to justify their barbarism whilst accusing their non-Muslim victims of some kind of proscribed debauchery such as just being a Jew or a Christian. Does the Koran provide good guidance? In truth, no other religion seems to have so many atrocities committed in its name as Islam, and currently the list grows daily. 95% of all terrorism in the world is Islamic; so who is debauched ?

The Koran confirms that;

13:27 *"Allah sendeth whom He will astray..."*

7:179 *"Already We have urged into hell many..."*

Does Islam lead people astray? The answer would clearly seem to be yes! Isn't it obvious that those who follow Allah are led astray and corrupted? Given the candidness of these passages how can there still be anyone pretending that Islam is "The Religion of Peace" and telling us stories of the great days of the Caliphate when different religions lived together in harmony under Islamic rule? Is there any truth in this version of history? So let's look at this in more depth.

We have already looked at the history of Islam and seen how it was born with a lot of bloodshed. Indeed, Mohammed himself led a genocide against the Jews in 627 AD at Banu Qurayza, killing between 700 and 800 men in a single day after they had surrendered. (see Ibn Ishaq 461-464 & Ibn Kathir) The property, women and children of those massacred were divided up between the victors with some of the women being taken off to be traded for horses for the cavalry (Ibn Ishaq 693). But later, when the expansion of the Islamic Caliphate slowed down, we are told of the heyday of Islamic culture and the so called *"Convivencia"*, a supposed time of great peace and harmony especially in the al-Andalus of Spain and North Africa, lasting from the Eighth Century until the Catholic Reconquest of Spain and the expulsion of the Muslims which started in 1499 and continued until 1609.

Now we know that in Islamic Spain, all non-Muslims had to pay a religious tax, like protection money, under Sharia Law to be able just to live, not to be converted by force or be put to death.

Verse 9:29 in the Koran instructs Muslims to

"fight those who believe not in Allah...until they pay Jizya (religious tribute tax) with willing submission and feel subjugated."

This tax could be as much as 50% of their wealth, as was the precedent set with the Jews at Khaybar (see Bukhari 5/59/550).

And of course, there were women and girls in sex-slavery all through that time. Very evidently, we are not talking about some kind of free, liberal egalitarian society here at all, so what more do we know about the truth? We know that there were many Christian martyrs in the Caliphate, including St Perfectus, and the other 48 Cordoba martyrs in the 9th Century, decapitated for professing their Christian faith, which under Sharia law was interpreted as blasphemy against Islam. Amongst their number was St Eulogius, executed for spreading the Gospel and for leading someone to their salvation.

Historian Bat Yeor, author of **"The Dhimmi, Jews and Christians under Islam"**, who has studied Jewish and Christian minorities living under Islamic rule throughout the ages, reports regular massacres, especially of Jews, for example at Fez in 1033, and in Granada in 1066. We also know of 3,000 (some say 9,000) Christian pilgrims killed in Jerusalem in 1065 by the Turcomans who had promised them safe passage in the period before the Crusades. She also mentions the Almohad persecutions in the Maghreb between 1130 and 1212 which effectively put an end to what remained of the Christian population in North Africa. In the Granada massacre, more than 4,000 Jews were killed in one day, and in Fez over 6,000 were killed. So sadly, the peaceful al-Andalus Convivencia never was real, it is no more than a dreamy myth.

On an individual level, things were very hard for Jews and Christians during that time. Maimonides, a well-respected Jewish historian was forced to flee Al-Andalus under threat of death for refusing to convert, and his experiences led him to conclude that Islam had inflicted more damage on the Jews than any other "nation".

History teaches us that through the ages Islamic rule has brought many pogroms and genocides and this continues to our day. Some have maybe even taken place without any real evidence being left, but many have taken place since the advent of news reporting, so today we have some accurate details of what happened in the following cases; -

Assyria 1843-46, Syria; Aleppo 1850, Damascus 1860, Armenia 1873-76, Bulgaria 1876, Persia 1894, the Balkans 1912-1913, the Ottoman Greeks 1913-1923, Armenia 1915, Assyria 1915-1918, Iraq 1933, Bosnia 1943, Syria 1947, Ottoman Greeks (Istanbul)1955, Cyprus 1960, India (Pakistan/ Bangladesh) 1971, Uganda 1971-1972, Cyprus 1974, Afghanistan 1979, Syria 1981-?, Iraq 1986-89, Afghanistan 1986-2001, Kashmir 1990-?, Libya 2011-?, Nigeria 2014-?, Iraq 2014-?

You can find details of all of these genocides on the web, including news reports from the time which tell us it wasn't just soldiers who did the killing and raping, it was very often ordinary Muslims. Many Islamic countries refuse to acknowledge that these atrocities even took place, despite the photographs, despite the journalistic records. Recently in 2015, there was controversy on the centenary of the start of the Armenian Genocide, in which about 1.5 million Christians were killed, because, despite all of the overwhelming evidence, a great many Muslims refuse to acknowledge that it really happened. And still today Islam is extinguishing Christian communities in the Middle East that have been there nearly 2,000 years. Despite the fall of the Islamic State in Iraq it continues. When will it all end?

Many of these massacres were the result of religious fatwas such as that issued in November 1914 issued by the Ottoman Caliphate proclaiming it; *"a sacred duty"*, to kill all infidels. In this case it specified Christians. It led directly to the Armenian and Assyrian genocides the following year. More recently, in Pakistan in 1971, as many as 2.4 million men, mostly Hindu, were killed and more than 200,000 women raped. The photographic records of this genocide give evidence of some of the most horrific things ever seen. This is all fruit of Mohammed and his Koran; hundreds of millions dead, many millions of others displaced from their homes, grieving lost loved ones or taken as sex-slaves. It will only end when the Koran is no longer viewed as being the word of God.

Millions of Muslims have died and suffered too. Shias and Sunnis see each other as apostates and thus unbelievers and so see the rules for killing unbelievers as applying to the other. Currently a deadly war between these two factions is being fought in Yemen. An even more deadly Shia/Sunni conflict is ongoing in Syria and Iraq where major world powers such as Iran and Saudi Arabia are shaping up for major confrontation. The recent execution by Saudi Arabia of a leading Shia cleric brought a severing of diplomatic ties, increasing hostility with Iran. Today, about 87%, estimates vary depending on the source, of the victims of Islamist terrorism are actually Muslims. Quite a paradox.

Surely any book that is truly from God would not lead people astray; but does the Koran lead people astray? Without a doubt, it does.

9:5 *"Slay the non-Muslims wherever you find them, seize them, besiege them, and be ready to ambush them"*

"the hour of resurrection will not be established unless you fight the Jews and kill them..."
(Bukhari 4/52/177, Sahih Muslim 49/6985)

When will all this destruction stop? All the fruit of Mohammed's revelations. Only when the Koran is no longer considered to be the word of God.

Jesus foresaw all this, let's look again at the Gospel of Matthew 7:15-16;

"Beware of false prophets, they come to you in sheep's clothing but inwardly they are ferocious wolves...by their fruit you will recognize them."

It is easy to see what kind of prophet Mohammed was! Indeed, as his religion is the second largest on Earth with 1.8 billion followers, behind Christianity with 2.4 billion, he is the most important false prophet of all time.

Could he be the False Prophet of the Book of Revelation?

If he is, we would expect to find untrue statements in his holy book.

Let's see...

Part Five - A false testament ?

"Such wisdom does not come from above, but is earthly, unspiritual, demonic." (James 3:15)

The Koran says; -

4:82 *"Will they (unbelievers) not then ponder on the Qur'an ? If it had been from other than Allah they would have found therein much incongruity."*

If you ponder on it, incongruity, error and falsity are what you will find. The Koran says of itself that it is perfect and infallible. It claims to be the word of an all-knowing, all-wise god; dictated through his chosen prophet. The Koran even arrogantly challenges us to look for errors in it. But we have found this to be a bluff to get Muslims to unquestioningly believe what it says. In fact, it contains a great many errors of fact, failures of logic and reason, and other imperfections besides. This Part of the book provides a selection of these. Let's be clear, if the Koran is not perfect, then the god who claimed to have created it is a phoney, a fake. Therefore, so must also be his prophet. And the simple truth is that there are dozens upon dozens of things in the Koran which are untrue. It gets many scientific, historical and literary facts wrong. The proof is here in this book for all to read.

So, if the Koran is not what it says it is, but is really a false word of god, a false testament, then where does that leave Islam? It is a falsity, the work of a false prophet, untenable to the intelligent mind. It is ready for the scrap heap of history.

In Deuteronomy 32:21 God promises to make Israel angry *"by a nation that has no understanding".* Given the lack of factual accuracy, logic and reason to be found in the Islamic holy books, you have to ask yourself; is the Lord talking about Islam here? Is there any other nation throughout all of history which has consistently and continually harassed and persecuted the Jewish people so much? Although the years of Islam's allies, the Third Reich, with the Holocaust were more intensely deadly, the duration was only a fraction of the 1,400 years of torment brought by Islam. The large absence of Jews from most of the Middle East, North Africa and Central Asia is the product of centuries of ethnic purging. We are now currently witnessing a similar cultural purging of Christians from Iraq, Syria, Northern Nigeria, and Pakistan. Today many Islamic nations and alliances would attack Israel and kill off all Jews if they thought they could get away with it. Look at the continual stream of anti-Jewish rhetoric coming forth from Iran, Syria, Palestine, from ISIS, Al-Qaeda, Boko Haram and others.

As you will see the Koran does not stand up to critical scrutiny. It is not perfect and infallible as Muslims claim. It is full of errors of many kinds. It cannot therefore be the word of God, and thus its author has to be counted as a false prophet. With regards to Islam we must continue the work of Christ described in 1 John 3:8 to *"destroy the works of the devil".*

Inconsistencies and self-contradictions

Muslims say that the Koran is perfect and infallible, but is this true? In the previous Part of this book, we have seen that Allah says repeatedly that He sends people astray, yet there are also a few verses which state the opposite, for example;

9:115 *"It was never Allah's part that He should send folk astray."*

This is evidently inconsistent with the numerous verses that clearly state that Allah does send people astray. However, this divergence can be understood if sending people astray was not Allah's original role or purpose, but for some reason he does it now as the bulk of the Koran's verses on the issue confirm. We'll discuss the true meaning of this later.

Again, in another section of this book on the question of forgiveness we have seen that Allah does not forgive, yet one verse says

39:53 *"Allah forgives all sins".*

Here there is a logical incongruity. Likewise, the other similar statements in verses

40:3 *"(Allah) The forgiver of sin..."*

4:110 *"whoso doeth evil or wrongeth, seeking pardon, will find Allah forgiving and merciful",*

are inconsistent with the statement in verse

63:6 *"whether forgiveness is asked for or not, Allah will not forgive them".*

It is logically inconsistent to say that Allah forgives all sins and that Allah will not forgive. If there is even a single sin that is not forgiven, then in verse 39:53 there is a false statement.

Do not all such self-contradictions in the Koran saying Allah will not forgive prove its falsity?

Many other statements in the Koran contradict others elsewhere in the book. Such contradictions show that the Koran is not "perfect and infallible" as it itself claims to be.

11:1 *"This Koran is a book whose verses have been perfected (in every sphere of knowledge, etc.) "*

But in fact, there are many such self-contradictions, like these;

39:12 *"And I (Mohammed) am commanded to be the first of those who are Muslims."*

5:111 *"(Jesus' disciples) said 'We have the faith, bear witness that we bow to Allah as Muslims."*

Jesus and his disciples lived 600 years before Islam existed, before the concept of being a Muslim existed. This verse is an absolute lie!

3:67 *"Ibrahim (Abraham) was neither a Jew nor a Christian, but he was a true Muslim"*

If Abraham was a true Muslim, 2,000 years before Mohammed lived, Mohammed was not the first! This last statement is in full contradiction to the first. They cannot both be true. Is the Koran perfect? No way!

Other contradictions involve the revelation of the Koran; -

44:3 *"Lo, We sent it (the Koran) down on a blessed night,"*

17:106 *"And We have sent it down progressively in stages..."*

It can't be both! Tradition and historical fact hold that the Koran was received by Mohammed over the period from 610 to 632 AD. Each contradiction proves that the Koran is neither perfect nor infallible.

Abrogation creates a similar problem; -

10:64 *"No alteration can there be to the words of Allah."*

2:106 *"We do not abrogate a verse or cause it to be forgotten except that We bring forth (one) better."*

But isn't abrogation a form of alteration? If it all came down in one night, then what is this abrogation? More proof that the Koran is not perfect!

And the Koran is supposed to be perfect and infallible...

10:37 *"The Quran is infallible...it comes from the Lord",*

4:82 *"Will they not ponder on the Koran, if it is from other than Allah they will find much incongruity."*

Have we found incongruity? What does inconsistency and self-contradiction say about the source of the Koran? With abrogation? It proves it is not from God!

Impossibilities!

The Koran says that Mohammed took a night journey, mentioned in verse 17:1, to *"the far distant place of worship"*, which Muslims say is the Al-Aqsa mosque on Temple Mount in Jerusalem. But Mohammed died in 632 and the Muslim armies did not take Jerusalem until 637. The construction of the mosque did not begin until 691 under Caliph Abdal Malik, following the creation of an open-air worship area by his predecessor Caliph Umar Ibn al-Khattab sometime around 666 AD. No mosque existed there during Mohammed's lifetime, so clearly it was impossible for him to have made such a visit. Tradition says that Mohammed made this journey on a winged horse called Burak, known as Pegasus in the West. Christians see this steed as a demonic messenger, a descendant of the ancient Greek deity Chaos.

Islamic tradition maintains that Abraham and his son Ishmael built the Ka'aba in Mecca as described in verses 22:26-33, 2:127, & 3:96;

"And when Ibrahim (Abraham) and Isma'il (Ishmael) were raising the foundations of the House (The Ka'aba in Mecca)..."

This was highly unlikely as Abraham died during the early part of the second millennia before Christ, the exact date is unknown, but it was sometime between 1750-1995 BC, in Canaan. His tomb, the Cave of Machpelah, can be visited in Hebron to this day. Furthermore, Abraham was a tent dweller and there is no record of him having acquired any building skills. Nor is there any archaeological evidence whatsoever that Mecca was inhabited before the 4th Century AD when trade routes were forged through a previously undeveloped area of Arabian desert. The earliest reliable information suggests that the pagan sanctuary at Mecca was founded sometime after that by the al-Amaliq (Amalekite) tribe. The length of the journey, over 1,200 Kilometres to a then undefined place, with no infrastructure for crossing great swathes of desert wilderness to get there, would have made it impossible on a practical level.

Whilst Islam pretends to be the spiritual heritage of Ishmael, and Mohammed claimed descendance from him, both he and his father Abraham worshipped the God *"El"* (Il in Arabic) not *"Allah"* (Al-ilah). El (il) is even part of Ishmael's name (Ismail in Arabic) which means *"El/Il (God) hears"*.

Other Koran verses talk of improbable things, Surah 18 verses 9-26 tell a tale of some youths who fell asleep in a cave and woke 309 years later.

18:25 *"and they remained in their cave for three hundred years and exceeded by nine"*

Is this believable? The Koran also says that Jews and Christians have been turned into apes and swine by Allah.

5:60 *"the recompense from Allah: those (Jews) who incurred the Curse of Allah and His Wrath, those of whom He transformed into monkeys and swine..."*

Really? Is reincarnation part of Islam?

Incorrect Facts?

It is claimed that the Koran is the word of God and therefore perfect and infallible. If it contains any incorrect fact, even just one, then it is neither perfect nor infallible. Non-Muslims say the book contains many statements which are scientifically or historically untrue, here are just a few examples; -

Koran Surah 19 claims that John (Yohanan in Hebrew, Yahya in Arabic) who baptised Jesus was the first to whom Allah gave that name,

19:7 *"We have given the same name to none before"*

However, the name had already been given to a King John (Yohanan/Yahya) of Israel, nicknamed "Hyrcanus", who lived from 164 BC to 104 BC, a century before John known as "The Baptist". This King John is remembered for having separated state governmental function away from the religious establishment, something Islam wants to undo.

Is the Koran perfect and infallible? It got that one wrong!

Elsewhere it claims, referring to the time of Moses;

7:137 *"We destroyed completely all the great works and buildings which Fir'aun (Pharaoh) and his people erected."*

Remnants remain of the original temples at Luxor which date from Moses' time, they were never completely destroyed. Are not the pyramids still there at Giza near Cairo with the Great Pyramid still remaining remarkably intact? Allah's statement appears to be untrue. Greek and Roman records show that the great buildings at Karnak, Heliopolis and elsewhere in Egypt were still in use after Moses time and it was only in the first and second centuries AD that they fell into disuse and were pillaged for building materials causing their ruin.

Once again, the Koran is wrong. It is also wrong concerning certain scientific statements; Surah 36 states;

36:40 *"It is not for the sun to overtake the moon, nor doth night outstrip the day. They float each in an orbit."*

It takes 24 hours, as the earth rotates, for us to see the sun again in the sky above the same longitudinal position but 24 hours and 49 minutes for the moon. Thus, the sun is seen to travel across the sky faster than the moon. Therefore, from an earthly perspective, the sun does overtake the moon, causing us sometimes to see solar eclipses. These are caused by the alignment of the moon directly between the earth and the sun so that we see the sun pass (overtaking) behind the moon.

And certainly, night outstrips day the closer one moves to the polar winter. In the Arctic and Antarctic Circles night completely outstrips day with no daylight at all on the winter solstices. This effect is greater the closer one moves towards the poles where there are longer periods of continuous night, even weeks or months long.

The sun does not float in an orbit around the earth. On the contrary, it is the earth that orbits the sun, taking a solar year of 365.256 days to complete an orbit. Therefore, the statement made in verse 36:40 is irrefutably incorrect. The Koran is proven imperfect and fallible.

God should know the facts, so is the Koran from an all-wise God, or was it written by a man of limited knowledge? There are other similar statements about the sun which are also untrue; one Surah talks of

18:86 *"the setting place of the sun....in a muddy spring"*

and this is expanded upon by in the Hadiths which confirms

"it sets in a spring of warm water" (Abu Dawud 3991).

Then according to the Prophet, it goes on to; *"prostrate itself underneath the Throne until it takes permission to rise again"*
(Sahih Bukhari 4/54/421).

This again is false, the place where the sun appears to set is relative to where you observe it from, and in different seasons it may seem to set in different places from the same viewing point. Even the people who laid the wooden guide foundations of Stonehenge 10,000 years ago knew that. In truth, the earth rotates in its orbit around the sun, and although an observer loses sight of the sun when it sets, it remains visible in the sky elsewhere. When the sun sets in Mecca, it is daylight in America. These days we can take a plane to the rest of the world and check it out.

A similar fallacy, this time including the moon. Can be found elsewhere in Surah 36

36:38-39 *"And the sun runneth on unto a resting-place for him. That is the measuring of the Mighty, the Wise. And for the moon We have appointed mansions till she return like an old shrivelled palm-leaf."*

It is just not scientifically true. What other verses say are also highly questionable;

17:16 *"And (Allah) hath made the moon a light"*

The moon is just a reflector and produces no light of its own, this is why we see different shapes in it, and is also why it becomes dark and disappears from view during the New Moon phase. If it was a light, we would always see it the same.

What about these verses?

50:7, 51:48 *"The earth We have spread out..."*

79:30 *"And the earth, after that He made it flat"*

The earth is not flat, although that was the predominant understanding in Mohammed's time. Once again, the Koran is wrong. So, who is speaking in the Koran, God or Mohammed?

Other verses are scientifically very incorrect;

86:5-7 *"So let man consider from what he is made, he is made from a gushing fluid that issued from between the loins and ribs."*

2:223 *"Your wives are a tilth (a place of sowing seed) for you..."*

Semen comes from the testicles, which are not between the loins and ribs, and it needs an egg, not a planting ground, to form an embryo. Another verse talks about the formation of the embryo;

23:14 *"The bones are formed, then the bones were clothed with flesh."*

The science of the Koran, again is untrue, the bones form inside the flesh of the foetus. Mohammed had no concept of genetics;

"And what makes a baby look like its father or mother?... And if a man's discharge proceeded that of the woman, then the child resembles the father, and if the woman's discharge proceeded that of the man, then the child resembles the mother." (Sahih Bukhari 6/60/7)

Other scientifically incorrect statements can be found elsewhere in the Koran too; -

24:45 *"Allah hath created every animal of water"*

Life is created of far more than just water, even the simplest organisms contain complex organic molecules such as DNA and RNA. All sorts of proteins, vitamins and trace elements are important to the proper functioning of any living body.

51:49 *"And of all things We created two mates"*

Again untrue; some life forms are purely asexual whilst the New Mexico Whiptail lizard (*Cnemidophorus neomexicanus*) only exists as females, reproducing solely by virgin birth. Many animals from sharks through to turkeys have also been proved to have offspring in this way, known academically as parthenogenesis. Honey-bees live in colonies, not pairs, with fertilized eggs from the queen bee developing into female worker bees and unfertilized (un-mated) eggs becoming drones or males. What about hermaphrodites, and gynandromorphs which have both sexes in one body? Certain species may even change gender during their lifetime, like the clownfish which does so when mates are in short supply. Chinese Moon Jellyfish (*Aurelia sp 1*), although they can reproduce sexually, normally produce hordes of clones from polyps which develop on their bodies, they don't have mates for this.

And Muslim men may have more than one wife plus sex-slaves.

That lizard, being only female, conclusively and definitively proves the Koran wrong.

13:3 *"And fruits of every kind He made therein in two sexes"*

Fruit, as such, doesn't have gender. In fact, many species of fruit trees, such as oranges, apples and mangoes reproduce asexually by a process called apomixis. Whilst certain fruiting plants bring forth both male and female flowers, some like bell peppers have flowers that are both, yet other fruits like kiwis and persimmons have plants which are effectively only male or female. Whichever way you look at it the Koran has missed the mark again.

Other untrue premises can be found in; -

7:147 *"Those who deny Our revelations...their works are fruitless"*

3:195 *"Never will I suffer to be lost the work of any of you"*

10:14 *"We appointed you viceroys in the earth"*

47:4 *"Now when ye meet in battle those who disbelieve, then it is smiting of their necks until ye have routed them... And those who are slain in the cause of Allah, He rendereth not their actions vain"*

61:9 *"that He may make it (Islam) conqueror of all religion"*

8:65 *"rouse the believers to the fight. If there are twenty amongst you, patient and persevering, they will vanquish two hundred: if a hundred, they will vanquish a thousand of the unbelievers: for these are a people without understanding"*

4:141 *"never will Allah grant to the disbelievers a way (to triumph) over the believers"*

Well what about the Battle of Poitiers (732), the Reconquista (711-1492), the Battle of Lepanto (1571), the Battle of Vienna (1683) and the defeat of the Ottoman Caliphate (1918)?

Didn't the non-Muslims achieve permanent and decisive victories over Muslims in all these battles. Has Mohammed's Allah got it wrong again?

In the near future, we can look forward to the full demise of the Islamic State which will be more proof of this.

Perfect? Infallible?

These are not the only incorrect "facts" found in the Koran, there are many more, but these are more than enough to clearly prove the point. If it had been dictated by God, then there would be no inaccuracy whatsoever. Even just one false statement proves that the Koran is neither perfect nor infallible. But we have several! You can check all the true facts out for yourself!

Failures of logic and reason

9:36   *"The number of months with Allah is twelve (lunar) months..."*

10:5   *"He made...the moon a light and determined for her stages, that ye might know the number of years..."*

The Islamic calendar is based on a year of 12 lunar months which does not stay aligned to the seasons. The solar year which does stay aligned to the annual seasons is longer, equivalent to 12.37 lunar months. Because of this discrepancy, Islamic dates fall about eleven days earlier each year relative to our standard solar calendar. This is unworkable for agriculture and other purposes in most parts of the world where temperatures, light levels and harvesting of crops are seasonal and the scheduling of economic activity needs to be tied to the seasonal months. Even those who like to plant and harvest by the moon need to consider the solar seasons.

In Islam months five and six are called **Jumaada Awal** (first freeze) and **Jumaada Thani** (second freeze). However, because of the shortcomings of the lunar calendar these Islamic months can fall in the Saudi Arabian summer months when there aren't any frosts and the record low night temperature is above 20 degrees Celsius. Once again whilst God surely knows his astronomy and the nature of the seasons, so it can only be by man's hand that Islamic culture has got out of chronological alignment.

Ramadan is a period of fasting and abstinence prescribed in the Koran verse 2:185 and elsewhere. The Ramadan fast, which is of pre-Islamic origin, takes place always in the ninth month of the Islamic calendar and so falls at different times each year. Eating, drinking any liquids, smoking, sex and lying are all forbidden during daylight hours the whole month.

This fasting during Ramadan is an obligation under Sharia law. Major problems arise with practising the fast in polar regions as these areas experience annual periods of constant daylight. In 2016, Ramadan started on June 6th and the festivities at the end of the fast went on until July 5th. In northern cities such as Norilsk in Russia, the continuous midsummer polar day lasts for more than six weeks from around the beginning of June until mid-July. Here it would have been impossible to undertake a total fast during the day, and then only eat at night, because there is no night during that period. If anyone did try to go without drinking anything during daylight hours, they would die of dehydration within a few days. Even in cold temperatures one could not live more than 4-5 days, certainly not a whole month, without taking in water in some form.

In reality, the Muslims in these places are obliged to cheat on the rules;

2:187 *"you shall maintain the fast until the night"*

and Hadith Khuzuymah; *"Allah has made it compulsory upon you to fast by day"*

because they are impossible. Instead they apply arbitrary sunset and sunrise times which have nothing to do with the actual hours of daylight there. Has the Koran failed again? Surely God wouldn't order Muslims to do something impossible as part of their faith, after all didn't He make the earth and therefore knows the polar seasons.

Or is the Islamic faith man made and not divine as many critics say, explaining easily these fallibilities?

18:1 *"Praise be to Allah Who hath revealed the Scripture unto His slave, and hath not placed therein any crookedness"*

It just isn't true.

Islamic inheritance law also fails the test of logic. Let's look at the full text of Koran verses 4:11-12 and 4:176;

"Allah instructs you concerning your children: for the male, what is equal to the share of two females. But if there are (only) daughters, two or more, for them is two thirds of one's estate. And if there is only one, for her is half. And for one's parents, to each one of them is a sixth of his estate if he left children. But if he had no children and the parents (alone) inherit from him, then for his mother is one third. And if he had brothers (or sisters), for his mother is a sixth, after any bequest he (may have) made or debt. Your parents or your children - you know not which

of them are nearest to you in benefit. (These shares are) an obligation (imposed) by Allah. Indeed, Allah is ever Knowing and Wise" (4:11)

"And for you is half of what your wives leave if they have no child. But if they have a child, for you is one fourth of what they leave, after any bequest they (may have) made or debt. And for the wives is one fourth if you leave no child. But if you leave a child, then for them is an eighth of what you leave, after any bequest you (may have) made or debt. And if a man or woman leaves neither ascendants nor descendants but has a brother or a sister, then for each one of them is a sixth. But if they are more than two, they share a third, after any bequest which was made or debt, as long as there is no detriment (caused). (This is) an ordinance from Allah, and Allah is Knowing and Forbearing" (4:12)

"Allah gives you a ruling concerning one having neither descendants nor ascendants (as heirs)." If a man dies, leaving no child but (only) a sister, she will have half of what he left. And he inherits from her if she (dies and) has no child. But if there are two sisters (or more), they will have two-thirds of what he left. If there are both brothers and sisters, the male will have the share of two females. Allah makes clear to you (His law), lest you go astray. And Allah is Knowing of all things" (4:176)

In the Sharia legal reference authority **"Islamic Inheritance Law"**, by Dr Jusuf Ziya Kavakci, p54-56, it admits that applying the inheritance share rules derived from the above verses can lead to complex situations where the total of prescribed shares due to inheritors can exceed 100% of the value of the estate to be divided.

Various websites both pro- and anti- Sharia Law give practical examples of how the sums of the shares just don't add up under these rules. Let's look at a practical example;

Applying the rules in verses 4:11-12 to the case of a man leaving a wife, one son and his parents. Concerning the son, he gets twice the amount for a female where a sole daughter would get one-half, so he gets 100% of the estate. Then on top of that, each of the parents gets 1/6 (approx. 16.67% each, 33.33% between them) and the wife gets 1/8 (12.5%). Adding up these shares gives a sum worth approximately 145.8% of the value of the estate to be distributed.

Impossible! The rules fail the test of logic. Sharia inheritance law just doesn't add up. And 4:176 says

"Allah makes it clear to you so you do not go wrong - Allah knows all things".

How could Allah get it so wrong? The only real explanation is that the Koran wasn't written by God. Even the syntax of the Koran calls its alleged God given origin into question. In Surah 1 in its entirety it is clearly Mohammed speaking to Allah and not Allah speaking to man.

Other verses likewise do not appear to be God speaking; -

6:104 *"Proofs have come unto you from your Lord, so whoso seeth, it is for his own good, and whoso is blind is blind to his own hurt. And I am not a keeper over you."*

This last phrase proves that this is clearly Mohammed speaking, other verses are similarly confused as to whom the grammatical subject is.

6:114 *"Shall I seek other than Allah for judge, when He it is Who hath revealed unto you (this) Scripture, fully explained ?"*

This simply cannot be Allah speaking, this is someone else speaking about him. Most of this chapter talks of Allah in the third person singular, he, whereas the majority of the verses have him talking in the first-person plural, "We". Chapter 3 is similarly confusing, it speaks both in the third person, then in the second person then afterwards also in the first-person plural, and then again in the first-person singular;

3:7 *"He it is Who hath revealed unto thee the Scripture wherein are clear revelations...No one knoweth its explanation save Allah...the whole is from our Lord..."*

3:8 *"Our Lord! Cause not our hearts to stray after Thou hast guided us..."*

3:151 *"We shall cast terror into the hearts of those who disbelieve"*

3:195 *"So those who fled and were driven forth from their homes and suffered damage for My cause, and fought and were slain, verily I shall remit their evil deeds from them"*

Try and workout the syntax in this passage; -

3:11 *"Like Pharaoh's folk and those who were before them, they disbelieved Our revelations and so Allah seized them for their sins. And Allah is severe in punishment"*

Allah is placed in the third person here, so who is this first-person plural who gave the revelations?

Clear revelations? That no one can understand but Allah. Surah 7 is just as confused;

7:180 "Allah's are the fairest names. Invoke Him by them"

7:181 "And of those whom We created..."

7:182 "And those who deny Our revelations - step by step We lead them on from whence they know not"

7:183 "I give them rein (for) lo! My scheme is strong"

7:184 "Have they not bethought them there is no madness in their comrade? He is but a plain warner"

7:185 "Have they not considered the dominion of the heavens and the earth, and what things Allah hath created"

7:186 "Those whom Allah sendeth astray...to wander blindly on in their contumacy"

He, We, I, just who is talking here? Chapter 13 is likewise flawed the text switching from *He* to *We*. Other verses are obviously humans speaking; -

37:164 "There is not one of us but hath his known position"

37:165 "O! we, even we are they who set the ranks"

37:166 "Lo! we, even we are they who hymn His praise"

37:169 "We would be single-minded slaves of Allah"

Sometimes Mohammed doesn't even hide the fact it is him talking;

51:50 "Therefore flee unto Allah; lo! I am a plain warner unto you from him"

All of chapter 84 seems to be his dialogue;

84:16 "Oh, I swear by the afterglow of sunset"

God doesn't need to swear by anything, He is all powerful, this again is just a man speaking.

81:15 "But nay! I swear by the stars"

The true God almighty doesn't talk like that! In Isaiah 45:23 He says;

"By myself I have sworn... "

And in verse 10:5 of the Koran there hides no little confession by Allah; -

"[Talking of the sun and moon]... Allah did not create this but in truth He explains the revelations in detail for people who have knowledge"

The logical conclusion from this is that Allah is not God!

"In the beginning, God created the heaven and the earth..."
(Torah, Book of Genesis 1:1)

And again, some of the Koran seems to be Mohammed just making up rules that suit himself; -

33:53 *"Enter not the dwellings of the Prophet for a meal without waiting for the proper time, unless permission be granted you. But if ye are invited, enter, and, when your meal is ended, then disperse. Linger not for conversation. Lo! that would cause annoyance to the Prophet... And it is not for you to cause annoyance to the messenger of Allah..."*

A book composed only of divine revelations or just a personal testament?

And more!

Please be aware that there are many other inconsistencies, fallacies and self-contradictions in the Koran besides those detailed here.

A simple internet search can reveal several lists of such problems, although to be fair some of the criticisms of the Koran that you will find mooted on the web are not valid. Those featured in this book all stand a strong test of reason, there are many others which are maybe not so clear at first glance, so they have been omitted from the preceding section of this book.

One such instance of a stated fact in the Koran which is a bit more complicated to verify concerns the family of Mary (Mariam in Hebrew, Maryam in Arabic) the mother of Jesus; -

19:27-28 *"O Maryam, sister of Haroun (Aaron)..."*

66:12   *"And Maryam, daughter of Imran (Amran)..."*

Now historians agree that Mary's parents were Joachim and Anna and there is no evidence of any siblings. The Gospel of Luke 1:5 says that Elizabeth, Mary's cousin, was a descendant of Aaron, so perhaps figuratively speaking she was a daughter of Aaron, but sister, definitely not! Aaron, her possible ancestor, did have a sister called Maryam and their father was called Amran (Imran in Arabic).

Could God have gotten confused and mixed them up? Would God have written it wrong in the Koran? No, it was illiterate Mohammed who got the story wrong.

It should be noted that there have been attempts to cover this problem up, one more recent English translation of the Koran verses reads

19:27-28   *"Sister of Haroun (Aaron) [not the brother of Musa (Moses) but he was another pious man at the time of Maryam (Mary)] ...",*

even though the part within the square brackets does not appear in the original Arabic. Other leading Islamic texts say that Imran is the Arabic form of Joachim, this is tactical lying because it is just not true.

Imran is the correct Arabic form of Amran, the name of the father of Aaron, Moses and Maryam.

Another trick to try to deal with this problem is to say that the term *"sister of Aaron",* is equivalent to saying; *"descendant of Aaron".* But a sister is not a descendant. The Islamic "experts" are obviously trying to cover up for Mohammed's mistake!

Furthermore, linguistic analysis of the Koran shows that the word "sister" is never used figuratively elsewhere in the book to mean "a descendant", it is always used to refer to contemporary relations.

It is quite clear that these statements about Mary are incorrect, yet the topic gives rise to such a tricky debate that it is included here only as an example of a whole large category of evidence which could have been included, but is superfluous here because the real question has already been answered. The Koran gets many things wrong.

Another similar problem arises with the name of John the Baptist. He was born son of a priest named Zechariah in Judea, who was visited by the Angel of the Lord and told before the birth to call him יוֹחָנָן , which transliterates into Johanan or Yochanan, and often translates as John in English. In Arabic, the corresponding name is Yuhanna (يوحنّا).

"Do not be afraid, Zechariah; your prayer has been heard. Your wife Elizabeth will bear you a son, and you are to call him John (Hebrew - Johanan). He will be a joy and delight to you, and many will rejoice because of his birth." (Luke 1:13-14)

This name has been in popular use since at least the 6th Century BC. You will find it in Jeremiah Chapters 40-41 where someone by this name appears in a prophetic story involving a character called Ishmael.

"When Johanan son of Kareah and all the commanders of the armies with him heard of all the evil that Ishmael son of Nethaniah had done, they took all their men and went to fight" (Jeremiah 41:11-12)

The name also occurs elsewhere in the Old Testament. However, when modern Muslim scholars translating the Koran found that verse (19:7), *"We have given the same name to none before"*, was untrue, they sought to cover it up by changing John the Baptist's name in Arabic from Yuhunna to Yahya (يحيى), the equivalent of the English "Jojo" which has no real Hebrew equivalent except perhaps as a diminutive form of the name Yosef (Joseph). Arthur Jeffery's study of **"The Foreign Vocabulary of the Qu'ran"** (Oriental Institute, 1938, p291) notes that the name Yahya is missing totally from early Islamic literature including early copies of the Koran.

This is yet another example of tactical deceit to hide the Koran's errors.

Only one imperfection is required to prove definitively that the Koran is not the perfect, infallible word of God, yet we have found many.

It is clearly imperfect and fallible.

If Mohammed and Allah say that the Koran is perfect and infallible, but it is easily proved not to be, then Mohammed and Allah have said something untrue.

And therefore, Mohammed is a false prophet and his Allah is a false god.

If the Koran is wrong, then Islam is wrong.

Part Six – The Bible and Koran compared

"test all things. Hold fast to what is good" (1 Thessalonians 5:21)

The Koran says that it confirms the Torah and the Gospels and that it is a *"detailed explanation"* (10:37) of former scripture. Thus, it pretends to confirm the Torah and Gospels and present a clear account of what they say. And based on this, Muslims are told that it in effect replaces, and renders redundant, the Bible. This lie has probably condemned more people to hell than any other since the Serpent's words to Eve in the Garden of Eden. The real reason for the Koran pretending to be a full explanation of God's Word is to prevent people from reading the Bible, lest they might find the truth and reject Islam. The reality is that Islam has little to do with the Hebraic and Christian covenants because the content of the Koran is not from the same god. We will deal with the issue of who Islamic Allah really is later on, but in this section, we make some direct comparisons between the content of the Bible and the Koran.

"To you it has been given to know the secrets of the kingdom of heaven, but to them it has not been given" (Matthew 13:11)

Now whilst it would be entirely possible to compare the whole texts of each of these sacred works and provide a very detailed point by point analysis of where and how they diverge, we have not felt it worthwhile to do so. Such long-winded apologetics would not serve any real purpose. In this book, it suffices to simply prove the Koran's statement to be untrue, to prove that it does not confirm or replace the Bible, and at the same time destroy the lie taught to Muslims that Islam supersedes Christianity. Unlike our relationship with God, Islam really is just a set of religious rules and practices. Islam seeks to take man back out of relationship with God and make him subject once more to the accuser and a written law. And just as Moses' Law could not bring salvation, Islam cannot.

"Because we know that a man is not justified by works of The Written Law, but by the faith of Jesus The Messiah... because no one is made right by the works of The Written Law" (Galatians 2:16)

In a few instances, we have gone further in our analysis to highlight particular issues and explain why Islam would try to change what the Bible says. The classic example is, of course, the denial in the Koran that Jesus died on the Cross, thereby trying to bury forever the Work of the Cross and the Resurrection. Islam does not want Muslims to find out the truth of Salvation in Christ but wants them to stay in ignorance. We need to break this lie and bring them the truth to see them saved and set free. Islam teaches a false Jesus, trying to make Him a secondary prophet behind Mohammed. It has to pretend that the Koran replaces the Gospels in order to stop Muslims from finding out the truth for themselves. How has this lie endured for centuries?

"Claiming to be wise, they became fools" (Romans 1:22)

Another area we look closely at, is the divergence between the original Bible stories and the Koran's versions, which we do to emphasize the differences between the overall messages of these books. For example, in re-telling the story of Cain and Abel, which we will consider later, the Koran reveals an Islamic Allah whose nature is very different from our Judeo-Christian God Almighty. This is a fundamental issue because we need to eradicate the lie that Muslims worship the same God and that Islam is just their way of doing it.

"it is not good for a person to be without knowledge" (Proverbs 19:2)

Then having adequately proven that the Koran does not confirm the Bible, we will not need to go into all the Koran's false versions of Bible stories in any greater depth. These only appear in the Koran to give it some purported historicity. The Koran does not come from the same origin as the Torah and the Bible. The illusion of a continuity through the Koran is a fabrication by Satan to lead people astray. The Koran contradicts the Bible with its murderous theology. What is of greater importance is to really understand who Islamic Allah is, and what Islam is from a Christian perspective. This we will do in the subsequent section.

Historical Confusion

Several verses in the Koran say that it confirms the Torah, the sacred Jewish writings of Moses (the term is often used to include other sacred Jewish texts too) and the Gospel, which comprises the four reliable accounts of the life of Jesus Christ which form part of the Christian Bible.

The full Christian Bible also includes the whole Torah which forms its first five books. These works pre-date the Koran by several hundreds of years, thousands of years in the case of Moses' writings, and there are quite a number of copies of them made well before Mohammed's time which are still in existence today, such as the Codex Sinaiticus from the 4th Century. Their contents can easily be verified.

3:3 *"He has sent down to you the Book in truth confirming what was before it...the Torah and the Gospel"*

5:48 *"And We have revealed to you the Book in truth confirming that which preceded it..."*

10:37 *'it was not possible for this Qur'an to be produced by any other than Allah as it is confirmation of what was before and a detailed explanation of former scripture, about which there is no doubt....'*

It should be noted that the Koran seems to infer that Jesus himself wrote a book called the Gospel, this is not true;

5:46 *"We gave Jesus...the Gospel".*

The four Gospels were written after the death of Jesus by four different writers including a doctor, Luke, who was commissioned by a Roman official to provide an account of Jesus' teachings and many healing miracles. Luke also wrote an account of those of Christ's followers too, "The Book of Acts". The other Gospels were written by Jesus' very close disciple John, another disciple Matthew, and Mark, a writer, who was a companion of St Peter, one of the founders of the Church.

The claim that the Koran confirms the Torah and Gospels is readily disproved by comparing their contents. To start with, the Torah makes it clear that Yahweh, not Allah, is God; -

"And they will know that I am Yahweh their God... I am Yahweh their God." (Exodus 29:46 - direct translation from Hebrew)

This difference is incontrovertible and incontestable.

But that's not the only divergence, one of the first stories in the Torah is that of Adam, the first man, in verse 2:19 in the Book of Genesis; -

"And out of the ground the LORD God formed every beast of the field, and every fowl of the air; and brought them unto Adam to see what he would call them: and whatsoever Adam called every living creature, that was the name thereof."

Whereas in the Koran on the same topic, it says; -

2:31 *"And He (Allah) taught Adam all the names..."*

The Torah and Koran versions of this story do not tally, there is no way they can both be right. The Koran cannot be said to confirm the Torah version because the two versions do not correspond. Either Adam named them or he did not. Indeed, even in the creation of man and woman the Torah and Koran differ, the Bible says (Genesis 5:2);

"Male and female He created them, and He blessed them and named them Man..."

In other words, in the Torah, both man and woman are equal and blessed, whereas as we have seen already in our Chapter on women, in the Koran the female is evil and worth less than the male.

Again, the differences between the Torah and Koran are irreconcilable.

The story of Adam and his mate Eve being punished and removed from the Garden of Eden is another example of the Koran being different from the previous scripture. In the Torah (Genesis 3:15) God puts enmity between Satan and the woman; -

"The LORD God said to the serpent (Satan), '...and I will put enmity Between you and the woman, And between your seed and her seed"

In other words, in the Bible, Satan and his demons become the enemies of all mankind. But in the Koran verse 2:36 Allah instead makes man and woman enemies of each other through Adam and Eve; -

"We (Allah) said 'Go down (from hence), one of you a foe unto the other"

The meanings of the two versions are very different, in the Torah the serpent (Satan) is made an enemy of mankind, whereas in the Koran men and women are made enemies of each other. This is a significant shift in meaning which reflects the misogyny that Mohammed and his Allah both show; -

"Woman has been created from a rib and will in no way be straightened...the most crooked part of the rib is the top"
(Sahih Muslim 8/3467-3468, Bukhari 7/62/113-114)

Verse 44:17 onwards in the Koran gives a partial account of the story found in the Torah of the Exodus of Jews from ancient Egypt. Its very reduced account fails to follow some of the key points in the original. For example, Koran Surah 44 has Moses' Lord saying; -

44:23   *"Take away My slaves by night. Lo I ye will be followed"*

whereas the Torah has God telling Moses that; -

"Pharaoh...will let you go from here, and when he does, he will drive you out completely". (Exodus 11:1)

The idea of the Hebrew slaves sneaking away by night is very different from the Torah account of a major confrontation between Moses and Pharaoh leading up to the departure of the Jews. The versions are not the same; the two books are just not telling the same story. The whole point of the Torah version is that God openly manifests His miraculous power to bring the Jews out of Egypt, but the Koran misses this fundamental point.

The Koran's statement in verse 10:37 that it is *"a detailed explanation of former scripture",* does not match the facts. The Torah and Gospels give many examples of God's supernatural intervention in human affairs which the Koran leaves out.

Many other Koran verses disagree with the histories given in the Torah and the Gospels, some just in minor ways, such as; -

5:78 *"the children of Israel who went astray were cursed by the tongue of David and of Jesus..."*

This verse is contradicted by the very books the Koran pretends to confirm; David was cursed by others as told in the First Book of Samuel 17:43 and in the Second Book of Samuel 16:10-11, and did once curse a family because its head killed one of his officials (Second Book of Samuel 3:29), he also cursed the Mountains of Gilboa (2 Samuel 1:21). He never cursed the Israelites with his tongue although unwittingly his actions once had the effect to bring on a curse. He repented of this later.

Islamic scholars quote sections of the Gospel of Matthew chapter 23 as being Jesus' alleged curse, especially this (verses 33-35);

"You serpents, you brood of vipers, how are you to escape being sentenced to hell ? Therefore, I send you prophets and wise men and scribes, some of whom you kill and crucify, and some you flog in your synagogues and persecute from town to town, so that on you may come all the righteous blood shed on earth..."

This clearly is not expressed as a curse but is a descriptive discourse, albeit colourfully allegoric, addressing the character and misdeeds of the religious leaders of the time. The meaning is clear if one reads from the beginning of that chapter. Jesus never cursed a person although He did prophetically curse a fig tree which bore no fruit for Him as a demonstration of his power for His disciples (Matthew 21:18-22).

In fact, in the Gospel of Matthew chapter 5 verse 22 Jesus says

"anyone who calls a brother or sister 'idiot' is answerable for it. 'And anyone who says 'you fool' risks hell-fire."

Jesus is explaining here that we should not curse another person even in the smallest way, but only bless them with the words of our mouths.

Indeed, this chapter begins (Matt 5:3) with Him blessing the lost, not cursing them;

"Blessed are the poor in spirit...."

In the Bible St Paul restates this; -

"Bless and do not curse" (Book of Romans 12:14)

Rather than confirming the previous scriptures the Koran seems to misinterpret them making it seem alright to curse people.

Other discrepancies in the Koran are more complex in nature; -

2:249 *"Saul set out with the army, he said to them; 'Allah will test you by the water. Whosoever drinks is not of me... save who takes it in the hollow of the hand"*

The selection of soldiers by how they drank is recorded in the Bible;

"So Gideon took the men down to the water. There the Lord told him; 'Separate those who.... drank from cupped hands...."
(Book of Judges 7:5-7)

Evidently, in the scriptures we have different versions of the same story told in different circumstances and with different actors, Saul and Gideon, ascribed to them. How can one know which is right? The answer is quite simple, the Book of Judges is estimated to have been written not too long after the event, about 1,050 to 1,000 BC, over one and a half millennia before Mohammed's Koran. It was written by people with knowledge of the Jewish culture, whereas Mohammed had no such direct knowledge. Because he was illiterate, he would not have been able to read up on the facts himself. Critics say that such inaccuracies in the Koran show that it is the work of man, an illiterate uninformed one, and not a work of God. They say Mohammed must have heard the story and remembered it wrong.

Look also at how the story is told in the Koran, the soldiers are told beforehand what the criterion of success will be, and that makes the test pointless, like giving out answers before an exam. It just doesn't make sense.

In the Bible version, only Gideon knows the criterion for success and so the scenario makes sense.

The Koran simply gets the Bible story wrong!

Similar divergences arise in many of the renditions of Bible stories in the Koran, just as we have seen in a previous chapter concerning statements about Jesus' mother Mary (Maryam). In one Koran verse recounting the story of Moses and Aaron; Pharaoh says;

7:124 *"Then I shall crucify every one of you"*

But archaeologists and historians agree that the ancient Egyptians of Moses' time did not carry out crucifixions, the first record of any crucifixion comes from around 479 BC, centuries later, carried out by the Persians (see Herodotus **"Histories"** ix 120-122).

Later in the same section about Moses;

7:143 *"And when his Lord revealed glory on the mountain (Mt Sinai) He sent it crashing down"*

this is quite different from the Torah account in the Book of Exodus chapter 19.

What does the historical evidence say? Well the mountain is still there today, there is no pile of rubble standing in its place, no sign of any of it crashing down. You can go visit it and prove the Koran wrong.

Some of the Koran versions of Torah histories are hard to follow, there are several other variants on the Moses story, and in chapter 28 of the Koran, Haman, otherwise only known from the Book of Esther, turns up several hundred years early in Moses and Pharaoh's time for a small cameo role.

The story of Cain and Abel gets mixed up too. In the Koran 5:31 Allah sends a raven to show Cain how to bury and hide his brother Abel's body after he had killed him, but in the Torah, Book of Genesis 4:10, God said to Cain;

"What have you done? Your brother's blood cries out to me from the ground."

Once again, the Koran fails and, instead of confirming the Torah, misses its message and presents another. We'll look at this story again later.

Surah 11:42-43 tells the tale of an unnamed fourth son of Noah who didn't make it onto the Ark and was drowned, whereas the Torah (Genesis 6:10) states clearly at the beginning of the episode that Noah had three sons and that all three survived the flood (Genesis 9:18-19).

Time and time again, the Koran doesn't confirm the Torah but changes its stories. In the Koran verse 29:14 version even Noah's age doesn't tally with the earlier account.

The Koran gives a short yet different version of the tale of Lot and the destruction of Sodom and Gomorrah. It has Lot being expelled from there;

27:56 *"Expel the household of Lot from your township..."*

but the Torah says that one of God's angels warned him to leave;

"one of them said, 'Flee for your lives ! Don't look back, and don't stop anywhere...'" (Genesis 19:17)

Koran verse 7:81 gives a different version of the fate of Lot's wife; *"his wife...stayed behind"*, whereas in the Torah (Genesis 19:26) she leaves but dies looking back; *"But Lot's wife looked back, and she became a pillar of salt"*.

Surah 12 gives a rather different version of Joseph's story to that found in the Torah, Genesis chapters 37-47, it says;

12:56 *"We gave power to Joseph in the land, he was the owner of it"*

That's another historically incorrect statement, not found in the Torah. The Pharaohs ruled and owned Egypt. Joseph's name does not appear in any list of Pharaohs, nor does any name like it.

The Koran versions are not true.

Surah 27:15 has a bizarre story of Solomon conversing with a talking ant, Surah 38 again gives stories of David, Solomon and Job quite different to the Bible, and Surah 87:19 talks of a **"Book of Abraham"** of which there is no record elsewhere save a book written centuries later in 1853 AD by Joseph Smith, founder of the Mormon movement, the contents of which have been widely discredited by historians.

Rather than confirming the Torah and the Gospels as the Koran itself claims, these passages prove their incompatibility. Many subjects are dealt with very differently by the Koran, where it says it is OK to beat women; -

4:34 *"As for those (women) from whom you fear disobedience... scourge them"*

38:44 *"take in your hand a green branch and beat her with it"*

but the Bible says men should care for women; -

"Husbands, love your wives...husbands should love their wives as their own bodies... and care for them" (St Paul, Letter to Ephesians 5:25)

Yet another area of disagreement is over prophecy, the Koran says;

33:40 *"Muhammad...the last of the prophets",*

but the Bible says all Christians have the potential to prophesy;

"For you can all prophesy in turn so that everyone may be instructed and encouraged" (St Paul, First Letter to the Corinthians 14:31)

In 1996 Kim Clement, a born-again Christian, prophesied in a public meeting what would happen on 11th September 2001 in New York and the war that would follow. You can find a recording of the actual prophecy on YouTube.

Near the end of May 2005 another Christian prophet Chuck Pierce said he saw in the spirit a sword hanging in the air over London which would fall at the end of forty days. On 7th July 2005, exactly forty days later the city was bombed by Islamists.

Both these prophets and many other Christians also accurately predicted Donald Trump being elected as President of the USA. Kim Clement even got his Christian name right.

There have been many true prophecies made since Mohammed's time, this present book even contains some prophecy about the future.

The Koran does not confirm, but truly misrepresents, contradicts and alters the meanings of the content taken from the Biblical texts.

The Koran does not confirm the Torah and the Gospels, and the allegation that it does is clearly not true. Because of this the Koran cannot replace the Bible as the Word of God.

Thus, Islam does not supersede Christianity or Judaism, but is a false religion theologically opposed to them.

Revisionism

Given that Mohammed was striving very hard to establish his new religion, we ought to take very seriously the possibility that the Koran, in saying it confirmed the Torah and Gospels, might just be feeding us a tactical lie. We must therefore also consider whether what the Koran says deliberately undermines Christianity and Judaism.

Surah 37, verse 83 onwards, gives a revisionist account of the Torah's story of the binding of Isaac found in the Book of Genesis 22:1-19. Certain details have been changed as the Koran verse shows;

37:102 *"And when he attained age to working with him, he said: O my son I surely I have seen in a dream that I should sacrifice you; consider then what you see. He said: O my father I do what you are commanded; if Allah please, you will find me of the patient ones"*

but the original says; -

"Then God said (to Abraham), 'Take your son, your only son, whom you love, Isaac, and go to the region of Moriah. Sacrifice him there as a burnt offering on a mountain I will show you."

"Isaac spoke up and said to his father Abraham, 'Father ?' 'Yes, my son ?' Abraham replied. 'The fire and wood are here,' Isaac said, 'but where is the lamb for the burnt offering ?" (Genesis 22:2/22:7)

What is different here is that the God of the Jews talks directly, clearly and in detail to the believer. Allah doesn't do this, and in the Koran Abraham just has a vivid nightmare and acts on it. The Koran here promotes an attitude of agreement to dying for Allah such as one finds in suicide bombers. Was it a dream? or did God speak directly to him? Was the son willing or unaware of what was going on? The Torah version was written nearly 2,000 years before the Koran and its truth was never questioned before the arrival of Islam.

Elsewhere in the Koran verse 9:30 asserts that; *"the Jews say Ezra is the son of Allah",* but the Bible (which includes both the Gospels and Torah) says of Jesus in the Gospel of John 3:16;

"But God loved the world so much that He gave his one and <u>only</u> Son, that whoever believes in Him shall not perish but have eternal life."

Again, the Koran fails to confirm the Torah and Gospels but instead misrepresents them. There is no historical evidence whatsoever in favour of the Koran's statement about Ezra.

Where someone takes pre-existing texts and changes them, this can only be described as revisionism.

Surah 19 renders an inaccurate version of Chapter One of the Gospel of Luke and includes the risible story of Mary climbing up a palm tree during childbirth. We have already seen the confusion in the Koran over Mary's lineage in 19:28 and untruth of 19:7. Remember that the Gospel of Luke was carefully compiled from living witnesses (see Luke 1:1-4) and that in his version of the naming of John the Baptist it was said;

"There is no one in your family who has that name." (Luke 1:61)

The Koran's replacing this with a statement saying that Allah had; *"given that same name to none before"*, in verse 19:7, shows that it has corrupted true scripture and replaced it with something which we know is not historically correct. Illiterate Mohammed could not go to source material to research what he said in the Koran and this gives rise to many mistakes.

Many of the mistakes are minor, such as Surah 6:74 which says Abraham's father was *"Azar"* whereas his father's true name was *"Terah"* (Genesis 11:26), and the *"red heifer"* in Torah Numbers 19:2-10 which becomes a bright *"yellow cow"* in the Koran verses 2:67-73.

Some verses of Torah stories become nonsensical in the Koran, like this one

34:12   *"Unto Solomon the wind, whereof the morning course was a month's journey and the evening course a month's journey, and We caused the fount of copper to gush forth for him, and certain of the jinn who worked before him"*

Other versions of stories are likewise garbled in the Koran, such as Surah 12 which recounts a very different version of the life of the Patriarch Joseph from the Book of Genesis chapters 37-47. In the Koran's rendition, many details are incorrect, as in verse 12:14 where Joseph's father Israel didn't want to send him out with his brothers *'lest the wolf devour him'*, whereas in the original (Genesis 37:13) the father sends him without any fear. In the Torah Joseph's brothers sell him to the Ishmaelite slave traders; *"for twenty shekels of silver"*, but the Koran 12:19 has the latter finding him by chance when looking for water;

"they sent their water drawer. He let down his pail (into the pit) then said 'Good luck! Here is a youth".

They then took him and sold him, making it OK under Sharia to take anyone you find, enslave them and sell them.

The Koran version (12:30) has the wife of Joseph's owner, who was trying to seduce him, not being believed when she said that he had taken advantage of her. Yet strangely he still had to go to prison. This just doesn't make sense. In the original (Genesis 39:16-19) she is fully believed and so Joseph being sent to prison thus makes sense. In the Koran, there is also a subplot not found in the Torah, inserted into this tale about women who cut their hands praising Allah;

12:31   *"(the women) cut their hands and said, 'Perfect is Allah"*

This a bit like today's Ashura self-harming rituals. So rather than being *"a detailed explanation of former scripture"* as Surah 10:37 claims, this is a darkly twisted bogus imitation of the Torah story that encourages people to harm themselves as a way of praising their god.

Surah 28 likewise mistells the story of Moses, verses 29-30 say;

"Then, when Moses had fulfilled the term, and was travelling with his housefolk, he saw in the distance a fire and said unto his housefolk: Bide ye (here). Lo I I see in the distance a fire; peradventure I shall bring you tidings thence, or a brand from the fire that ye may warm yourselves. And when he reached it, he was called from the right side of the valley in the blessed field, from the tree: O Moses I Lo I I, even I, am Allah, the Lord of the Worlds"

The original version of the story of the encounter with God in the burning bush (Exodus 3:1-2) says;

"Meanwhile, Moses was shepherding the flock of his father-in-law Jethro, the priest of Midian. He led the flock to the far side of the wilderness and came to Horeb, the mountain of God. There the Angel of the LORD appeared to him in flames of fire from within a bush. Moses saw that though the bush was on fire it did not burn up"

These versions are so different as you can see, the Koran version then jumps ahead to the next chapter of Exodus (4:3) when God turned his staff into a serpent. This cuts out the conversation that God has with Moses about the promised land, where the State of Israel stands today, that He is giving to the Jews;

"So I have come down to deliver them from the power of the Egyptians, and to bring them up from that land to a good and spacious land, to a land flowing with milk and honey, to the place of the Canaanite..."
(Exodus 3:8)

This God given promise to the Jews is the principal reason for the existence of the modern State of Israel where it is today. Yet many

Muslims and Muslim nations want to destroy it. This is a very serious issue. God said to Moses that the land of Canaan was being given by Him to the children of Israel. The Koran does not confirm this. This revisionism, the editing out by Mohammed of this Word of God from the story of Moses has very serious consequences today. The existence of the State of Israel, in the place where God said it would be, has been a major bone of contention ever since it was established. Surrounded by Muslim neighbours who are under the anti-Semitic influence of their holy books, there has been constant tension often leading to war. Mohammed's failure to confirm the Torah has cost many lives. If the Koran had included a true confirmation of the Torah, then the Middle East would not be the battleground it is today.

But God's will cannot be blocked; -

"Who has ever heard of such a thing? And who ever sees such things? Can a country be born in a single day, or can a nation be brought forth in a single moment? Yet no sooner was Zion in labour than she delivered her children" (Isaiah 66:8)

The state of Israel was born in a single day on 14th May 1948 as the result of a United Nations Resolution.

A prophetic word in the Bible come remarkably true, now that's the mark of a true prophet.

Corrupted Scripture

Within all the scriptural incongruity there are verses in the Koran and the Hadiths which say the Torah and Gospels have been corrupted;

2:59 *"But the transgressors changed the Word from that which had been given them."*;

2:75-79; *"...a party of them..... perverted it knowingly.... woe to those who write the Book with their own hands..."*;

"Allah has told you that the people of the Scripture changed their book and distorted it and wrote with their own hands."
(Bukhari 9/92/461 & 9/93/614)

Yet it is the Koran which was written later and so would be a misrepresentation of the earlier Torah and Gospels. And this is what we find in fact, it is the Koran which has corrupted the previous scriptures. It is not *"a detailed explanation"* of them, it has inaccurate, doctored, and twisted versions of just some parts of them. The Koran's claim is untrue.

Tactical lying may also explain why these verses contradict others found in the Koran that say that the Torah and Gospels we have are true;

> 5:46 *"...they (the Jews) have the Torah which is the Command of God".*

> 5:50 *"And let the People of the Gospel judge by what God has revealed in it."*

Both of these verses are referring to the Torah and Gospels available at Mohammed's time, and we know with certainty that their contents have not changed since that time because there exist full original copies from before his era. In fact, studying in depth the alleged corruption of the previous scriptures, which is really just a smokescreen for not addressing the inaccuracies of the Koran, the whole issue seems to be limited to a question of whether or not adulterers should be allowed to live. Sharia law wants them all stoned to death and says that the punishment has been trafficked in the Gospels to overrule the rule in Leviticus 20:10 that adulterers *"shall surely be put to death"*. Islam seeks to negate Jesus living example of mercy towards such sinners that we see in the Gospel of John Chapter 8. Sahih Muslim 17/4206 gives an example of how Mohammed dealt with adultery; -

"There came to him (the Holy Prophet) a woman from Ghamid and said: 'Allah's Messenger, I have committed adultery, so purify me'...then Muhammad pronounced punishment; And she was put in a ditch up to her chest and he commanded people and they stoned her. Khalid bin Walid came forward with a stone which he flung at her head and there spurted blood on the face of Khalid and so he abused her....and she was buried."

But didn't the Ten Commandments say; *"Thou shalt not kill"*?

Isn't God supposed to be merciful?

Jesus in the Gospels had a more humane response (Gospel of John 8:4-11),

"The teachers of the law and the Pharisees brought in a woman caught in adultery. They made her stand before the group and said to Jesus, 'Teacher, this woman was caught in the act of adultery. In the Law Moses commanded us to stone such women. Now what do you say?' They were using this question as a trap, in order to have a basis for accusing Him. But Jesus bent down and started to write on the ground with his finger. When they kept on questioning Him, He straightened up and said to them, 'Let any one of you who is without sin be the first to throw a stone at her...' Again He stooped down and wrote on the

ground. At this, those who heard began to go away one at a time, the older ones first, until only Jesus was left, with the woman still standing there. Jesus straightened up and asked her, 'Woman, where are your accusers? Has no one condemned you ?' 'No one, Sir,' she said. 'Then neither do I condemn you,' Jesus declared. 'Go now and sin no more.'

Some of the statements in the Koran give the impression that Mohammed did not have any real grasp of Christianity. Koran verse 5:116 implies that Jesus said

"take me and my mother for two gods besides Allah."

The Jesus of the Gospel did not say this and would never have said it because this is another statement based on a false understanding of Christianity. Christians pray to the Holy Trinity of the "Father" God, the "Son" Jesus Christ and the Holy Spirit. This is in line with what Jesus said;

"Therefore go and make disciples of all nations, baptising them in the name of the Father and of the Son and of the Holy Spirit."
(Gospel of Matthew 28:19)

So, Koranic Surah 5:73 says that Christians are wrong about the Trinity when in fact the Koran has got it wrong. Mohammed evidently had no understanding of the Triune (three-in-One) nature of God; the more abstract, some might say harder to reach, Father, with Jesus the accessible human face easy to find in prayer, and the Holy Spirit who we can receive as a part of God to live inside us when we align with God's way for us. They are all facets of the same Godhead. So once again the Koran has misreported the Gospels and Torah, misrepresenting the pre-existing Jewish and Christian covenants.

This is clearly the work of a man, not of God.

The Koran also says in verse 5:17;

"They have certainly disbelieved those who say Allah is Christ",

meaning that Jesus Christ is not God, whereas Jesus said in the Gospel of John 10:30;

"I and the Father (God) are one".

Later in the Gospel, after Jesus had been resurrected, Apostle Thomas said of Him;

"My Lord and my God" (John 20:28).

Certainly, Jesus is very different from Islamic Allah. Muslims have little idea of what the Gospels truly say. Clearly again the Koran does not confirm them but tells a very different story. The Koran gives a distorted view of Christ and Christianity. Even Mohammed's physical descriptions when saying he saw Jesus during his night journey are very different from the Biblical accounts. Here's a passage of Hadith expanding the content of the Koran Surah 17 (Bukhari 4/55/607);

"Allah's Apostle said, 'On the night of my ascension to heaven, I saw (the Prophet) Moses who was a thin person with lank hair, looking like one of the men of the tribe of Shanua; and I saw Jesus who was of average height with a red face as if he had just come out of the bathroom. And I resemble prophet Abraham more than any of his offspring does..."

Another (Bukhari 4/55/650) says;

"the Prophet did not tell that Jesus was of red complexion but said, "While I was asleep circumambulating the Ka'ba (in my dream), suddenly I saw a man of brown complexion and lank hair walking between two men, and water was dropping from his head. I asked, 'Who is this?' The people said, 'He is the son of Mary, Jesus"

And yet another (Bukhari 4/55/648) says;

"The Prophet said, 'I saw Moses, Jesus and Abraham (on the night of my Ascension to the heavens). Jesus was of red complexion, curly hair and a broad chest. Moses was of brown complexion, straight hair and tall stature as if he was from the people of Az-Zutt."

Compare these to the first-hand account of Jesus' close disciple John in the Book of Revelation which says he saw Jesus in heaven,

"clothed with a long robe and with a golden sash around his chest. The hairs of his head were white, like white wool, like snow. His eyes were like a flame of fire, his feet were like burnished bronze, refined in a furnace, and his voice was like the roar of many waters. In his right hand he held seven stars, from his mouth came a sharp two-edged sword, and his face was like the sun shining in full strength."
(Revelation 1:13-16)

These accounts don't seem to be talking about the same Jesus.

One of the key doctrines in Christianity is **"the work of the Cross"**, but the writer of the Koran is unaware of this subject and even tries to deny that the Crucifixion of Jesus took place at all. Of course, the four Gospels give much detail, like John Chapter 19;

"the soldiers took Him away. Carrying His own cross, He went out to The Place of the Skull, which in Aramaic is called Golgotha. There they crucified Him" (Gospel of John 19:16-18)

But the Koran says;

4:157 *"they slew him not nor crucified him..."*,

but Jesus' death on the Cross was witnessed by many, with several accredited historians writing of it. The Jewish authorities kept records of it in the Talmud, b Sanhedrin 43a;

"On the eve of Passover Yeshua (Jesus) was hanged (crucified)... Since nothing (evidence) was brought forward in his favour he was hanged on the eve of Passover"

and the Romans kept records in their annals (Cornelius Tacitus xv. 44);

"Christus...was executed at the hands of the Procurator Pontius Pilate"

and the Historian Josephus wrote in the First Century in "The Antiquities of the Jews (18.3);

"Now there was about this time, Jesus, a wise man... Pilate condemned Him to the cross".

The Romans were great record keepers, hundreds of other documents recording the Crucifixion are to be found in the Vatican Library in Rome and in other major libraries around the world. Who should we believe, the Bible, the official records and the historians of the time, or illiterate Mohammed who, over five centuries later, did not give even one single reliable reference to any official or academic source material in the whole Koran?

No one in their right mind would chose Mohammed's version over the Bible, which is confirmed by the official chronicles and respected historians of the time.

In denying the Crucifixion, the Koran's revisionism openly gives us proof that it is a work of spiritual deception and that Mohammed did not understand even the most basic precepts of Christianity.

This *"work of the Cross"* according to the apostle St Paul is

"of first importance: that Jesus Christ died for our sins according to the scriptures." (First Letter to the Corinthians 15:3)

Jesus died so that we, upon accepting His self-sacrifice, upon accepting our salvation in Him, could no longer be condemned for any sin. Following His death on the Cross, He descended to hell (Acts 2:31) overcoming Satan and taking all power over heaven and earth, hell and death. After His Resurrection, He appeared to St John and the other disciples saying; -

"I am He that liveth, and was dead; and, behold, I am alive for evermore, amen; and have the keys of hell and of death" (Revelation 1:18)

"All authority in heaven and on earth has been given to Me" (Matthew 28:18)

That means that Jesus has authority higher than Islamic Allah, and as we shall see in the coming chapters, this is what the reality is. The Jesus, called; *"Isa"* in Arabic, taught in Islam is a false depiction.

Here the lie that the Koran confirms the Gospels is fully exposed for what it is. The Koran's allegation that the Torah and Gospels have been corrupted is proven by the fact that the Koran itself contains corrupted versions of parts of their texts. Thus, it is, in fact, the Koran which is the corrupted scripture, and it therefore cannot supersede nor replace either the Torah or the Gospels.

Text analysis of the Christian New Testament, which includes the Gospels, shows it to be far less violent than both the Old Testament (including the Torah) and the Koran. In fact, many observers say that the Koran is no more than a disguised attempt to undo Christianity and replace it with another legalistic spirituality akin to Moses's Law of sin and death.

This is an important debate and can only be understood by comparing key doctrines of Christianity with what the Koran says.

The Koran portrays a very different ideology from that of the Bible, even the nature of its god is different.

In the West, we are free to read the Gospels for ourselves, they are banned in most Muslim nations.

Fight the Good Fight, or Terrorize?

The Koran says;

5:46   *"And... We sent Jesus... confirming the law that had gone before..."*

but the Bible explains that;

"no one will be declared righteous in God's sight through the works of the law, but rather, through the law we become conscious of our sin," (Letter to the Romans 3:20)

"you are no longer under the requirements of the law; you live under the freedom of God's grace." (Romans 6:14)

and St Paul goes on to explain that with the Work of the Cross,

"the Spirit of life in Christ Jesus has set you free from the law..." (Romans 8:2).

The Bible clarifies;

"So the law was our guardian until Christ came that we might be justified by faith" (Galatians 3:24),

"Through Him (Christ Jesus) everyone who believes is set free from every sin, a justification you were unable to obtain under the law" (Acts 13:39)

"For the law made nothing perfect, and a better hope is introduced..." (Hebrews 7:19).

This doesn't look like Jesus confirming Mosaic law, does it? Furthermore, the Bible explains that under the Old Testament law we were like children or slaves who needed to follow rules, but when we come to maturity we become free. We no longer require being told what to do, but instead can learn to live in real freedom, to live by principles. (for a fuller explanation of this please see the Bible chapter; Galatians 4)

As mature followers of God, we are not called to blindly obey a set of rules, but to work spiritually and intellectually to destroy mindsets that promote evil. We do not have to kill people who disagree with us, but instead destroy the mindsets and spiritual forces that oppose God's will.

St Paul, who wrote several parts of the Bible, had the greatest understanding of the Christian way and he explained it thus;

"We fight not against flesh and blood, but against the rulers, authorities and powers of this dark world, and against the spiritual forces of evil in the heavenly realms" (Letter to the Ephesians 6:12),

"we do not wage war as the world does. The weapons we fight with are not the weapons of the world, on the contrary, they (our spiritual

weapons) have the power to demolish strongholds (in the mind). We demolish arguments and every pretension..." (2nd Corinthians 10:3-5)

How can this be confirmed by a book whose abrogated word says to physically kill or terrorize? Look again at all the commands in the chapter on terrorism;

(9:5) *"slay the unbelievers wherever you find them"*

And this present book is not about hating or wanting to harm Muslims, but is about destroying the ideology that has poisoned and imprisoned their minds. We need to help them to see Islam for the demonic influence that it truly is, so they can understand they need to get free of it. This will never be done by violence, but must be done out of love and respect for them.

Mohammed, it would seem, had no grasp of Christianity and only said his new religion replaced all previous faiths as a ruse to try to stop Muslims comparing them in real terms;

3:85 *"religion other than Islam, shall not be accepted."*

So rather than;

5:48 *"confirming that which preceded it and as a criterion over it",*

the Koran in fact falls a long way short of the spirit, soul, mind & body awareness that previous scripture has.

In an earlier chapter of this book we have already read a long list of the Koran's scriptures which incite violence and terrorism.

9:29 *"Fight those who do not believe in Allah..."*

2:191 *"And kill them wherever you find them..."*

The Gospels on the other hand record that Jesus preached the Gospel of Peace.

"Love your enemies and pray for those who persecute you"
(Matthew 5:44)

"bless those who curse you, pray for those who mistreat you"
(Gospel of Luke 6:28)

Unlike the Koran, which carries messages of hatred and mistrust, the Gospels carry a universal command to love.

Compare the miraculous healings and the message of love and peace in Jesus life to the violence and bloodshed of Mohammed's, are they not poles apart? Jesus healed people as the Gospel of John 9:1-12 recalls;

"neighbours and those who had formerly seen him begging asked, 'Isn't this the same (blind) man who used to sit and beg?' Some claimed that he was. Others said, 'No, he only looks like him.' But he himself insisted, 'I am the man'. 'How then were your eyes opened?' they asked. He replied, 'The man they call Jesus made some mud and put it on my eyes. He told me to go to Siloam and wash. So I went and washed, and then I could see."

His healing people was not an isolated event;

"when Jesus went out He saw a large crowd, and He was moved with compassion for them, and healed their sick"
(Gospel of Matthew 14:14)

"great multitudes followed Him, and He healed them all"
(Gospel of Matthew 12:15)

And He even raised the dead;

"a large crowd... found out that Jesus was there and came, not only because of Him but also to see Lazarus, whom he had raised from the dead"
(John 12:9)

When Jesus was arrested before being condemned to the cross, one of His followers drew a sword and attacked the High Priest's men who had come to take Him, slicing off a man's ear. Jesus responded saying;

"Stop, no more of this I' and touching the man's ear healed him."
(Gospel of Luke 22:51)

The Koran does not confirm this way of doing things. And instead of a body of law, Jesus left only simple commandments;

"Love the Lord your God with all your heart, with all your soul, all your mind and strength...Love your neighbour as yourself...There is no greater commandment than these" (Gospel of Mark 12:30-31),

"love one another, just as I have loved you, you also are to love one another" (Gospel of John 13:34).

"God is spirit, and those who worship Him must worship in spirit and truth" (Gospel of John 4:24)

When Jesus sent his followers out He told them to

"Heal the sick, raise the dead, cleanse the lepers and cast out demons. Freely you received, freely give" (Matthew 10:8).

"Then he sent them out to tell everybody about the Kingdom of God and heal the sick" (Luke 9:2)

"So they set out and went from village to village, proclaiming the good news and healing people everywhere" (Luke 9:6).

Very evidently all religions are not equal. What would any sane person prefer to see on our streets; people trying to live out what the Bible says?

"True religion in the eyes of God is caring for orphans and widows in their distress..." (Letter of James 1:27)

or what the Koran says?

28:86	*"Never be a helper to the unbelievers"*
8:12	*"instil terror into the hearts of the non-Muslims"*

No Salvation, no Holy Spirit

"Salvation is found in no one else, for there is no other name under heaven given to mankind by which we must be saved" (Acts 4:12)

As we have seen in a previous section of this book, Allah can't make up his mind whether he is all-forgiving or unforgiving. Given this clear self-contradiction, how can any Muslim be sure of salvation?

Osama Bin Laden summed up his beliefs on gaining forgiveness and attaining paradise in his first fatwa (August 1996); -

"A martyr's privileges are guaranteed by Allah; forgiveness with the first gush of blood, he will be shown his seat in paradise, he will be decorated with the jewels of belief, married off to the beautiful ones, protected from the test in the grave, assured security in the Day of Judgement, crowned with the crown of dignity, a ruby which is better than this whole world and its entire content, wedded to seventy-two of

the pure Houris (beautiful virgins) and his intercession on behalf of seventy of his relatives will be accepted"

Koran verse 3:195 promises;

"those who... fought and were slain, verily I shall remit their evil deeds from them and verily I shall bring them into Gardens underneath which rivers flow - A reward from Allah"

This explains why suicide bombers want to die! But is this really what Islam teaches? The Koran says (4:17-18);

"Forgiveness is only incumbent on Allah towards those who do evil out of ignorance and then turn quickly (repenting) to Allah. Toward them will Allah turn in mercy.... Forgiveness is not for those who do ill until death faces them and then say 'Lo! I repent now', nor for disbelievers."

4:168-169   "Those who disbelieve or deal in wrong, Allah will never forgive them, neither will He guide them unto a road, except the pathway to hell"

19:71   "There is not one of you who can avoid it (hell), this is an ordinance of your Lord Allah..."

Even Mohammed did not know whether he would be spared hell; -

"By Allah, though I am the Apostle of Allah, yet I do not know what Allah will do to me..." (Sahih Bukhari 5/58/266)

This is a far cry from the universal promise of salvation in the Gospels;

"For God so loved the world that He gave His only begotten Son, that whoever believes in Him shall not perish but have eternal life. For God did not send the Son into the world to judge it, but that the world might be saved through Him..." (Gospel of John 3:16-17)

"Jesus said... 'I am the resurrection and the life, he who believes in Me will live (eternally), even if he dies (physically), so everyone who believes in Me will never die. (spiritually) Do you believe this?" (John 11:25-26)

"This is love: not that we loved God but that He loved us and sent us His Son as an atoning sacrifice for our sins." (First Epistle of John 4:10)

Once again, we clearly see that the Koran does not confirm what the Gospels say. Time and time again the Koran is wrong, another example is how the blood sacrifice of Jesus on the Cross removes the need for ritual killing of animals such as is required under the Law of the Torah and the Sharia Law equivalents. It also removes the need for kamikaze self-sacrifice. So, Koran verses,

61:6 *"Jesus....confirming what came before in the Torah"*

5:46 *"We sent Jesus...confirming what was before Him in the Torah..."*

are untrue because Jesus did away with all of the requirements of ritual killing of animals prescribed in the Torah; -

"The animals...sheep or goats...keep them until the fourteenth day of the month when the whole peoples of Israel must sacrifice them at twilight" (Exodus 12:5-6)

"If the priest that is anointed do sin according to the sin of the people; then let him bring for his sin, which he hath sinned, a young bullock without blemish unto the LORD for a sin offering" (Leviticus 4:3)

"The guilt offering is to be slaughtered in the place where the burnt offering is slaughtered, and its blood is to be splashed against the sides of the altar" (Leviticus 7:2)

Jesus, by sacrificing Himself on the Cross, brought the end to the need for religious ritual animal slaughter; -

"Unlike other High Priests, He does not need to offer sacrifices day after day.... He did not enter by means of the blood of goats and calves...This Priest (Jesus) offered, for all time, one sacrifice...the sacrifice of the body of Jesus Christ, once, for all." (Hebrews 7:27, 9:12, 10:12 & 10:10)

"Jesus Christ...He is the atoning sacrifice for our sins, and not only for ours but also for the sins of the whole world." (1 John 2:1-2)

Thus, Jesus did not confirm the Torah, instead He brought a better covenant.

"the covenant He mediates is superior and is founded on better promises. If the first covenant had been faultless, there would have been no need for a second covenant to replace it." (Hebrews 8:6-7)

The Koran however reinstates ritual killing, called *"halal"*;-

(22:34) *"And for all religion We have appointed a rite of sacrifice that they must mention the name of Allah over what He has provided for them as meat."*

Yet again more proof that the Koran's allegation that it confirms the Gospels is untrue, because Jesus had already done away with ritual killing. As we will see in a following chapter, halal ritual killings are sacrifices made to demons.

As already noted, another lie in the Koran concerns the alleged prediction of the coming of Mohammed; Koran 61:6 says;

"when Jesus the son of Mary said, 'O children of Israel, indeed I am the messenger of Allah to you confirming what came before me of the Torah and bringing good tidings of a messenger to come, whose name is Ahmad".

Many Muslims say that this is in the Gospel of John verse 14:16,

"I will ask the Father to send another helper who will be with you always"

But we all know this verse is about the Holy Spirit. Yet nearly all Muslim scholars continue to claim this verse refers to Mohammed. It clearly does not, and reading on in this passage Jesus explains more through the following verses with John 14:26 unambiguously identifying the coming helper,

"the helper, who is the Holy Spirit...will teach you all things and remind you of everything I have said..."

The Greek word used here means helper, or perhaps advocate, it certainly does not say *"Ahmad"* (praised one). And this verse had already been fulfilled when the Holy Spirit came on the day of Pentecost (Acts Chapter 2), centuries before Mohammed was born. The Koran tells lies.

And did Mohammed remind us of everything Jesus said? No, he most certainly did not. Is the Koran a fully detailed explanation of previous scripture as it claims?

10:37 *"And it was not [possible] for this Qur'an to be produced by other than Allah, but [it is] a confirmation of what was before it [i.e. the Taurat (Torah), and the Injeel (Gospel), etc.] and a detailed explanation of the [former] Scripture,"*

12:111 *"Indeed in their stories, there is a lesson for men of understanding. It (the Quran) is not a forged statement but a confirmation of the Allah's existing Books [the Taurat (Torah), the Injeel (Gospel) and other Scriptures of Allah] and a <u>detailed explanation of everything</u> and a guide and a Mercy for the people who believe."*

Very clearly it is not a detailed explanation of everything; it gets simple facts wrong. Nor is it a detailed explanation and confirmation of the Torah and Gospels. Most likely Mohammed deliberately misrepresented the Gospels for his own ends to try to give himself and his new religion more credibility. He never understood them and certainly missed the transformational aspect of the coming of the Holy Spirit.

"Do you not know that your body is a temple of the Holy Spirit, whom you have from God" (St Paul's Letter to the Corinthians 6:19)

This attests to the very spirit of God living inside of you once you have accepted Christ as your Saviour and received the baptism of the Holy Spirit.

You thus become transformed and

"renewed in the spirit of your mind, and put on your new self, which is in the likeness of God" (Letter to Ephesians 4:23-24).

The Holy Spirit, also known as the Holy Ghost, helps you in many ways as the Bible describes; -

"God has poured out His love into our hearts by the Holy Spirit Whom He has given us" (Romans 5:5)

"you will abound in hope by the power of the Holy Spirit" (Romans 15:13)

"The Spirit helps us in our weakness....the Spirit himself intercedes for us" (Romans 8:26-27)

"He will guide you in all truth...and He will tell you what is to come" (John 16:13)

"who comforts us in all our troubles, so that we can comfort those in trouble" (2 Corinthians 1:4)

"the mind set on the Spirit is life and peace" (Romans 8:6)

"the fruit of God's Spirit is love, joy, peace, patience, kindness, goodness, faithfulness, gentleness, self-control" (Galatians 5:22-23)

The Holy Spirit also brings us spiritual gifts, words of knowledge and wisdom, faith, healing, miracles, prophecy, discernment, speaking and interpreting different languages as described by St Paul in his First Letter to the Corinthians Chapter 12.

Who would you rather have as your helper, Mohammed or the Holy Spirit?

Islam has no equivalent of the Holy Spirit. It is God's covenant plan that all mankind receives the blessing of the Holy Spirit.

Personal Demons

"I am saying that these sacrifices are offered to demons, not to God" (1st Corinthians 10:20)

Islam has been criticized by some Christians as being demonic in nature, let's see whether it is or not.

"There is not one of you (Muslims) who does not have a jinn (a demon, an attaché of the devil) appointed to be his constant companion... Even me!" (Sahih Muslim 39/6757, 52/62/2814).

Mohammed said unequivocally that every single Muslim has a demon, we have it right from the Prophet's mouth. This statement, without the shadow of a doubt, proves Islam to be a demonic religion. Next time someone gets accused of "demonising" Muslims, you can quote this! It was Mohammed who really demonised them!

This demonic element of Islam seems to be confirmed by UN statistics, the **World Health Report 2015** (p112) recorded a significantly higher incidence of mental disorders (which is how social scientists would label demonic oppression), amongst under 19's in the Middle East/North Africa area, a part of the World which is, save Israel, almost exclusively Islamic. In the UK one in seven prison inmates is Muslim, compared to a general population level of only one in twenty. Other minorities in the UK do not have such high rates of criminality, so this would seem to be another physical confirmation of this spiritual phenomena.

The Koran and Hadiths tell us that Islamic Allah empowers the demons; -

"Whomever Allah will, He gives them (the demons) power over him...with the permission of Allah." (Hadith Al Basri)

34:12 *"(We gave him) certain of the jinn (demons)... by permission of Lord Allah..."*

6:128 *"o ye...jinn...much of mankind did ye seduce..."*

Many Islamic teachings confirm that, with Allah's permission, the jinn have control over a Muslim and, in some cases, can even enter their bodies and live inside them. Unlike Christianity, where demons are enemies of God, in the Koran they appear to be aligned with Allah. Mohammed even said how much the demons like the Koran

72:1 *"the jinn (demons) listened and they said, 'what a wonderful Quran".*

The demons like the Koran, and they like Islam because it gives them power over people. Sahih Muslim 4/0903 confirms that Halal sacrifices feed the demons.

"They (the demons) asked him (the Holy Prophet Mohammed) about their provision and he said: 'Every bone on which the name of Allah is recited is your provision... these are the food of your brothers (fellow demons)."

This appears to be a demonic covenant whereby the demons are rewarded for their part in all this. This ties in with Surah 22:36 of the Koran;

"And the Budn (cows, oxen, or camels driven to be offered as sacrifices)... mention the Name of Allah over them when they are drawn up (for sacrifice)"

In other words, Mohammed said that each Muslim has a demon as a constant companion, and they must eat Halal meat to feed the demons;

6:118 *"You shall eat from that upon which Allah's name has been pronounced..."*

Thus, the demonic element of Islam is evident and unquestionable. An amazing testimony on the Bibles for Mideast website illustrates further. It tells of an Imam who was dying, aware of demons coming to take his soul to hell, saying they had the right to do so. But Jesus appeared, causing the demons to flee; and He gave the man's his life back so he could serve Him and be His witness. The man is now the leader of a church. This confirms the true demon-overcoming power of Christ. In the Gospel of Mark 5:1-20, there is an account of Him meeting a demon-possessed man who;

"...lived in the tombs. No one was able to restrain him, even with chains, because he often had been bound with shackles and chains but had snapped off the chains and smashed the shackles. No one was able to subdue him, and always, night and day, he was crying out among the tombs and cutting himself with stones. When he saw Jesus he ran and

knelt down before Him. And he cried out with a loud voice 'What do you have to do with me, Jesus, Son of the Most High God? I beg You before God, don't torment me!' 'Come out of the man unclean spirit!" Jesus ordered the demons to come out of the man and they left him"

Jesus cast the demons out. This same power has been given to us, His followers. In chapter 16:15-18 of the Gospel of Mark, Jesus confirmed;

"Whoever believes and is baptised will be saved... And these signs shall accompany those who believe; in My Name they will drive out demons, they will speak in new tongues... they will lay hands on the sick and they will recover".

And when they had put this to the practical test, His disciples found and reported back to Him;

"even the demons submit to us in Your Name" (Gospel of Luke 10:17)

Looking at all this logically it is evident that we Christians enjoy a more powerful spirituality than Islam's submission to Allah. This clearly proves the claim in Surah 9:33 that Islam is *"superior over all religions"* to be wrong. Muslims submit to their demons because Allah has given the demons power over them, yet Christians have power over all demons through Jesus' Name.

This also answers the question; is Jesus and His Name more powerful than Mohammed's Allah? Even if Allah gave a demon permission over a person, a Christian using Jesus' name could drive it out.

The use of the name of Jesus is therefore more powerful than Allah's permission; and thus, Koran verse;

6:34 *"There is none to alter the decisions of Allah"*

is proved wrong too.

In fact, many Muslims know there is something wrong in their lives but are so brainwashed and indoctrinated that they blame everything but Islam for their malaise. As Muslims each have a personal demon, but we Christians can drive demons out, shouldn't we help them?

Mohammed's Allah cannot be God if Jesus and us, his followers, have greater power.

Who then is this Allah?

Part Seven - Is Allah the same God?

"You shall have no foreign god among you; you shall not worship any god other than Me." (Psalm 81:9)

The Koran contains many descriptions of Islam's god Allah who is identified by name from the very first verses., The term "Lord" is also used extensively in the text. Other names and descriptive terms are used less frequently but there is no equivalence whatsoever to the name **Yahweh** (Jehovah) which our God used when revealing himself face to face to Moses. Given the total absence of this name, *"the Name"*, which appears time and again throughout the Bible, the issue seems pretty clear-cut from the start.

"For I know that Yahweh is great; our Lord is greater than all gods" (Psalm 135:5)

Putting aside the confusion that is caused by the fact that Arabic word Allah just means **"god"** in the most general sense, we can compare the content of the Bible and Koran to compare the attributes of our God and Islam's Allah. Whilst of course, one could tally up the number of times each of the various names and descriptions occur in the Koran and Bible and try to make sense of that, what is clearly more fruitful is to look at Islamic Allah's overall aim in the Koran and compare it to God's redemptive plan for mankind revealed in the Bible. We ought to say we were quite surprised to find Allah's overall aim stated so openly where he says he *"will fill hell with demons and mankind"*. That rather gives the game away doesn't it, but nonetheless we diligently went through some of Allah's other stated objectives and these too revealed great doom and destruction. Remember than Satan, when as Lucifer, he fell, described in Isaiah 14:14 he said; *"I will ascend above the heights of the clouds; I will make myself like the Most High"*. He wants to be worshipped like God, he established Islam for this; to have his own holy book the Koran, and to have houses of worship to him, mosques all over the earth. But then doesn't God say in verse 15; *"but you are brought down to the realm of the dead, to the depths of the pit"*. This all ties in with Koran verse (9:115) that says; *"it was never Allah's part that he should send people astray"*. As Lucifer that was not his role but when he fell he took on that role. Has Allah come forth from the Pit of Hell? We'll answer that later.

"Do not invoke the names of other gods; do not let them be heard on your lips" (Exodus 23:13)

To be quite honest what surprised us greatly was that Islam has been able to keep Islamic Allah's true nature under wraps and hidden for so long. In the 7th Century when Islam was born, Christian scholars thought it was a heresy because of its false claims to continue the Judeo-Christian heritage. They were blinded to the truth that Islam is far more dangerous than that. But then remembering back to the first time we opened a copy of the Koran to read it, we found so much witchcraft coming off the words that our heads began to spin. Many Muslims say that if you try to study the Koran on your own, *"it will eat your mind"*. It was not easy going reading through the whole Koran and systematically making notes for our work. For example, there are groups of letters spelled out at the beginning of many of the chapters of the Koran, these are spells. They obviously make it hard for the Koran's readers to take in the reality of what it says. Because of this, we obviously implore all our readers to exercise extreme caution when trying to read the Koran for yourselves. You'd best have someone from your church praying for you if you try to read much, and use an academic translation rather than an Islamic one. We have powerfully prayed for the true spirit of God to cover and protect you as you read the Koran verses quoted in this book, so you need fear nothing reading them here.

"But you, beloved, by building yourselves up in your most holy faith and praying in the Holy Spirit, keep yourselves in the love of God" (Jude 1:20-21)

When we were working on this book we prayed after each session to be delivered of everything bad that we had encountered in our work; -

"Heavenly Father, Lord Jesus Christ and Holy Spirit, we thank you for delivering us completely from every unclean thing we have seen and thought about, we thank you for washing us clean with your precious blood Jesus, for cleansing our eyes, our brains and our memories of every ungodly thing that has touched them, in Jesus Name, amen."

There is further confirmation of Islamic Allah's true identity in the Book of Revelation which we discuss in Part 8. Having uncovered this identity of Islamic Allah it is very worthwhile to look at how Islam works spiritually. Bear in mind always that we fight not against flesh and blood

"For our struggle is not against flesh and blood, but against the rulers, against the powers, against the world forces of this darkness, against the spiritual forces of wickedness in the heavenly places." (Ephesians 6:12)

There is no indictment of individual Muslims in all this, they are mostly humble caring people who have been misled. What we, as Christians, must destroy is the hierarchical demonic system that ensnares all Muslims in the belief of things untrue. We must help them get free; when you see a woman in a hijab, can you see freedom? Muslims need to be set free from a false belief system and the demons that hold that system in place.

Jesus called us to cast out demons in Matthew 10:8;

"Heal the sick, raise the dead, cleanse the lepers, cast out demons"

We are in times when this is very relevant, because every Muslim has a personal demon. We are called to cast out these Islamic demons, to make them flee and therewith bring forth the largest harvest of souls that history has ever known. It's in the Bible and we are called to do it. Although it sounds a bit hard and scary, there are many different means to accomplish it. We'll talk about this more in the last Part of this book.

"There is an appointed time for everything. And there is a time for every event under heaven... A time to be silent and a time to speak"
(Ecclesiastes 3:1,7)

Clearly the first step is to awaken Muslims to the truth. Our book **"Islamic Apocalypse"** has been written in such a way that a Muslim can read it without finding any real cause for offence save that they will find out they have been lied to. Recommend it to people. Our free e-booklet "The Undoing" is available for everyone. You could even print up copies to hand out. All we need do is to convince people to read them, you can use social media, personal emails or leave copies with them. Don't worry about political correctness issues, God's Will is more important. If anyone does threaten action against this kind of activity, then it is an opportunity to put the Koran and Islam with all its hate speech in the spotlight so it can be truly uncovered for all to see. The Father has chosen this time, as we approach the 1,400th anniversary of the start of Islam to set Muslims free. His love never fails. Be bold for Him.

"I can do all things through him who strengthens me" (Philippians 4:13)

Moving onto the revelations concerning the true spiritual nature of Islam, which we discuss in this section of the book; it has to be said that in the light of Mohammed's connections with the pagan Ka'aba sanctuary at Mecca, with his training as a medium whom the jinn demons could talk through, it is no real surprise that his religion is no more than Arabian jinn paganism repackaged for a monotheistic age. The old war goddess *"Akhbar"* (Venus), her image, the Black Stone, remains even today in the Ka'aba. It is still an idol, it is still venerated in the Hajj with pilgrims circling around it, bowing to it, touching and kissing it. And Muslims still point themselves towards this idol at every prayer time. You can find film of the Hajj on YouTube and see for yourself that this truly is idol worship. The whole ritual pilgrimage, including the circling and kissing the Black Stone, are pre-Islamic in origin and are probably still the same as when Mohammed was a child. Another part of the Hajj celebrates the appearing of Satan near Mecca. The Muslims go there to throw stones at Satan, perhaps he is still there because regularly there are deadly stampedes with hundreds, sometimes even thousands, being trampled to death. This place is not far from the cave where Mohammed received his first visitations.

"Finally, my brethren, be strong in the Lord, and in the power of his might" (Ephesians 6:10)

"so that you may be blameless and pure, children of God without fault in a crooked and perverse generation, in which you shine as lights in the world as you hold forth the word of life" (Philippians 2:15-16)

One of our friends goes regularly to East Africa on mission, spending several months of each year there. A few years ago, he had a great breakthrough when a local Imam came to him one evening and said; *"I know you Christians have something more than what we Muslims have, teach me how it works"*. So, over the following months, our friend taught him the Gospel, explained to him about the Holy Spirit and God's redemptive plan for mankind. The now ex-Imam also shared and explained how Islam worked in that part of the world. He told that when he had been selected to be an Imam he had to undergo a demonic initiation lasting three months. During this time, he was left alone on a "haunted" island where each night for the three months a different demon visited him and taught him different aspects of marabouting (Islamic witchcraft). He was taught how to make and break curses, how to initiate pseudo-healing and deliverance by releasing a person from their jinn demon and assigning another more powerful demon of a different type in its place. (It is because of rumours of such demonic initiations that most countries in the West now insist that their Imams are home trained.) Needless to say, our friend learnt a great deal from this encounter, a reality about Islam most Muslims would not want to admit. The Imam also explained how it worked economically, how the zakat charity payments made at the mosques each week were gathered up and driven to an airfield where they were put on planes to Yemen. No accounting was ever done and the ex-Imam had been free to help himself to whatever he wanted for the coming week. In fact, he was very disappointed when he found that his new found Christian friends wanted him to be financially accountable.

One God, or different deities?

"You say you have faith, for you believe that there is one God. Good for you! Even the demons believe this, and they tremble in terror..." (James 2:19)

The Arabic word *"Allah"* today simply means **"the god"** or **"the deity"**, so religions other than Islam also use this word to refer to their gods. This does not mean though that they are talking about the same spiritual entity. We should consider the attributes of the different gods as revealed in their sacred writings to discover whether or not they are the same entity.

Compare the following passages from the Koran (7:97-99); -

"Are the people of the townships then secure from the coming of Our wrath upon them as a night-raid while they sleep? Or are the people of the townships then secure from the coming of Our wrath upon them in the daytime while they play? Are they then secure from Allah's scheme? None deemeth himself secure from Allah's scheme save folk that perish"

and from the Bible, (Psalm 91:1-3,5); -

"Whoever dwells in the shelter of the Most High will rest in the shadow of the Almighty. I will say of the LORD, 'He is my refuge and my fortress, my God, in whom I trust. He will cover you with his feathers, and under his wings you will find refuge; his faithfulness will be your shield and rampart. You will not fear the terror of night, nor the arrow that flies by day"

The content of each of these passages appears to be saying the very opposite to the other. Islamic Allah seems to want everyone to live in fear of him and our Judeo-Christian God wants you to live in peace under His protection. They appear to be quite opposite in character.

The Koran reveals a number of other attributes of the Islamic god Allah and whilst the first Chapter calls

1:1-4 *"Allah, the Beneficent, the Merciful, Lord of Worlds and Master of the Day of Judgement"*

other parts of the book paint a very different picture. In the earlier Chapter on Fatalism we have looked at how Islamic Allah leads people astray; here's some more similar verses; -

6:25 *"We have placed veils upon their hearts, lest they understand, and in their ears deafness..."*

18:57 *"Lo I on their hearts We have placed coverings so that they understand not and in their ears a deafness.... that they can never be led right"*

74:31 *"Allah sendeth astray whom He will and whom He will He guideth"*

40:34	*"Allah deceiveth him who is a transgressor or doubter"*
19:83	*"We have set the devils on the disbelievers to confound them with confusion ?"*
86:16	*"And... plot a plot (against them)"*
7:94	*"We overtook its people with distress and affliction"*
7:182	*"We will progressively lead them (to destruction)"*
95:5	*"We reduced him (mankind) to the lowest of the low"*
68:44	*"We gradually draw them to destruction..."*

"were it not for the affliction (that Allah sent) ... the women of this world... would be intelligent", (Al Tabari 1/110 p281)

Islamic Allah goes on to explain his goal; -

22:6	*"Allah quickeneth the dead"*
41:39	*"Lo ! He who quickeneth it is verily the Quickener of the dead"*
42:9	*"He quickeneth the dead"*
16:70	*"Allah...causeth you to die"*
10:56, 44:8	*"He quickeneth and giveth death"*
50:43	*"Lo ! We it is who quicken and give death..."*
19:86	*"...and drive the sinners to hell"*
11:119	*"Verily the Word of thy Lord be fulfilled. I shall fill hell with jinn (demons) and mankind together"*
32:13	*"I will fill hell with the jinn and mankind together"*

7:179 *"Already We have urged into hell many of the jinn and mankind"*

"Out of 99 women, one is in paradise and the rest are in hell" (Hadith Kanz al-`Ummal 22/10)

"The Messenger of God said, 'Everyone that God admits into paradise will be married to 72 wives; two of them are houris (black eyed nymphs) and seventy of his inheritance of the [female] dwellers of hell. All of them will have libidinous sex organs and he will have an ever-erect penis" (Sunan Ibn Majah, Zuhd 39)

This is one of the infamous Hadiths which is said to be key to recruiting suicide bombers, but isn't it clear from the wording that this Islamic paradise is actually hell. It is a place of perpetual torment where the inhabitants are in permanent burning desire and cannot find any gratification. According to the Bible there is no marriage in heaven.

In fact, much of the Koran is about doom, destruction and hell-fire, nearly a twelfth of its verses talk of the hell and the punishments that Allah has in store for mankind. From such verses, it is very apparent that Islamic Allah is not the same as the God of the Gospels.

"For God did not send His Son into the world to condemn it, but to save the world through him"
(Gospel of John 3:17)

and the Gospel of Mark explained who His Father God is; -

"He is not the God of the dead but of the living". (Mark 12:27)

St Paul explained it like this;

"God did not appoint us to suffer wrath but to receive salvation through our Lord Jesus Christ". (First Letter to the Thessalonians 5:9-10)

Our God does not seek destruction;

"For I know the plans I have for you' declares the Lord, 'plans to prosper you and not harm you, plans to give you a hope and a future."
(Jeremiah 29:11)

If the Christian God is so loving that He wants everyone to have the opportunity of salvation and eternal life, and Islamic Allah leads people astray and wants to fill hell with mankind, then is it not abundantly clear that we are dealing with very different spiritual entities?

The Koran says Allah is the creator of evil; -

9:2 *"ye cannot escape Allah..."*

113:2 *"...the evil He created"*

74:56 *"He is the fount of fear"*

The God of the Bible is described very differently; -

"And fear not them who kill the body, but are not able to kill the soul" (Matthew 10:28)

"God is love" (1 John 4:8)

"For God is not a God of confusion but of peace" (1 Corinthians 14:43)

"Peace I leave with you; my peace I give to you. Not as the world gives do I give to you. Let not your hearts be troubled, neither let them be afraid" (John 14:27)

Fear and love are opposites, fear leads to negative feelings, to avoidance and causes worry, whilst love brings positive sentiments, it attracts and manifests peace.

If there is one Koran verse which definitively proves that the nature of Islam's Allah is opposite to that of our Christian God, then it must be this;

(80:17) *"Perish man !"*

Allah says he wants mankind to perish! Compare this to The Gospel;

"For God so loved the world that He gave His only begotten Son that whosoever believeth in Him should not perish but have eternal life" (Gospel of John 3:16)

It is clear that our God wants no one to perish, offering a universal salvation for all through Christ Jesus. So logically, the Koran's Allah and the God of the Bible want the very opposite to each other.

Did Mohammed just create his god in his own image? Just like Mohammed from the start of his time in Medina, the Islamic State today lives from the spoils of jihad, from killing, stealing and destroying.

They say it's Allah's way! Islam's Allah is very clearly not the same as our God of righteousness and justice.

There is no god but God - so who is Islam's Allah?

"there will be false teachers among you. They will secretly introduce destructive heresies, even denying the sovereign Lord" (2 Peter 2:1)

Some writers have tried to identify Islamic Allah with other known deities, one popular candidate is Hubal, one of the Ba'als which were the pagan's spiritual lords reigning over particular locations, such as Canaan and Phoenicia. Pre-Islamic worship, including temple prostitution and human sacrifices to Hubal, certainly took place in the Ka'aba but given the worldwide impact of Islam it would seem unlikely that this Allah is just a local demi-god.

Other commentators have suggested similarities between Allah and the Hindu god Shiva, the Destroyer, who also bears the name "the Beneficent", this makes a better fit of attributes and there is some very interesting linguistic evidence that some Islamic concepts and practices evolved from Hinduism. There is certainly a lot of verses about doom and destruction in the Koran.

However, further comparison of the Koran with Biblical scripture seems to provide an even better answer for who he is, the Koran says; -

8:1	*"The spoils of war belong to Allah..."*
48:20	*"Allah promiseth you much booty that you will capture..."*
9:5	*"Kill the unbelievers..."*
2:191	*"Slay them wherever you find them..."*
6:6	*"many a generation We destroyed..."*
7:4	*"How many a township have We destroyed / As a raid by night or while they slept at noon, Our terror came to them"*

Now compare those statements to this verse from the Bible; -

"The Thief (Satan) comes only to steal, kill and destroy, I (Jesus) come that they may have life abundantly."
(Gospel of John 10:10)

Steal, kill and destroy! It rather seems like Allah and Satan have got some things in common.

Let's look at some more Koran verses;

7:136   *"We took retribution...We drowned them in the sea"*

10:13   *"We destroyed the generations before you..."*

17:16   *"when We would destroy a township... we annihilate it with complete annihilation..."*

17:58   *"There is not a township that We shall not destroy...this is set forth in the Book."*

17:17, 18:59, 19:98, 20:128, 21:6, 22:45, 28:43, 28:58 32:26, 36:31, 38:3, 46:10, 46:27, 47:13, and 50:36 all contain more boasts of generations and townships destroyed by Allah;

54:51   *"We have destroyed your fellows... does no one remember?"*

77:16   *"Did We not destroy the men of old?"*

57:22   *"No calamity befalls the earth unless We decree it in a book before We send it, it is truly easy for Allah."*

21:42   *"Who guards you in the night or in the day from the Beneficent (Allah)?"*

7:78,91,95   *"Then We seized them unawares. So the earthquake seized them and morning found them dead in their homes"*

13:13   *"He is severe in punishing"*

25:14   *"Pray for many destructions..."*

2:30   *"the Lord (Allah) said... 'I am about to place a Viceroy in the earth...one who will do harm therein and will shed blood..."*

13:27   *"Allah causes to go astray whom he will"*

4:142   *"The hypocrites seek to deceive...but it is He (Allah) who is deceiving them!"*

40:34   *"Allah deceiveth him who is a transgressor or doubter"*

14:27   *"Allah leads wrongdoers into error"*

42:50   *"He maketh barren whom He will"*

Compare all those statements with the Bible; -

"I have plans... for well-being (to prosper you), not for calamity, they are plans to give you a future and a hope." (Jeremiah 29:11)

"Satan, the Deceiver, who leads the world astray..." (Revelation 12:9)

"It is impossible for God to lie." (Hebrews 6:18)

"the devil (Satan)... was a murderer from the beginning... he is a liar and the father of all lies" (John 8:44)

And look at what Allah says in these Koran verses;

7:24, 2:36   *"I shall make you (man and woman) a foe unto the other..."*

64:14   *"among your wives and children there are enemies for you, therefore beware of them..."*

64:15   *"Your children are only a temptation..."*

7:179   *"Already We have urged into hell many..."*

11:119   *"Verily I shall fill hell with the jinn and mankind."*

32:13   *"I will fill hell with jinn and mankind together..."*

This again is in total contradiction to what our God says;

"Husbands, love your wives, never treat them harshly." (Colossians 3:19)

"Children are a gift from the Lord", "children are a blessing" (Psalms 127:3/37:26)

"Save others by snatching them out of the fire (of going to hell)"
(Jude 1:23)

"Everyone who calls on the name of the Lord (Jesus Christ) will be saved (from hell)" (Romans 10:13)

What Allah wants is clearly the opposite of what our God promises. This confirms that the Koran's Allah is a good match for Satan. We can see that Allah hates women, bringing terrible suffering upon them through sex-slavery, FGM and wife-beating. The Bible says; -

"And I will put enmity between thee (Satan) and the woman"
(Genesis 3:15)

So, is Allah the Satan of the Bible? As we have seen Allah admits urging people into hell, he and his fallen angels are in charge there; -

74:30 *"have We not only appointed angels to be wardens of the Fire..."*

We know also that he assigns a demon to each Muslim and thus fits Satan's description as *"Beelzebub, Prince of Demons"* given by Jesus in Luke 11:15. In the Koran, Allah confirms he is in charge of the demons;

7:27 *"We appointed devils as companions..."*

Even Mohammed's angelic visitations fit the bill; -

"Satan masquerades as an angel of light, his servants disguise themselves as servants of righteousness" (2nd Corinthians 11:14-15).

Remember that Mohammed could not tell the difference between Jibril's revelations and Satan's inspiration, as the Satanic verses incident proves.

St Paul, prophetically, ahead of time, summed it all up well;

"the one whose coming is in accord with the activity of Satan, with all power and signs and false wonders, and with all the deception of wickedness for those who perish (who are going to hell), because they did not receive the love of the truth, so as to be saved."
(Second Letter to the Thessalonians 2:9-10)

Islam's false promise of salvation by Allah is one of the devil's cruellest tricks, duping people into a religion that leads them to hell.

Looking again at the dissimilitude between the Koranic and Biblical versions of recounted events confirms Islamic Allah's satanic identity. Let's reconsider the different versions of the story of Cain murdering his brother Abel, Koran verse 5:31 says,

"Then Allah sent a crow scratching in the ground to show him (Cain) how to hide the disgrace of his (murdered) brother. He said, 'O woe to me! Have I failed to be like this crow and hide the body of my brother?' And he became regretful"

But in the Bible, Book of Genesis 4:10, God said to Cain;

"What have you done? The voice of your brother's blood cries out to Me from the ground",

and God then punishes him.

Analysing the intent of Allah and of our Judeo-Christian God in the different versions of this scenario, we see that Allah in the Koran was clearly trying to guide Cain in how to cover up Abel's body so He could help him get away with the murder of his brother. Yahweh, the God of the Torah and Gospels on the other hand, being all knowing, comes to do justice by bringing judgement against Cain to banish him from the Garden of Eden.

The difference again is manifest; Islamic Allah inspires murderers but the true living God brings justice. Much of the Koran, including all those terrorist verses that call for killing, the enmity to women, and its anti-Jewish, anti-Christian message are more easily understood with this revelation that Mohammed's Allah is the Bible's Satan.

Sex-slavery, stoning to death, child marriage, terrorism and FGM are all altars to Satan.

Other things Mohammed said confirm that Allah desires sin; -

"If you were sinless, Allah would sweep you out of existence and replace you with people who commit sin..." (Sahih Muslim 37/6622)

Allah, like Satan, wants people to sin and admits it in the Koran;

6:137 *"(Pagans), the killing of their children... in their religion. And if Allah had willed, they would have not done so."*

and even to kill their children. This is horrific !

Satan is not all powerful and he is subject to the will of God Almighty.

This explains the start of Surah 14; -

14:1 *"This Scripture which We have revealed unto thee...by the permission of their Lord, in the way of the Almighty..."*

Allah needed permission from above! More proof he is not God because God doesn't need anyone's permission for anything. Compare this statement to the Bible;

"I am God and there is none beside me." (Isaiah 45:5)

Yahweh is God, Islam's Allah is not.

The Star and Crescent

"They abandoned the house of the LORD, the God of their fathers, and served the Asherim (goddesses) and the idols" (2nd Chronicles 24:18)

The satanic verses incident gives us insight into how Islam works spiritually. In these verses, Mohammed named three pre-Islamic pagan goddesses, **Allat**, **al-Uzza**, and **Manat**, recommending they should be prayed to as divine intercessors between man and Allah. The original Koran verse as recorded by Tabari said (Volume 6 p107);

"These exalted... verily their intercession is accepted with approval".

These divinities correspond to those known to us today as Venus, Jezebel and Diana. They are spirits of the Nephilim (giants) who form an intermediate part of the demonic hierarchy over Islam, with Satan plus his fallen angels (see Matthew 25:41 & Revelation 12:7) at the top, and demons ruling over each Muslim at the bottom.

"The Nephilim were on the earth at that time (and afterward), when those divine beings (fallen ones) were having sexual relations with those human women, who gave birth to children for them. These children became the heroes and legendary figures of ancient times." (Genesis 6:4)

The First Book of Enoch, Chapter Seven, tells of these giants, the offspring of women and fallen angels, who taught mankind war and weapon making;

"And they became pregnant and they bare giants...who consumed the acquisitions of men. And when men could no longer sustain them, the giants turned against them and devoured mankind... they began to sin....and devour one another's flesh and consume the blood. Then the earth laid accusation against the lawless ones."

These three goddess spirits can be seen in Islam today, most Muslim flags feature the Star of Venus, the Crescent Moon of Diana and the green of Jezebel. Their respective characteristics of war, trickery and violation of women (Venus), Queen of the dead, destruction, and moon adoration (Diana), or stealing, lying and false authority (Jezebel), are readily apparent in the Mohammed's original Islam, in the Islamic State and elsewhere. Other colours often used in Islam are black, which signifies death, rebellion, anarchy, piracy and powers of darkness, and red representing bloodshed, revolution and anti-Christ.

The origin of the Star and Crescent iconography goes back to at least 2,200 BC, to the **Stele of Ur-Nammu** when it was used to symbolize the moon god Nanna, also known as Sin, father of goddess Inanna (the Sumerian equivalent of Diana), and Ningal the star goddess (Venus). Interestingly some of the Sumerian laws given by these two pre-Islamic gods are equivalent to Sharia law, such as the rules on being put to death for adultery and the laws of retaliation.

In early Christian times, one of the "Seven Wonders of the Ancient World", was what the Bible described as *"the temple of great Artemis, of her image (idol) which fell from heaven"* in Ephesus, modern Turkey (Book of Acts 19:35). Artemis is the Greek name for the moon goddess Diana and the image was similar to Mecca's Black Stone. What a coincidence!

The Islamic calendar and major events such as Ramadan are all determined by moon watching. The appearance of the crescent moon after a new moon is the start of each lunar month, the basis of the Islamic calendar. Other elements in Islam have a strong imprint of paganism, including ritual blood sacrifices. *"Halal"* meat is prepared subject to Sharia rules whereby Allah's name must be invoked at the time of slaughter. FGM, circumcision, Eid al-Adha sacrifices and the Ashura self-cutting or flagellation rituals are other blood rites carried out in Allah's name, and such blood sacrifices whilst invoking a god's name echo pre-Islamic pagan Arabian rites and Satanism.

22:36 *"And the Budn (cows, oxen, or camels driven to be offered as sacrifices) ... mention the Name of Allah over them when they are drawn up (for sacrifice)"*

With the Islamic State, we have also seen the return of ritual killing whilst shouting *"Allahu-Akbar"* (intending *"Allah is great"*). This cry has been heard being shouted by many terrorists, as, for example, during the attack on Charlie Hebdo in Paris. We know this is actually a pre-Islamic chant because Mohammed's grandfather, guardian of the pagan idols at the Ka'aba sanctuary, is recorded as having shouted it when he discovered the Zamzam well there.

Commonly found in the Middle East and North Africa, is the *"Hamsa"* (Arabic for "five") image, also known as the Hand of Fatima, after Mohammed's daughter. It is said to represent the Five Pillars of Islam. In truth, it is another occult symbol which goes right back to the pre-Islamic times. It was associated with the Carthaginian goddess Tanit, to whom young girls were sacrificed. The design also has some associations with Egyptian deity Isis and her Roman counterpart Venus.

Mainstream Islam too is full of various pre-Islamic practices, the ritual prayer positions in Islam can be seen on pre-Islamic archaeological remains together with the crescent moon symbol. Praying five times a day and having a month of daylight fasting are also pre-Islamic. The timing of the five daily prayers seems to have been inherited from the Sabeans who followed Hindu Vedic practices, as does the ritual cleansing before prayer. The annual "Hajj" pilgrimage to Mecca continues many practices which are of pre-Mohammedan origin. The circling around the Ka'aba seven times is a demonstration of pagan practice.

The Black Stone which is the object of veneration at the centre of the circling is an idol that in earlier times was addressed as a female deity. John of Damascus in the Fount of Knowledge tells that the Black Stone of Ephesus had the likeness of Aphrodite (the Greek name for Venus), *"who they (the Arabs) named Akbar in their own language".* Hence that Islamist shout of *"Allahu-Akbar"* really is an invocation of the ancient goddess of war Venus. Ironically the Egyptian equivalent of this goddess was called Isis.

Although idol worship is in theory forbidden in Islam, pilgrims touch and kiss the Black Stone in Mecca, bow down and prostrate themselves before it, as pagans would do with any other idol. During WW2 author John Van Ess visiting the Ka'aba noted;

"in one corner is the Black Stone, probably a meteorite, the kissing of which is now an essential part of the pilgrimage".

Sahih Muslim 7/2913 tells of Mohammed himself kissing this stone idol.

"I saw Allah's Messenger kissing you, that is why I kiss you"

This is essentially the same as the idol worship which took place in Ephesus, mentioned above, and referred to in the Book of Acts 19:35.

"what man is there after all who does not know that the city... is guardian of the temple of the great goddess... of the image which fell down from heaven ?"

It is really very surprising that the annual Hajj pilgrimage does not go to Medina, the real birthplace of Islam, where the first mosque was built and where Mohammed is buried. Instead the pilgrims make almost the same pilgrimage as the pre-Mohammedan pagans going to the Ka'aba, circling around the Black Stone and venerating it.

If the Hajj Pilgrimage and the direction of prayer of all Muslims are focussed on this egg-shaped idol, once addressed as a female pagan deity, then it is evident, as many experts maintain, that Islam is actually paganism packaged as monotheism.

But the idolatry doesn't stop there, just as Christians praise Jesus, whom they believe to be divine, Muslims praise Mohammed even going as far as writing *"Praise Be Unto Him"* or *"PBUH"* every time his name is written. The regular Tashah-Hud prayer even includes words addressed directly to Muhammed rather than Allah.

This is a form of Ba'al worship, and at the time of the Crusades the name "Baphomet" (short for the French; *Ba'al Prophète Mahomet*, in English; *"Lord Prophet Mohammed"*) was coined to describe it. In visual appearance Baphomet also corresponds to the description of the two horned Second Beast in Chapter 13 of the Apocalypse.

Many Knights Templar and Masons had encounters with this Ba'al spirit, and that is what corrupted them away from Christianity. In 1312 **Pope Clement V's Decree**, paragraph 25, specifically refers to and bans Mohammedan worship. As Freemasonry grew out of the Knights Templar movement, it aligned itself with Islam. The Scot's Rite Lodges have been particularly shaped by the influence of Turkish Dolmeh Muslim Jews; Zevi Sabbatai and Jacob Frank. The Islamic agenda for war is still there. At the Great Masonic Temple in London, the "Mother of all Temples", Masons worship at an Altar of War. The recent attempt to get a statue of Baphomet placed at the US Supreme Court precinct in Ohio could be seen as a spiritual ploy to spiritually open the way for Sharia law in America. And even the fun-loving, charitably-minded Shriner Masons wear hats with the Star and Crescent of Islam on them.

Let's add all this up;

Islam pretends to be against idolatry yet the focus of prayer and pilgrimage, which all Muslims bow down to, is a pre-Islamic pagan idol.

It pretends to be a religion of peace but preaches killing, it condones killing, enslaving and raping those who don't agree with it.

It says the Koran is perfect and infallible but that book actually contains many errors of fact, inconsistencies and self-contradictions.

It pretends that the Koran confirms the earlier Judeo-Christian scriptures, whereas, in reality, it actually carries corrupted versions of their content.

Islam also pretends to continue and supersede all Judeo-Christian heritage, but it is not actually a part of it. It is a monotheist repackaging of Amalekite paganism.

Indeed, Islam's heritage of sex-slavery from Mohammed right through to ISIS today echoes the stealing of women by the Amalekites at Ziklag in the time of King David as described in the Bible;

"the Amalekites had made a raid on the Negev and on Ziklag, and had overthrown Ziklag and burned it with fire; and they took captive the women, young and old, not killing them, but carried them off and went on their way " (1 Samuel 30:1-2)

And its genocidal nature is foreseen in Haman in the Book of Esther who was a descendant of Agag (see Esther 3:1), an Amalekite King who Saul spared in disobedience to God's command in the First Samuel, Chapter15.

"Haman looked for a way to destroy all Mordecai's people, the Jews, throughout the whole kingdom of Xerxes" (Esther 3:6)

The Amalekites were perpetual enemies of Israel. In T.P. Hughes **Dictionary of Islam** it notes that Muslim scholars believe Goliath was of Amalekite origin. Their pagan gods opposed God's people. It is not surprising then that close examination of the Islamic sacred texts proves Allah not to be the same as the God of the Jews and Christians.

Islam pretends to guide people but misleads them.

Looking again at the Koran we can see how sneaky this is;

7:182 *"And those who deny Our revelations - We progressively lead them to destruction in ways they perceive not..."*

Mohammed's Allah admits to trickery here, saying that people don't even know when he is leading them astray.

So, what are these revelations which are denied, are they not all the things we looked at in this book; the presence of the terrorist verses in the Koran, the boasts of destructions, the degradation of women, the xenophobia of unbelievers, et cetera.

It is clear most moderate Muslims publicly deny these things.

Another of these revelations is that Allah deliberately leads people astray, the Koran says it over twenty times so it must be important.

45:23 *"Allah sendest them astray purposely..."*

13:27 *"Lo, Allah sendeth whom He will astray..."*

So syllogistically putting these three verses together you get this logical conclusion; -

If one denies, as Muslims do, that Allah leads people astray, then step by step they are being unknowingly led into error by him.

Thus, they would not even know themselves that he was leading them astray.

This therefore applies to the moderate Muslims' denial that Islam is a terrorist religion or that it degrades women and so on. They are thus in denial of Allah's revelations, and so Allah has the right to lead them astray under the terms of verse 7:182 quoted above.

He is leading them astray and they don't realize.

Allah's purpose is clear;

32:13 *"I will fill hell with...mankind"*

Most Muslims openly say they are led by Allah, and say that those who are not led by him go to hell, but this is not what these verses say at all.

Muslims are in denial that Allah leads them astray. So, by denying that Allah's leading leads to hell, they deny his revelations, and he thus leads them unknowingly astray on the path to hell. There's a brain buster for you.

Whichever way one looks at it, with Allah all roads lead to hell. And Islam with its terror and sex-slavery creates hell on earth.

The only way out is to choose instead the God who promises you salvation;

"Believe in the Lord Jesus, and you will be saved" (Book of Acts 16:31)

Part Eight – Islam and the Apocalypse

"Now the Spirit expressly states that in later times some will abandon the faith to follow deceitful spirits and the teachings of demons"
(1 Timothy 4:1)

When we are young children at school we accept what we are taught and unquestioningly believe it to be true. Then as we grow and progress further, we learn that in many things there are different camps with differing views vying to impose their vision on the world. Part of our growing up is learning how to research the truth for ourselves and how to discuss and debate it with others. But there is a time of even greater wisdom when one begins to realise that much of what one has been taught in earlier years is opinionated, short-sighted, incorrect or even just plain wrong.

"Remember ye not the former things, neither consider the things of old"
(Isaiah 43:18-19)

Take, for example, what my generation was taught about the coming of Christianity to Britain, we were told that St Augustine of Canterbury arrived in the land in 597 AD and began to establish the faith there. But this is not really true, because Christianity arrived at Glastonbury only a few years after Christ's death on the Cross, brought by Jesus' uncle Joseph of Arimathea. Legend has it that he planted his staff in the ground where it flowered and took root. A descendant of this thorn tree can still be found in the grounds of Glastonbury Abbey which was built on the site where he established the first ever church in Britain. DNA tests of the thorn tree have shown that it is of a species normally only found in the Holy Land. The Christian faith was rapidly accepted by the people and a vibrant "Celtic" Church established. It is said by the reputed historian Bede, that King Lucius converted to Christianity in the middle of the Second Century, with him dedicating his whole land to Christ. Certainly, Roman writer Tertullian noted that by about 208 AD that the new faith had even spread to parts of Britain outside of Roman control. The truth is, that when Augustine arrived, Britain already had a large network on non-hierarchical churches across much of the land. In fact, what Augustine did was to impose a Roman hierarchy over the existing churches, within a hundred years effectively wiping out the Holy Spirit driven British Celtic Church and replacing it with imperial organisational religion. Local fivefold-ministry church leadership was removed, and overseeing Bishops, Archbishops and Cardinals appointed in its place. Old English was replaced by Latin which few people spoke. And after 664, the celebration of Christ's resurrection during Passover was abandoned, replaced by the semi-pagan festival of Easter, (named after the pagan goddess ***"Eostre" - Ishtar***). With these changes, the miraculous healings stopped and the glory of that initial move of God in the land vanished, its very presence hidden by history. But now British Christians are again celebrating Passover and a new great awakening is stirring. So you see, it is so important to find things out for oneself and this knowledge has been exceedingly useful for those praying for the fulfilment of God's original covenant plan for the British Isles.

"The one who scatters has come up against you. Man the fortress, watch the road; Strengthen your back, summon all your strength." (Nahum 2:1)

So, with regards to Islam, almost none of us have been taught much about it. If we had known the truth about Mohammed's true-life story, and how that inspired centuries of violent conquest in the name of Islam, then we never would have allowed Mohammedan religion any place in our society. When you understand that the growth of Islam, until the era of European colonialism which halted it, was only achieved by massive slaughter of all types of non-Muslim, we would have sooner resisted it. But we are where we are now, and it is Biblical prophecy, and not history, on which we must rely to guide ourselves forward.

"I will give you the keys of the kingdom of heaven" (Matthew 16:19)

The interpretation of end-times events you will find in this book is a little different from that found elsewhere. Importantly, under the strict guidance of the Holy Spirit, we have reconciled Christ's command to *"love our enemies"*, and St Paul's directive that we *"fight not against flesh and blood"*, with the very militaristic prophecies of Armageddon. Yes, Islam wants war but Jesus, the Prince of Peace, will have a harvest of souls. Jihadis want World War III but the earth will have a Third Great Awakening. And so, as you will read, Armageddon becomes a prophetic symbol of the fall of the rule of the Islamic Caliphate, and this time around, as the Islamic State falls, the Lord will guide the Muslim world into the Valley of Decision. Intellectually and morally we must bring Muslims to the realisation that their religion is not from God, that the Koran is not true. The true Word of God, the Bible says;

"For though we live in the world, we do not wage war as the world does. The weapons we fight with are not the weapons of the world. On the contrary, they have divine power to demolish strongholds. We demolish arguments and every pretension that sets itself up against the knowledge of God, and we take captive every thought to make it obedient to Christ." (2nd Corinthians 10:3-5)

We must bring them the truth of the Gospel. We the Body of Christ, the worldwide church, all those who stand for the truth, have a mandate for this in our time. God is with us.

"... For I will contend with him who contends with you..." (Isaiah 49:25)

Besides the Book of Revelation, the Books of Daniel, Ezekiel, Isaiah and other prophets, the Torah gives us an interesting view of what is happening now. **The Song of Moses** at Deuteronomy 32:21 not only explains that Israel will be driven to jealousy by Christians walking in truly Christ-like miraculous power (see Romans 11:11), but there will also be a *"foolish nation"*, the nation of Islam, which drives Israel to anger. The Song of Moses prophecy goes on to give some detail about this nation. Verse 22 talks of this nation being born from hell, from Satan's pit, growing to touch the whole earth. Verses 28-33 go on to give a description of this nation;

"They are a nation without sense, there is no discernment in them... Their vine comes from the vine of Sodom and from the fields of Gomorrah. Their grapes are filled with poison, and their clusters with bitterness. Their wine is the venom of serpents, the deadly poison of cobras..."

But God will destroy the nation of Islam; *"Vengeance is Mine, and retribution, in due time their foot will slip; for the day of their calamity is near, and the impending things are hastening upon them."* (Deuteronomy 32:35)

The fall of Islam will be quick and the Lord will bring His harvest (recompense) out of its fall. It is our work as the Body of Christ to prepare the world for the Valley of Decision. We do it by declaring the true Gospel and by proving false the testament of the Koran.

Revelation 13:8 - A World Caliphate?

"All the inhabitants of the Earth will worship the Beast, all whose names are not written in the Lamb's Book of Life" (Revelation 13:8)

Surveys have consistently shown that a clear majority of Muslims around the world would like to live under a worldwide Islamic Caliphate governed in accordance with the principles of Sharia Law. Professor Ruud Koopmans at the Berlin Social Sciences Centre found that even in Western Europe, 65% of Muslims immigrants thought Islamic religious rules were more important than the laws of the country they were living in. They want to live under a Sharia ruled Caliphate.

The name **"Caliphate"** is derived from *"Khalifah"*, the Arabic word for successor, because Mohammed promised;

24:55   *"He will make them Caliphs (successors) in the world...He will firmly establish the religion (Islam) for them..."*

and they must govern by Sharia, by applying what the Koran says;

5:49 *"So govern between the people by that which Allah has revealed...".*

Before dying Mohammed named his successor (see Sahih Muslim 31/5879) and sent the Muslim armies out to conquer the whole world for Islam. The true Caliphates were established by war and were only brought to an end with the military defeat of the Ottoman Empire. Author of the book **"Political Islam"**, Bill Warner estimates that the total number of non-Muslims killed throughout history in the name of the Caliphate exceeds 270 million. Other estimates go as high as 890 million.

Whilst the true figure is impossible to verify, we do know that the numbers involved are enormous, just check back to the list of recent genocides such as the killing of a million and a half Christians in Armenia only a century ago reported by the newspapers of the time. Or check out Tamerlane, who in 1400 AD had 90,000 men killed in one single day (the women were taken into slavery of course).

The genocides of Hindus in the Islamisation of India were probably the largest in all time, as historian Will Durant writes in 'The Story of Civilization; Our Oriental Heritage'; *"The Islamic conquest of India is probably the bloodiest story in history. It is a discouraging tale, for its evident moral is that civilization is a precious good, whose delicate complex order and freedom can at any moment be overthrown by barbarians."* Even conservative estimates put the number of Hindus killed at around 80 million since the time of Mahmud of Ghazni's first raids into India from Khorasan to the present day. Some commentators put the figure at over 400 million based quotes in Firishta's *"Tarikh-i Firishta"* ("The History of India, as Told by its Own Historians" Vol. 6 "The **Mohammedan Period"**, Cambridge) and the speeches of Swami Vivikananda (Prabuddha Bharata **"On the Bounds of Hinduism"** 1899).

The origin of the Caliphate also brought with it, by implication, the Islamic concept of *"Dar al-harb"* which means the *"territories of war"* meaning that everywhere outside the control of the Caliphate are where war should be waged overtly or covertly to bring in Islamic rule. The full extent of just how this quest for world domination shapes Islamic eschatology is examined by J P Filiu in his book **"Apocalypse in Islam"** (translated by DeBevoise, University of California Press). At the end of the first chapter he observes;

"...the modern (re-)discovery of the end of the world sees itself as a return to sources... one concerned with textual justification, the other in support of armed combat..."

Interestingly there is a Hadith which predicted the demise and later return of the Caliphate (As-Silsilah as-Shahihah 1/5) and just over a year ago, the Islamic State declared this new reign of Islamic rule with an ongoing display of killing, violence and abuse of women. Every day our news-media carry stories of beheadings of enemy fighters, brutal executions of gays, the enslaving and rape of non-Muslim women and more. Thousands of Muslim volunteers from around the globe rushed to be part of this new Caliphate. The Islamic State has openly tried to emulate Mohammed's original Islam, following his example. So just as Mohammed killed people for not attending prayer, the Islamic State just did the same executing a 16-year-old for not attending Friday prayers.

Perhaps all this is not surprising given the millions of dollars of oil revenue that the Gulf States and other Muslim countries have invested around the world in building mosques, Islamic schools and funding preachers who are actually just spreading true Mohammedan Islam. The ultimate aim of all Islam and of all true Muslims is to bring the whole world under Islamic government and Sharia law, to be governed by the Koran. It is therefore obvious that if groups like the Islamic State and Al Qaeda want this, the Koran is compatible with their extreme views.

Indeed, the resurgence of violent jihad in recent years is linked directly to the availability of the Koran. Its availability on the web in every language has caused many to become radicalized. The Islamic State uses its online Dabiq magazine to emphasize the terrorist verses. A recently convicted terrorist in London had on him, at the time of his arrest, a copy of the Koran with such verses highlighted.

Nearly all of the nations of the West have vowed to destroy this new Islamic Caliphate, and its territory is now shrinking in Iraq and Syria. But it is growing elsewhere, in the Philippines and Nigeria. Sadly, all the World's superpowers seem to be able to think of, is bombing it out of existence with much collateral damage to civilians rather than eradicating the very basis of its ideology. Yes, we need to wage war to protect our homelands, but belief systems are only made stronger by martyrdom and war. Even the threat of nuclear weapons will not eradicate the Islamist mindset, it must be undone ideologically.

When the Islamic State falls, other jihadi groups will continue to rise up and take their place until the Islamist mindset is eradicated. That will not be achieved by killing people nor by closing down mosques and banning the Koran. All it takes is proving, in public debate, the Koran to be untrue. Proving categorically that the Koran is not perfect and infallible, as this book does, will destroy people's reliance on it as the command of God.

When people realise that Islamic Allah's way leads to hell they will abandon it very quickly. Why are we so touchy about confronting Islamic beliefs, nobody threatens World War III when Christian or other ideals are put in question? Keep it as a war of ideas and ideals then Islam has no excuse for violence.

Let's not pretend it will happen overnight, but if done properly, it can be done in a few decades. And it needs to be done quickly because there are millions of Muslims around the world brainwashed to kill for their religion. Not standing up against the tyranny just lets the whole problem deteriorate. Failing to address the true causes of Islamism means that the situation will get worse and worse. Do we want to put it off for a few years until Muslims outnumber every other people group on the planet, and more countries submit to Sharia, as current projections suggest? Do we want to wait until terrorists blow up a whole Cathedral full of us Christians? They are already trying to do it! Circumstances demand that we act right away. Kill the hatred before it kills you.

Commentators frequently employ the term "apocalyptic" to describe what is taking place today, but is there more than just a poetic justification to the use of this word?

Are we heading into an Islamic Apocalypse?

666 - The Mark of the Beast

"After this I looked, and there before me was a door standing open in heaven. And the voice I had first heard speaking to me like a trumpet said, 'Come up here, and I will show you what must take place after this."
(Revelation 4:1)

The Book of Revelation tells us much about what will take place in the last days. The Islamic sacred books also contain a number of references to the end of the age, the Apocalypse;

"The Last Hour will not come unless the Muslims fight against the Jews, and the Muslims would kill them..." (Sahih Muslim 49/6981)

but most mentions of the end times in Islamic texts are vague like

"Great cities will be destroyed..."
(Al-Muttaqi al-Hindi, Al-Burhan fi Alamat al-Mahdi Akhir al-Zaman)

The Bible gives us much more detail and contains a significant amount of prophecy concerning the last days which has caused much debate over the centuries since it was written.

In the years since the bombing of the World Trade Centre in New York on 11th September 2001, there has been a resurgence of interest in trying to interpret and understand this complex prophetic material. Of particular interest has been the predicted coming of a False Prophet, a Beast with a severed head rising from the sea, and the personification of the "Anti-Christ". The Book of Revelation, "The Apocalypse", and the Gospels, together with the books of Daniel, Joel, Ezekiel, Isaiah and other Jewish prophets, give us many clues as to who or what these are and what will happen in the tumult of the end of days.

Historically there has been much conjecture about the identity of these enemies of God, much of it more fanciful than informed. For example, even the Catholic Church, the Pope and the European Union have been touted as candidates for these roles even though all of them fall short of the brutal quality implied by the term *"the Beast".*

It is certainly not part of their fundamental charters and mandates that all who don't believe in them must be killed. But it is in Islam's Koran;

2:191, 9:5   *"Kill the unbelievers wherever you find them"*

8:39   *"Make war until... all religion is that of Allah"*

It is only more recently that Islam has been suggested as the first great Beast, and we do now see this inherently brutal nature in the Islamic State, in the history of Islam and in the life of Mohammed. There is some supporting evidence in favour of this idea that the first beast that rises out of the sea of humanity is Islam. Indeed, the word *"Apocalypse"* is Greek for the uncovering, the unveiling, which gives us a big clue because the veiled woman is the most visible sign of Islam.

Another important pointer is found in Revelation 17:10-11;

"And there are seven kings: five are fallen, and one is, and the other is not yet come... And the beast that was, and is not, even he is the eighth, and is of the seven, and goeth into perdition"

This refers to the unholy empires that will rule over Jerusalem through the ages, Egypt, Assyria, Babylon, Medo-Persia and Greece are the five which had then been and gone. Rome is the one at the time of St John writing and the Islamic Caliphate was the seventh and looks like it wants to be the eighth again.

The relationships between the First Beast, the False Prophet and the Antichrist are also important indicators. As we have seen in previous chapters of this book, Islam is an anti-Christ religion because it denies the divinity of Jesus the Messiah, the Christ, the Anointed One. And the

Koran does contain untrue statements, false words that would qualify Mohammed as the False Prophet. Indeed, he says Jesus spoke of him in the Gospels, but the only coming prophets Jesus mentions are false.

"For false messiahs and false prophets will appear and perform great signs and wonders to deceive, if possible, even the elect" (Matt 24:24)

The Second Beast, rising out of the earth and thus symbolizing a man rising to power, is also the False Prophet in verse 19:20 in the Revelation.

"the false prophet who had performed signs on his behalf, by which he deceived those who had the mark of the beast and worshiped its image"

"he had two horns like a lamb, but he sounded like a dragon. He exercised all the authority of the first beast on its behalf..." "The second beast was permitted to give breath to the image of the first beast, so that the image would also speak and cause all who refused to worship it to be killed." (Revelation 13:11-12,15)

The visual description corresponds to that of the Baphomet (Ba'al Prophet Mohammed) spirit. Look at the fit; the image projected by the Beast is Allah, and Mohammed's words do certainly command the killing of all who will not worship that image; the Koran clearly says,

9:5 *"Kill the unbelievers wherever you find them..."*

Are you aware of any other religion which orders its followers to kill everyone else? Revelation 20:4 even says the Christian martyrs will be *"beheaded"*, which is what the Koran commands and ISIS have done;

47:4 *"Therefore, when you meet the non-Muslims, smite at their necks..."*

8:12 *"I will cast terror into the hearts of those who disbelieve. Therefore strike off their heads..."*

Certainly, we hear many people now saying, *"How do we stop Islam taking over?"* which reflects St John's prophecy in Revelation chapter 13;

"Who is like the Beast ? Who can wage war against it ?" (Revelation 13:4)

In the Koran, Islamic Allah confirms being behind the Second Beast, the False Prophet, agreeing with Revelation 13:11 which describes it as *"another Beast coming up out of the Earth"*.

27:82 *"when the Word is fulfilled...We shall bring forth a Beast of the Earth... ".*

On top of that, according to tradition, Muslims will rush to be scratched on their foreheads and receive a mark from it which will consign them to paradise or hell. (see Qurtubi, Jami` al-Ahkam al-Qur'an)

Another clue to the identity of the First Beast comes from the Book of Revelation verses 13:16-18 which culminates in the statement;

"Here is wisdom. Let him who has understanding calculate the number of the Beast, for it is the multitude of a man and its number is 666".

The Greek symbols for 666 were handwritten on St John's original manuscript of the book and in early copies such as the Codex Vaticanus and are uncannily similar to the Arabic words *"Bism-illah"* which means *"in the name of Allah".*

In fact, the handwritten Greek symbols for *"666"* appear to contain a rotated mirror-image of this accompanied by two crossed swords, a symbol for both Islam and jihad.

Why a mirror image you might ask?

Simple, because Arabic reads from right to left whereas Greek, like English, reads from left to right.

These Arabic symbols are frequently worn by jihadis and Islamic fundamentalists on headbands and armbands fulfilling the prophetic vision of Revelation verse 13:16;

"It causes them...to have a mark (a sign) on their right arms or foreheads."

St John was clearly seeing these things in the future and writing down what he saw. It is a true sign and wonder that he was able to see in the Spirit so clearly! And Islam is Mohammed's multitude, it really is a one man show, and most Muslims are so caught in it they ritually say; *"praise be unto him"* every time they speak his name. This is Baphomet Baal worship.

Only our true God is worthy of our praise and worship.

Now for those of you who love coincidences, 666 is also the number of Nautical Miles from Temple Mount in Jerusalem to the Ka'aba in Mecca. And if you think this really is just a spooky coincidence, then consider this one too; the London Stone is 1,948 Nautical Miles from Temple Mount, and London was the place from which Jerusalem and its surrounding area was governed until the Jews returned and proclaimed the State of Israel, gaining independence in, you guessed it, 1948 AD.

God Likes to give us signs! So that we understand!

Anyway, St John tells us that this beast has a severe head wound that was once fatal but has been healed, could this be the Ottoman Caliphate which was killed off but is returning?

"And I saw a Beast coming out of the sea. It had ten horns and seven heads, with ten crowns on its horns, and on each head a blasphemous name...One of the heads of the Beast seemed to have had a fatal wound, but the fatal wound had been healed" (Revelation 13:1,3)

In recent years, we have seen Turkey, which once was the head of the Caliphate but then became a secular state after its fall, has become increasingly re-Islamized. The current President and ruling party appear intent to make the country fully Islamic again. After his recent election victory, he promised constitutional change having previously said he would like to have the sovereign status of a monarch. Historically in Turkey this would mean becoming a Caliph, and he has even started sitting on the old Ottoman thrones in political photo opportunities. In March 2016, a **"Caliphate Conference"** was held in Ankara where a pledge was made to Allah to restore the Turkish Caliphate. As we write constitutional reforms have been agreed by a national referendum, the country is on the way to re-becoming an Islamic dictatorship. The fatally wounded head of the Beast is being restored... These constitutional reforms have opened the way for the appearance of the Antichrist.

The blasphemous names on each head of the Beast are the flags and mottos of the leading Islamic nations which all have proclamations that Allah is god. This is blasphemy to Yahweh the real God. As for the identity of the Antichrist, this is more difficult to pin down because his time has not yet come. Prophecy tells us that he will proclaim himself as having divine authority, setting up an idol or false altar in a rebuilt Jewish Temple on Temple Mount in Jerusalem.

As that re-building has not yet taken place, he has not yet been revealed (for more see Book of Daniel 9:27 & St Paul's Second Letter to the Thessalonians 2:3-4). Once the Temple starts to be rebuilt it is time to look for him.

Many minds throughout history have pondered on the characteristics given by the Scriptures of this Antichrist, although he is far from being the only one. Antiochus Epiphanes, even before Jesus' time was one, Hitler and Stalin were other Antichrists. But the final Antichrist seems to have the attributes of a false Messiah, and writers as diverse as Hyppolytus of Rome (170-235 AD) and Arthur Pink (1886-1952) have identified him with the *"King of Assyria"*, expecting him to come from somewhere in the Middle East. Assyria is the area where the Islamic State is currently most active. He will be powerfully evident when he comes, deceiving some, but reviled by others.

The Revelation of St John 16:13-16 says that when the *"Dragon"* (Satan/Allah), the *"Beast"* (Islam) and the *"False Prophet"* (Mohammed) speak, frogs come out of their mouths, signifying that demons will proceed from them to execute whatever they command. Their purpose is to prepare the world for Armageddon. This is a clear sign of the demonic nature of their works and as we have read Islam is a demonic hierarchy that holds all Muslims in submission

Iran and other Islamic nations are even now relying on Islamic Apocalyptic writings to guide their foreign and military policies. This a scary prospect in a time when Iran is also clearly trying to build nuclear weapons. Israel who they seek to destroy, already has them whilst Saudi Arabia probably has them from their close ally Pakistan.

Islamic traditions hold that the *"Mahdi"*, an Islamic Messiah, will come at around the time of Jesus' Second Coming and unite all Muslims. But it ought to be said that the Koran does not mention him, and the other sources on which this prophetic character are based are generally deemed as being of questionable authenticity. Nonetheless he is a powerful figure in the Islamic imagination, a recent President of Iran, Ahmadinejad, said he had come to pave the way for the Mahdi.

We learn that the Mahdi is a descendant of Mohammed, will bear the same name, and will suddenly appear in Mecca after a period of great chaos. There is great chaos in the Middle East now. He will fight the *"Dajjall"*, a sort of strange one-eyed antichrist figure. But Islam itself is anti-Christ because it denies that Jesus is Christ, the true Messiah So, really, this *"Dajjall"* is a sort of contradiction in terms. Some call the Mahdi the 12th Imam and calculate Abu Bakr al-Baghdadi of the Islamic State to be the Eighth. But this is pure conjecture as there have in effect already been more than 12 Caliphs.

The Mahdi will wage jihad against the whole world, covert at first, and then will go on to reign for Islam from Jerusalem for seven years, aided by the "discovery" of the Ark of the Covenant with the "original" Torah inside it which will convince many of his spiritual authority.

It is predicted, he will destroy the holy places of Islam in Mecca and Medina, then will seduce many Jews into siding with him because he will say that the religious legalism of Mosaic Law and of Islam are essentially the same. This is part of the deceit which enables him to rise to great power. Many of the descriptions of the Mahdi tally with those of the Bible's Antichrist. Author Joel Richardson lists several similitudes between the Antichrist and the Mahdi in his book **"Islamic Antichrist"**.

Both the Mahdi and the Biblical Antichrist kill Jews and Christians but will make a false peace treaty (Hudna) with Israel for seven years and then break it half way through. He will rule for seven years and make his seat of religious, political and military power on Temple Mount in Jerusalem. He will work with the Beast to behead and kill unbelievers and will oversee the prohibition of all economic activity for those who refuse to take the Mark of the Beast.

Jesus will then return and this is where the two versions of the end times diverge again. In the Bible He goes on to win Armageddon and destroys the Antichrist, but in Islam, Jesus allegedly becomes a Muslim and kills all the Jews and Christians who won't convert to it. More proof that Islam teaches a false Jesus.

We'll return to the Battle of Armageddon in the next section.

Another important character in the Apocalypse is the Woman riding the Beast. She is the *"Great Whore of Babylon"*, the economically driven world capitalist system which has become drunk and prostituted because it has failed to stand up against the Beast and has thus sold its soul to it. She was born in Babylon when the Shekel was established as the first tradeable currency, and she is now whoring over the seven mountains, the seven key arenas of life; - government, business, religion, education, the media, entertainment, and lifestyle, which affect us all.

We have all put our hands in hers, and consumed the fruit of her prostitution, whether it is by wearing clothes produced with child labour, or by using high-tech goods, the production of which pollutes the planet. All down the line fundamental moral issues are ignored, clean technologies suppressed in favour of cheap oil, weapons are sold to repressive regimes, and meanwhile the planet's ecosystems choke and destabilize into impending disaster.

And what's at the foundation of today's industrial economy? Oil. And who has most of the oil reserves? Islamic countries. So, whatever happens don't upset the Muslims because they've got most of the reserves. Wasn't it said at the end of WWII that American foreign policy was all about oil from then on? So just don't criticize Islam, and if the Oil Sheiks want to spend their money building mosques and madrassas for teaching the world all those terrorist verses in the Koran, we'll turn a blind eye to it. And to the Islamic State too, with its lovely cheap oil prices!

The West took a very long time to use its military capability which could have quickly wiped the Islamic State off the map. Many question why this was? Russian leader Vladimir Putin was the first world leader to have really used much military might to try to destroy it. He accused Turkey of being a gateway where cheap oil from the Islamic State was being exported for sale, and did bomb hundreds of oil tanker lorries on their way to the Turkish border. But afterwards he stopped short of eradicating it and has since started selling weapons to Turkey. Very evidently, the cheaper oil prices have benefited the economies of many developed countries, the real question is just how much did the cheap oil override other issues in the corridors of power?

So, even if there's a problem with terrorism don't say that it is Islam. Except that doesn't work...

And it is all changing now.

World War III and Satan's Throne

First the good news, where chapter 13 (verses 8 & 12) of the Book of Revelation talk of *"all on the earth"* worshipping the Beast, the word for Earth may have been mistranslated from the Greek word *"Gés"*, which means more realistically in this context means *"the land"* in the sense of a region or territory. There are many instances of the use of this Greek word where it cannot possibly mean the whole Earth, such as in Acts Chapter 7 where it appears three times, each time meaning a country or a region. The whole Earth will never become wholly Islamic. But it is certainly already true that in the Middle East region most of the inhabitants are Muslim and worship Islam and Allah.

And the bad news; - well it seems like the end of days' events are already unravelling. In the Book of Isaiah Chapter 19 we read of a coming drought in Egypt (verses 5-6);

"the waters shall fail...the river shall be wasted and dried up...the rivers shall be emptied far away...the (irrigation) canals shall dry up".

This is happening now; the Aswan Dam has already significantly reduced the flow of the Egyptian Nile but a new dam is under construction just inside the Ethiopian border which may spell disaster downstream. Some estimates say that 2 million farmers downstream may lose their livelihoods during the period when the dam is being filled. And in the hot tropical climate loss of water due to evaporation can be extremely high too, reducing flow downstream by over 10% at each dam.

The prophecy tells of civil war, ecological and economic failure at the same time as a despotic power reigning over the land. The election of the Muslim Brotherhood candidate Mohammed Morsi following the Arab Spring, led to great turmoil which shows no signs of abating yet. No one knows when stability will return to the land. Egyptian-American author Nonie Darwish in her book **"The Devil We Don't Know: The Dark Side of Revolutions in the Middle East"** (Wiley and Sons) has closely analysed the ongoing changes and what may follow. To quote her conclusion;

"The epidemic of Islamic terrorism, civil unrest, wars and revolutions is nothing but a symptom of panic over Islam's downfall...If it were not for petro-dollars, Islam would have died a natural death after World War II, together with Nazi ideology. Petro-dollars have come to the rescue and sustained it. Yet despite their wealth from oil, Muslim countries have again reached an alarming level of stagnation, poverty and demoralization..."

Only time will tell where this all leads but God has already started pouring out His Spirit in Egypt and we now hear reports of people there having had some miraculous encounters with the living God. Indeed, it was during a time of non-stop 24/7 Christian prayer meetings that Morsi was overthrown and imprisoned, showing how much religious affiliation in Egypt is shifting.

Another end time prophecy that is materialising is chapter 13 of Isaiah which talks about Babylon, which today we call Iraq, verse 16 says;

"Their children will be smashed to death before their eyes; their houses will be looted, and their wives raped."

This is exactly what the Islamic State have been doing, Canon Andrew White, widely known as the Vicar of Baghdad, has told of children being sawn in half in front of their Christian parents because they will not convert to Islam. These families are driven out of their homes the possessions seized as booty, the fathers killed too, with the mothers and daughters enslaved and then raped. Later verses in that Chapter of Isaiah talk about places becoming deserted, and we have seen millions flee the area to seek refuge.

The fourteenth Chapter of the Book of Zechariah, another Old Testament Jewish prophet, seems to follow on from this;

"I will gather all the nations against Jerusalem for battle. The city will be captured, the houses looted, and the women raped. Half the city will go into exile, but the rest of the people will not be removed from the city. Then the LORD will go out and fight against those nations, as he fights on a day of battle." (Zechariah 14:2-3)

The build up to the apocalypse is taking place before our very eyes. What is to come?

As noted above, the Mahdi/Antichrist will lead jihad against all of the non-Muslims of the world and Islamic scholars see this as leading up to a grand final battle, Islam versus the rest of the world. But before this there will be strife in the Islamic world. According to some the rising of the Mahdi will be foreshadowed by the rise of a lesser figure called *"The Sufiani"* leading an alliance of *"Three Flags"*, three powers fighting to gain control in the Middle East. Then a confederacy of *"Ten Flags"*, fighting with the Mahdi, will arise and overcome the Three Flag alliance and this is how the Mahdi gains great international power and influence.

Iranian officials have said that the situation is now ripe for them to extend their Islamic Revolution to all Shias across the Middle East from Iran through Iraq and Syria to Lebanon. Already Iranian Revolutionary Guards are present fighting against the Sunni Islamic State in Iraq and Syria. A full Iranian invasion of these lands could lead to a great war between Shias and Sunnis for dominance in the Muslim world. Possibly a nuclear one, if Iran manages to succeed with its not so hidden agenda to make an atomic bomb. Is this the Three Flag Alliance?

One of the signs of the Mahdi's coming, according to some sources, is an army with black banners arising east of Israel which he will join with and reconquer that land for Islam. (see Ibn Izzat & Arif; **"Al Mahdi and the End of Time"**) Some think this army with black banners will come out of Khorasan which refers to Iran or Afghanistan but this reference could be historic, relating to the Islamization of India.

"Black standards will come from Khorasan, nothing shall turn them back until they are planted in Jerusalem" (Sunan At-Tirmidhi 2269)

This perhaps tallies with the prophecies in the Book of Daniel chapter 8 which many interpret as being that Iranian alliance arising, which is here eventually defeated by the confederacy led by Turkey (Ionia).

Some Bibles have mistranslated Ionia to mean Greece thinking this referred to the Greco-Medean wars but it specifically relates to the end times (see verse 26) and Ionia specifically designates the area around Izmir province, thus indicating Turkey.

"And out of one of them came forth a little Horn, which waxed exceeding great, toward the south, and toward the east, and toward the pleasant land. And it waxed great, even to the host of heaven; and it cast down some of the host and of the stars to the ground, and stamped upon them. Yea, he magnified himself even to the prince of the host, and by him the daily sacrifice was taken away, and the place of his sanctuary was cast down. And an host was given him against the daily sacrifice by reason of transgression, and it cast down the truth to the ground; and it practised, and prospered. Then I heard one saint speaking, and another saint said unto that certain saint which spake, 'How long shall be the vision concerning the daily sacrifice, and the transgression of desolation, to give both the sanctuary and the host to be trodden under foot?' And he said unto me, 'Unto two thousand and three hundred days; then shall the sanctuary be cleansed."
(Daniel 8:9-14)

The angel Gabriel explained the vision to Daniel;

"a king of fierce countenance, and understanding dark sentences, shall stand up. And his power shall be mighty, but not by his own power: and he shall destroy wonderfully, and shall prosper, and practise, and shall destroy the mighty and the holy people. And through his policy also he shall cause craft to prosper in his hand; and he shall magnify himself in his heart, and by peace shall destroy many: he shall also stand up against the Prince of princes; but he shall be broken without hand"
(Daniel 8:23-25)

The horn, representing power, is that of the *"first king"*, in other words the power of the Mohammed which returns with this king of fierce countenance. Will the Mahdi's Turkey win a war for Muslim supremacy?

Against Iran's Three Flag alliance? they have sided with Lebanon's Hezbollah and Assad's Russian backed Syria in the ongoing wars in Syria and Iraq. What's more Sunni clerics in Saudi Arabia have issued a fatwa that all Muslims should take up arms to defeat this essentially Shia alliance. The execution by beheading in Saudi Arabia of a leading Shia Imam accused of terrorism and the war in Yemen have brought matters towards a flashpoint. Saudi Arabia sees Shia's as terrorists.

Russia itself is driven by a Russian Orthodox prophecy that it will one day capture Constantinople, Istanbul, as it is currently known.

Many Muslims including the Iranian Ayatollahs believe that the Mahdi would first appear in 2016 and that he will come to Israel in 2022.

The 12th December 2022!

But it is the Ten-country alliance, which Daniel saw come out of Turkey, that is with the Mahdi and takes supremacy. Certainly, the Ten Flags representing nations is equivalent to the Beast of Revelation's ten horns;

"The dragon stood on the shore of the sea. And I saw a beast coming out of the sea. It had ten horns and seven heads, with ten crowns on its horns, and on each head a blasphemous name" (Revelation 13:1)

"The ten horns are ten kings who will come from this kingdom. After them another king will arise, different from the earlier ones; he will subdue three kings" (Daniel 7:24)

Each of the first Ten Kings is one of the Islamic Caliphs. Are the Three Kings to be subdued, the leaders of the Three Flag Alliance? It is interesting that Daniel in his prophecies should specifically say that this last king is *"King of Ionia"* (Daniel 8:21) from Izmir province in Turkey because the Book of Revelation also mentions that area in chapter 2 verses 12-13;

"Pergamum... where Satan's throne is... where Satan dwells"

Pergamum, known today as Bergama, in Izmir province, Turkey, was home to the Pergamum Altar, which is what St John was referring here to as being Satan's throne and even his dwelling place.

This satanic throne has an interesting history; it dates back to the ancient Greek empire and was used for human sacrifices to the pagan gods until the Fourth Century AD, then was later abandoned until its remains were discovered by German archaeologists in 1878.

By agreement with the Ottoman authorities, the vestiges of the altar were taken piece by piece to Berlin where it was restored, and a special museum was built to house it, which opened in 1901. Due to structural problems supporting the great weight of the exhibit, the first museum had to close and a newer museum built opening in 1930.

Then towards the end of World War II the Russians captured Berlin and took away the altar to the Hermitage Museum in Leningrad.

In 1958, some parts were returned to East Germany, then with the fall of the Soviet Union in the 1980's much of the rest of the altar was returned to Berlin, although some parts still remain in the Pushkin and Hermitage Museums in Russia.

In recent years Turkey has been asking for the return of the altar to be rebuilt in its original location but Germany has refused saying it obtained the relic legally.

The Pergamum Museum in Berlin which houses it is currently closed for structural improvements and the Turkish government has said several times that it intends to build a replica of the shrine on the original site in Bergama.

What is particularly noteworthy is that within 40 years of the shrine being removed from Turkey, the Ottoman Turkish Caliphate fell. The altar then was in Berlin in Germany which was centrally involved in both World Wars, the design of Hitler's podium in the Zeppelin Field where the Nuremberg Nazi rallies were held was deliberately modelled on it. It then went to Russia during the darkest years of Cold War Sovietism when Stalin was in power.

It does seem to carry a very dark heritage with it, all of the countries where it resided have seen repressive regimes which arose who persecuted Christians and, even more so, Jews. It really seems to carry Satan's power wherever it has been. And now Turkey wants to rebuild it in its original place and form. What's more, they want to set up a special museum containing all the original statues of ancient gods that came from the area, so this would probably look something like the original pagan Ka'aba idol sanctuary in Mecca.

Can't we get the Islamic State to blow this evil throne to smithereens?

So anyway, it looks like a Turkish-led confederacy under the Mahdi might well lead the end times assault on Israel in the battle of Armageddon. Muslim scholars say a great final battle will ensue in Dabiq, Syria (see Sahih Muslim 41/6924) and the Islamic State has taunted the United States to come and do battle with them there. The Bible however puts this final battle nearly 1,000 Kilometres away at Megiddo in northern Israel, and this place name is at the origin of the term *"Armageddon"* used for this great final showdown.

Wherever this last battle is fought, the overall scenario however is the same; a building conflict between the people of the Beast, the armies of Islam, and the non-Muslim peoples. Indeed, we are already in that war, it is wrongly called the *"war on terror"*, but it really is a sort of war between Islam and the "West", a war of ideas and ideals.

As the true Islam of Mohammed with his Koran are the very root of this terror, (and don't forget that over 95% of all terrorism in the world is Islamist), we are currently in a World War III of ideas and ideals under another name.

A spiritual and intellectual war of ideas and ideals. And a physical one too.

Certainly, we now know from recently discovered documents that both Al Qaeda and the Islamic State have deliberately sought to use terrorism to provoke a worldwide military conflict between Islam and the rest of the world. The Islamic State's monthly magazine is even called Dabiq and they have recently released a fantasy video of them destroying Rome, showing just how much they are driven by Apocalyptic thinking.

There are some Islamic nations too, as well as these groups, which are being driven by Apocalyptic theology. Author Timothy Furnish has researched this in great depth in his book **"Ten Years' Captivation with the Mahdi's Camps"**. These Muslims deeply believe that it is their duty to Allah to push the world towards a final great Armageddon where according to the Book of Revelation (9:13-21) a great army of 200 million men will assemble after four angels bound at the Euphrates River in Iraq are loosed.

These military forces in the Book of Revelation are carried along on spiritual warhorses which have the appearance of being godly, having faces like lions but which from behind can be seen to be demonic, looking like serpents. Their spiritual breastplates are fire and brimstone, showing that they believe they are executing God's judgement whereas in fact it is He that has summoned them to this place to bring judgement against them. (see Book of Joel 3:1-21)

Some commentators seeing the size of this 200-million-man army believe it can only be from China, but a recent study, **"The World's Muslims: Religion, Politics and Society"** in 2013 has shown that 28% of Muslims worldwide believe in violent jihad. Many of these believers in Islam see jihad as their only guaranteed way of assuring a place in paradise. This would mean that about 360 million adult men and women are keen and willing to war on behalf of Islam. Discounting mothers with children and the elderly, there would still remain enough manpower to muster an army of 200 million under the flag of jihad.

Even 19% of American Muslims believe in violent jihad, so there alone is huge army of potential warriors. A 2015 study by the Sun newspaper in the UK came up with a similar percentage, 20% there, who believe in violent jihad. In Brussels hundreds of young Muslims came out on the streets to openly celebrate the 2016 airport and metro bombings with dancing which later turned to rioting.

And the situation seems to be deteriorating, a collated study of statistics by Raheem Kassam published on the Breitbart news website entitled **"Data, Young Muslims in the West are a Ticking Time Bomb, Increasingly Sympathizing with Radicals, Terror"**, showed that the number of young Muslims in the West expressing support for violent jihad is growing.

Elsewhere the figures are astonishing as the article points out;

"And this number pales in comparison to global Muslim population figures. According to World Public Opinion (2009) at the University of Maryland, 61 per cent of Egyptians, 32 per cent of Indonesians, 41 per cent of Pakistanis, 38 per cent of Moroccans, 83 per cent of Palestinians, 62 per cent of Jordanians, and 42 per cent of Turks appear to endorse or sympathise with attacks on Americans or American groups."

So, the figure of 200 million for this great army is entirely feasible. The ancient Prophet Ezekiel lists the confederacy that will come against Israel for this great battle, Chapter 38 verses 1-6 list the main nations who will take part in this invasion and Chapter 39 addresses *"Gog"* (Turkey) as leader with the other nations being *"Magog"* (Chechnya/Caucasus), *"Persia"* (Iran), *"Cush"* (Sudan), and *"Put"* (Libya).

These are all Muslim nations today. Noticeably Egypt, Syria, Iraq and Jordan, surprisingly, are missing from this list, but the Book of Isaiah Chapter 19:21-25 has already given us the answer indicating that God will visit them and they will become predominantly Christian lands.

Biblical prophet Zechariah in chapter 9 of his book seems to be talking about the current tumult in Syria and Palestine, connecting it to Christ's reappearance.

"Behold, the Lord will dispossess her and cast her wealth into the sea; And she will be consumed with fire." (Zechariah 9:4)

Another ancient Jewish Prophet, Joel, talks of the final confrontation of God's enemies in the valley of decision meaning that Christ will come down in judgement and intervene to end the war.

"Proclaim this among the nations: Prepare for holy war; rouse the warriors; let all the men of war advance and attack! ...Let the nations be roused and come to the Valley of Jehoshaphat, for there I will sit down to judge all the surrounding nations.... Multitudes, multitudes in the valley of decision! For the day of the LORD is near in the valley of decision." (Joel 3:9,12,14)

God would prefer to destroy evil without bloodshed and save the souls of those who sow destruction because it is Satan who has stirred them up for war.

Can Jesus' peaceful intervention prevent a great bloody battle to end all battles?

Well he did say to us *"Love your enemies".* (Matthew 5:44/Luke 6:27)

Don't forget that this great final showdown really comes with the first resurrection and the rapture when all the true believers in Yahweh are lifted up;

"For the Lord himself shall descend from heaven with a shout, with the voice of the archangel, and with the trump of God, and the dead in Christ shall rise first. Then we who are alive and remain shall be caught up together with them in the clouds, to meet the Lord..."
(1 Thessalonians 4:16-17)

At this time, the Book of Revelation tells us, the Beast and False Prophet, (Islam and Mohammed/Baphomet) are defeated whilst Satan is bound and cast into the abyss bringing about Christ's reign for 1,000 years.

"Then I saw the beast, the kings of the earth, and their armies gathered together to wage war... the beast was captured, and with it the false prophet... The two of them were thrown alive into the fiery lake of burning sulphur." (Revelation 19:19-20)

Only after this does Satan return to be finally defeated;

"When the thousand years are completed, Satan will be released from his prison and will go out to deceive the nations from the four corners of the earth, Gog and Magog, and to gather them for battle... And the devil, who deceived them, was thrown into the lake of burning sulphur, where the beast and the false prophet had been thrown..."
(Revelation 20:7-8,10)

Armageddon; The Valley of Decision

"The God of peace will soon crush Satan under your feet. The grace of our Lord Jesus be with you" (Romans 16:20)

Sorry to disappoint some of you, but in fact it may be that the physical Battle of Armageddon has already been fought!

Following the prophetic capture of Jerusalem by General Allenby towards the end of 1917, he set about consolidating the victory. Further strongholds in the region, like Jericho, were taken in the months that followed and the British were able to build up superior forces which, with total air superiority, could not be resisted by the Ottoman Turks.

The British army went on to rout the Turkish forces around Megiddo (Armageddon) in September 1918, before sweeping through Damascus, Beirut, Tripoli and Aleppo starting a chain of events which led to the complete downfall of the Ottoman Empire and its Caliphate.

Just over a month later the Ottoman rulers surrendered, with the British taking possession of Constantinople on 10th November 1918. The Caliphate ceased to exist a few years later, the first time there had been no Caliphate since Mohammed's time.

Armageddon was thus the decisive battle of the war and the death sentence of the Caliphate.

No real Caliphate has existed since apart from the recently declared Islamic State which many Muslims do not publicly recognize as having true authority.

The Battle of Dabiq has already been fought too, some 400 years earlier than Megiddo when the Ottomans themselves were victorious and went on to establish the Caliphate's religious control over Jerusalem in 1517.

Thus, Armageddon and Dabiq are just prophetic symbols for either side's ultimate victory and are thus no longer battles waiting to be fought.

But that doesn't mean that things aren't going to get very, very hot in the Middle East.

Great armies are already in Assyria, the Syria and Iraq region, even now the Russians, Iranians, Americans, British, French, Saudis and others are all fighting there.

These apocalyptic visions we have been considering in this part of the book are a very powerful driving force in the religious doctrines of some Islamic groups, right from the official Ayatollahs in Iran to the self-proclaimed Caliphate of the Islamic State. They are all working towards killing all Jews to bring forth the Day of Judgement.

"The last hour would not come unless the Muslims will fight against the Jews and the Muslims would kill them..."
(Sahih Muslim 49/6981)

We are in a real war with the Islamic State and the new Caliphate, but God would still prefer to undo Islam in a peaceful way, with us fighting it intellectually and spiritually in preference to military war.

As St Paul said; *"We fight not against flesh and blood",* so we in the West should act accordingly as far as is possible.

But do not forget that Al-Qaeda leader Osama bin Laden admitted that when they attacked New York on 11th September 2001 they were deliberately planning to ignite a worldwide conflict.

The Islamic State wants to do the same. The Islamist agenda has always been to provoke armed conflict. Satan's agenda is to kill, steal and destroy, and this includes trying to provoke a third World War between Islam and the rest of the World.

But God's agenda is a third Great Awakening, already stirring in many places. A great revival of Christian faith that will bring a new Reformation of society aligned with Christ's Kingdom principles.

Thus, God has another way. And in the light of this, the Islamic prophecy about the final battle being fought at Dabiq has an interesting conclusion. So, ignoring the facts that Dabiq has already been fought, and that Constantinople is already Muslim, let's look at how it finishes.

According to Sahih Muslim 41/6924;

> *"The Last Hour would not come until the Romans land at al-A'maq or in Dabiq...they will arrange themselves in ranks, the Romans...would say: 'Do not stand between us and those who took prisoners from amongst us. Let us fight with them;' and the Muslims would say: 'Nay, by Allah, we would never get aside from you and from our brethren that you may fight them'.*
> *They will then fight and a third of the army would run away, whom Allah will never forgive. A third would be constituted of excellent martyrs in Allah's eye and would be killed, and the third who would...be conquerors of Constantinople...*
> *then Jesus... would descend and would lead them in prayer. When the enemy...sees Him, it would (disappear) just as the salt dissolves itself in water and if He (Jesus) were not to confront them at all...Allah would kill them by his hand and he would show them their blood on his lance"*

Jesus will appear and pray; this causes the mighty army which opposes God to melt away even though Allah would have preferred having them killed.

Common sense would interpret this passage to mean that upon seeing Jesus they will become Christian which is how they can come to pray with Him.

They will now seek peace, no longer following Islam's way of war. That is why Allah would want them killed.

This largely corresponds to the Biblical interpretation of Jesus' return at the end of the age.

"You shall hear of wars and rumours of war...for these things must come to pass..."
(Gospel of Matthew 24:6)

"Multitudes, multitudes in the valley of decision! For the day of the LORD is near in the valley of decision..."
(Book of Joel 3:13-14)

"And then shall appear the sign of the Son of Man in heaven: and then shall all the tribes of the earth wail, and they shall see the Son of man coming in the clouds of heaven with power and great glory."
(Gospel of Matthew 24:30)

"And after these things I heard a great voice of a multitude in heaven saying, 'Alleluia; Salvation and glory and honour and power, unto our God, for true and righteous are His judgments: for He hath judged the great whore, which did corrupt the earth with her fornication, and hath avenged the blood of His servants at her hand...'

And I saw heaven opened, and behold a white horse; and He that sat upon it was called Faithful and True...in righteousness He doth judge and make war. His eyes were as a flame of fire, and on His head were many crowns...and He hath on his vesture...a name written, King of Kings and Lord of Lords...

And I saw the beast, and the kings of the earth, and their armies, gathered together to make war against Him that sat on the horse and against His army...

And the Beast was taken, and with him the False Prophet that wrought miracles before him, with which he deceived those who had the Mark of the Beast and worshipped its image. These were both cast alive into the lake of fire...and the remnant were slain (in the Spirit) with the Sword which proceeded out of the mouth of Him that sat upon the horse..."
(The Apocalypse (Revelation of St John) Chapter 19 abridged)

"The Sword of the Spirit which is the Word of God...", "For the Word of God is alive and active. Sharper than any double-edged sword, it penetrates even to dividing soul and spirit...it judges the thoughts and attitudes of the heart..."
(Book of Ephesians 6:17, Book of Hebrews 4:12)

Muslims in explaining their view of all this say that Jesus will become a Muslim but this is impossible because He is the truth. Because the Koran contains statements which are not true, Jesus cannot hold it up as the Word of God, and therefore can never accept the first Pillar of Islam.

"Jesus answered, 'I am the Way and the Truth and the Life. No one comes to the Father except through Me" (Gospel of John 14:6)

Note that it is the true Word of God, the Sword that proceeds out of Jesus' mouth, that destroys His enemies. We must wield the Word of God and kill the Beast. We must behead it, and destroy it ideologically and in so doing, bring Christ's salvation to individual Muslims. Every Muslim saved is a nail in Islam's coffin. Islam is intellectually very, very weak; and as we have seen in previous parts of this book, its core text the Koran does not stand up to close analytical scrutiny. The religion's fragility can be seen in the fact there has to be a threat of death to stop people leaving it. That is also why Muslims can be so threatening about what they call blasphemy, they are obliged to protect Islam from the criticism that would show it for what it truly is.

"Stand your ground, putting on the belt of truth and the body armour of God's righteousness. For shoes, put on the peace that comes from the Good News so that you will be fully prepared. In addition to all of these, hold up the shield of faith to stop the fiery arrows of the devil. Put on salvation as your helmet, and take the sword of the Spirit, which is the Word of God. Pray in the Spirit at all times and on every occasion"
(Ephesians 6:14-18)

It has been very easy to incontrovertibly prove that the Koran is not perfect and infallible. It has also been exceedingly easy to show that it contains false statements, thus making Mohammed a false prophet and Allah a false god. Islam is not the religion of the one true all-wise, all-knowing God.

If symbolically Armageddon now means the downfall of the rule of Islam, then the world's Muslims will be brought in this time to the *"Valley of Decision",* where they can discover who the true God really is. The Islamic Apocalypse brings the whole Islamic world into that place where each must decide whether to embrace the truth that the Koran is not from God, or to continue in its violent ways.

Nations will also go through the *"Valley of Decision",* in deciding how they will deal with the growing Islamist problem. Terrorism has recently become an almost daily event around the world, and riots, Muslim *"Intifadas",* have been started by Muslims in Western countries. The rising level of anti-Semitic attacks has already caused some Jews in the West to start hiding their identity and even consider re-locating to Israel. Indeed, thousands have already left.

"God, who began the good work within you, will continue his work until it is finally finished on the day when Christ Jesus returns."
(Philippians 1:6)

The Valley of Decision is the culmination of God's redemptive plan for mankind.

The first book of the Bible tells us of the plan of God to bless humanity through the line of Abraham. That includes today's Muslims;

"in you (Abraham) all the families of the earth shall be blessed."
(Genesis 12:3)

Jews, Christians and Muslims all link their spiritual inheritance back to him. He had two sons, Ishmael and Isaac, and it is Isaac, his younger son through whom the Jews and Christians trace back their covenants. Mohammed is said to be a direct descendant of Ishmael and thus Islam is part of the Abrahamic inheritance. As first born, Ishmael was born to Hagar, the Egyptian slave of Abraham's wife Sarah, who had suggested using her as a surrogate. This was a legal and common practice under Hammurabi's Babylonian Law Code which Abraham would have known. Any child born in such circumstances would be deemed a lawful heir to the slave owner. This is a spiritual root of Islam's sex-slavery.

After Isaac was born, Ishmael was rather harshly sent away from Abraham's family and would have died in the wilderness had it not been for the intervention of God. This episode left Ishmael with a heavy spirit of rejection which remained in his bloodline. Islam is tainted by this spirit which is why the religion is so rejecting of non-Muslims and especially Jews and Christians, the inheritance of his younger brother Isaac.

Other aspects of the faith can also be seen augured in the Bible. In the Book of Genesis, it says that the Angel of the Lord told Hagar about her then unborn son Ishmael;

"He will be a wild donkey of a man; his hand will be against everyone and everyone's hand against him, and he will live in hostility toward all his brothers." (Genesis 16:12)

This is a very interesting prophecy which is worth looking at closer.

Wild can mean full of lust and violent, and a donkey in the Bible often symbolizes something prophetic as with Issachar, Balaam, Job and even Jesus' triumphal entry into Jerusalem. Is the Angel of the Lord perhaps predicting a violent prophet? Is it talking of Ishmael's descendant Mohammed?

The rest of the prophecy is easily evident in Mohammed's life and in Islam itself. Islam is against everyone who doesn't believe in it and hostile towards Jews and Christians, brothers in the Abrahamic inheritance. It is very harsh on Muslims too with its Sharia constraints. Islam is probably the most divisive thing in the world today. With it now spreading around the world, this prophecy has reached its fullness.

It is interesting that Jacob/Israel's brother Esau married into the Ishmaelite line (Genesis 28:9), and he had received this blessing from their father Isaac; *"Behold, away from the fertility of the earth shall be your dwelling, And away from the dew of heaven from above. By your sword you shall live..."* (Genesis 27:39-40) This suggests a violent, desert-dwelling heritage which we see in the history of the Arab race, from which Mohammed was issue. We see the sword on the flags of many Islamic nations. And Esau's descendants are *"Edom"* as the Book of Genesis Chapter 36, verse 1, explains where there are several interesting prophecies in the Bible concerning them. The prophet Amos speaks of the Lord's punishment *"because he pursued his brother with the sword and cast off all pity, and his anger tore perpetually, and he kept his wrath forever"* (Amos 1:11) and the Edomites became bitter enemies of Israel. Several prophecies focus on the foretelling of Edom's destruction including Psalm 137, Isaiah 34, Jeremiah 49, Ezekiel 25 & 35, Obadiah 1, and Malachi 1.

"Because you maintained an ancient hatred and handed over the Israelites to the power of the sword in the time of their disaster, the time of final punishment, therefore as surely as I live, declares the Sovereign LORD, I will give you over to bloodshed and it will pursue you. Since you did not hate bloodshed, bloodshed will pursue you..." "you will become a desolation, Mount Seir, and so will all Edom in its entirety. Then they will know that I am Yahweh" (Ezekiel 35:5-6,15)

The Amalekites who built the original pagan sanctuary at the Ka'aba in Mecca were descendants of Edom (Genesis 36:12). Islam is their spiritual heritage. It will ultimately be destroyed. But God the Father wants to see all of Abraham's descendance redeemed.

As we have seen, the last book of the Bible, the Revelation of St John talks of the Apocalypse. This is the place of final confrontation which puts Muslims in the Valley of Decision where they must choose either Islam, the way of the False Prophet, or the true way of salvation and peace through Christ. In this last book of the Bible we can see the fulfilment of what was started in the first book. We await the reconciliation of the offspring of Abraham so they can receive the Father's blessing. With a repentant and loving heart, we must each offer an olive branch to the other branch of our spiritual family.

The salvation of all Muslims is important to God.

They must pass through the Valley of Decision to come out of Islam.

We must lead them to it and through it.

Whilst there may be some initial anger from a few Muslims at the unveiling of the truth of what their religion really is, very soon all level-headed Muslims who find out about it will realize that what we Christians believe in is true and will quickly want to leave Islam.

Many are already disgusted at terrorism, sex-slavery, FGM, intolerance and xenophobia, but do not understand that Islam actively teaches and propagates these things.

We must help them see the light and leave their demonic religion.

Quite definitely, Mohammed prophesied a falling away of Islam in the last days, saying;

"There will come a time for my people when there will remain nothing of the Qur'an except its outward form and nothing of Islam except its name..." (Hadiths Ibn Babuya, Thawab ul-A'mal, Al Bihar by Al-Majlisi 13/155, Kanz Al-amal 766)

Part Nine - The Undoing

"Let Him make speed, let Him hasten His work, that we may see it; And let the purpose of the Holy One of Israel draw near and come to pass, that we may know it !" Woe to those who call evil good, and good evil; who substitute darkness for light and light for darkness; who substitute bitter for sweet and sweet for bitter ! Woe to those who are wise in their own eyes and clever in their own sight !" (Isaiah 5:19-21)

Now we are sorry to be the bearers of bad news, but it does have to be said that not everybody is happy when you start speaking the truth about Islam. So, now that you are armed with the truth, and ready to do your bit to propagate it, desiring to see Muslims set free, you do need to be aware that there are some who are only too ready to brand any Christian as an Islamophobe, inferring you are fearful of Islam. And it is not just Muslims who will make this accusation, what's more! This is so ironic because it is the opposite of the truth. Islam is afraid of us knowing the truth, and scared of the truth that sets people free. Yet there are some who would try to silence that truth. We have to say we have had web pages taken down without a word by service providers who are too cowardly to even enter into dialogue about it. Forgive them Lord they know not what they do. They treat us as if we are the ones making hate remarks, whereas in fact we are the ones trying to stop Islam's hate speech. Anyway, it only takes a couple of hours work to put up another site to touch thousands of people. God's work cannot be stopped. Perhaps the saddest thing is that some of those who try to block the truth about Islam, genuinely think they are doing good. Some think they are making the world a better place, whereas in fact they are doing the opposite, making it much easier for Islam to propagate hatred through its sacred texts. They have thus sided with anti-Semitism, terrorism and the degradation of women which are all irremovable parts of the basic Islamic belief system all held in place by the Koran. These things can thus never be removed from Islam and never be overruled within it. To Muslims these words are Sharia and must be obeyed.

"Blessed are you when people hate you, when they exclude you and insult you and reject your name as evil, because of the Son of Man" (Luke 6:22)

Those who stifle proper informed debate about Islamic beliefs are actually exhibiting either total ignorance of the issues, or true fear of Islam. They must be frightened of it otherwise why would they stop people speaking the truth about it? Instead of there being proper open public discussion, Islamic anti-social behaviour is excused and whitewashed over. This creates resentment in those who see a people who will not assimilate into our society being given special treatment.

Where is the rebuke for the xenophobia, learnt from the Koran, that is so openly exhibited by some Muslims? And the resentment of this, instead of finding its proper expression through debate and discussion, flares up into demonstrations of anti-Muslim violence. This is wrong; in a peaceful democratic society, the pressure valve of reasoned, justified debate must be kept open. Closing it off creates a climate ripe for inter-cultural violence. The recent massacre in Orlando proves that there is an issue over conflicting cultural ideas and ideals that has to be resolved. Only a fool would try to ignore the fact that nearly all Muslims in certain immigrant communities think apostates, adulterers and homosexuals should be killed, because that is what Sharia law proscribes. Our democratically established laws say they shouldn't be killed. There is evidently, a conflict of values. Studies have also shown that many Muslim immigrants in the West believe Sharia is more important for them to follow than our national laws. Such issues cannot be swept under the carpet, they will not go away on their own. And there is only one resolution for the arguments, Sharia Islamic values should be debated and proved wrong, otherwise we risk being forced to accept them.

"For such is the will of God that by doing right you may silence the ignorance of foolish men" (1 Peter 2:15)

Some of the public policies of governmental authority in both Europe and the USA have shown a tendency to try to bury the problem of Islamism rather than let public debate run through to its logical outcome. Certainly, there is repeated proof of this in statements from people like former US Secretary of State Hillary Clinton, who said that it is unwise to imply that Islam is a problem. Clearly the fear of the Islamic reaction is the reason for this attitude which hinders and blocks proper debate on the issue. European governments have even taken to pressurizing social media providers to take down anti-Islamic content from the web as well as anything that criticizes the European Union policies. This has happened in Europe at the hands of the European Commission even though the European Union is subject to the European Convention on Human Rights which is supposed to guarantee freedom of speech and artistic expression. The convention was established after World War II to prevent the rise of totalitarianism in Europe in the future, yet the European Commission has ridden roughshod over it without any real informed debate on Islam in the European or any national Parliament. It is a frightening sign of the times.

"Blessed are those who are persecuted because of righteousness, for theirs is the kingdom of heaven" (Matthew 5:10)

But as we have already said so many times, God's work will be done and only a fool would try to stifle free speech and free debate in the smartphone age. Already those who inhibit free speech about Islam and other topics, whilst saying they are trying to prevent hate speech, they are actually proving themselves to be the totalitarian extremists by their acts of self-righteous and self-motivated censorship of others. There is no disclosure or discussion of what the criteria are for this censorship. And there never can be, because if there was open discussion, then the hate verses in the Koran would have to be outlawed. And they don't have the courage to do that. There is no appeal to a higher authority, or any authority at all, there is, in short, a total disrespect for the statutory safeguards that our constitutions have put in place. But beyond this, if we allow the web to be censored, then it should only be done by a proper constitutionally authorised publicly accountable body, it should not be done arbitrarily. There ought to be full open debate and public agreement as to what the criteria of censorship are, if any. Anything else is authoritarianism, fascism, unjust and unjustified control of freedom of speech. It is crazy that a terrorist was able to livestream his atrocity on social media, whilst those who were seriously discussing the true reasons why he did it had their accounts taken down. You can recognize an extremist because they don't want anyone with a different viewpoint to have means to express it. All extremes are wrong whether they be religious, political or anything else. Freedom of speech is an absolute. The truth protects.

"They sacrificed unto devils, not to God" (Deuteronomy 32:17)

This freedom of speech debate even affects what we say inside church. In 2015, a pastor in Northern Ireland was prosecuted for having said that Islam is demonic and Satanic, after a recording of part of a Church service appeared on the web. Fortunately, the pastor was acquitted but it shows how our right of freedom of expression even inside the Church is under threat. At least now, having uncovered the proof of Mohammed's own admission that every Muslim has a demon which is fed by halal sacrifices, the issue is put beyond doubt and any further attack on such a comment should really metamorphose into Islam itself being put on trial. And again in 2017 Christians have faced similar prosecution for comments made during street evangelism. Whilst their right to free speech and freedom of religious expression were finally upheld, it does show just how much we are obliged to fight to keep our freedom.

"He who justifies the wicked and he who condemns the righteous are both alike an abomination to the LORD" (Proverbs 17:15)

You can always recognize tyranny, whether right wing, left wing or religious, by its mode of government. One of the biggest tell-tale signs of trouble is when there are attempts to stifle debate and free speech. Mohammed's Islam is totalitarian, its stifles all criticism by calling it blasphemy against Islam, its prophet or its god. Even in our society the accusation of Islamophobia, in fact a covert application of Sharia blasphemy rules, is used to prevent the truth being told. Why does Islam do this? The answer is very simple, the religion does not stand the test of reasonable criticism. Cutting off free speech is the only way it can survive. Look at how the Bible is banned in most Muslim majority countries. Why? Because it contains truths that can prove the Koran to be wrong. We need to fight to stop this kind of suppression of the truth from taking a hold in our society. It is up to us in the Body of Christ to steer our society back to being anchored once again in the truth, back to open and free debate and discussion of all societal issues. Britain, USA, Canada, Australia and their allies did not stand together and fight fascism seventy-five years ago to give us a world where one lot of people could dictate to all others what we can or cannot say!

"When the enemy comes in like a flood, the Spirit of the LORD shall lift up a standard against him" (Isaiah 59:19)

This is an urgent matter; we must act now to continue to protect free speech, so that the day never comes when one could no longer talk of the Work of the Cross or the Resurrection because it might offend some Muslim somewhere. We must also act to maintain a state of law in our nations. It has come to light that numerous criminal enquiries into sexual abuse and rape by members of Muslim communities, in several countries, have been stalled, even officially blocked, because of accusations of Islamophobia. This is so tragic, will our forces of order no longer stand up to protect the orphans, the weak and defenceless? Will these young girls, even in our lands, because of political correctness, be given up as sacrifices on the altar of sexual jihad? Look at what happened with the "grooming gangs" in Rotherham in the UK. Wikipedia has a clear account of it, telling how vulnerable young girls were abused for decades and abandoned by the authorities who should have protected them. The same is happening in many cities around the world.

"Father, forgive them, for they know not what they do" (Luke 23:34)

It is important to understand how this works spiritually. There is a principle in the demonic realms that the person with the bigger demon gets power over those with lesser demons. They work in hierarchies. That is how someone like Mohammed, or Hitler, or Pol Pot, can rise to power, and that is how the Antichrist in the end times will rise to political supremacy. What is happening in the West now is that the politicians, judges, journalists and others in positions of influence who have entered into agreement with communism, ultra-leftism, revolutionary socialism, freemasonry, and other demonically inspired anti-Christ ideologies, have all fallen under the influence of the greater demonic power of Islam and come into alignment with it. They are no longer able to say anything of any consequence against Islam and Sharia law, and they are even so bound that they work to silence all criticism of them. They are incapable of acting against those demonic forces. Horrific crimes such as the sexual mutilation of young girls in their thousands goes unprosecuted, not just because of fear of upsetting religious sensitivities, but because of the demonic power behind these outrages. We see similar alignment with Islam in the political left wings all across the West. Some political parties have even entered into this to such an extent that they hold meetings where the sexes are segregated and some have lost leading members through them making blatant anti-Semitic remarks in public and being forced to then resign. President Obama was publicly criticized in the media for failing to acknowledge the Islamic motive in the recent Orlando terrorist attacks. Indeed, the Obama administration worked hard to try to distance Islam from such terrorism.

"Don't participate in the fruitless works of darkness, but instead expose them" (Ephesians 5:11)

Islam is responsible for 95% of the world's terrorism, more than all the other religions, political parties and other alignments put together. Islam and terrorism are inextricably linked. You have already read many of the commands to terror from the Koran. Terrorism is at the heart of Islam, it cannot be isolated from it and surgically removed. Besides, a significant percentage of Muslims, about 20%, around the world believe in violent jihad and Islamism, that's hundreds of millions. But the truth is that Islam has no answer to the critique expounded in this book. It is incapable of adaptation or change because it is rooted only in the 7th Century testaments of its false prophet Mohammed. As it cannot change it will fall. But for now, it survives by blocking all rational debate about it.

Let's recap what has been covered in this book so far.

In Part One of this book we looked generally at what Islam is and in Part Two we considered certain basic Islamic beliefs.

We saw that inequality and violence against women, including FGM, are condoned by the Koran and Hadiths.

We learned that democracy and Islam are mutually incompatible.

It showed too that Sharia law and other aspects of Islamic culture block social and economic progress.

We also read through the lists of violent, xenophobic and racist/anti-Semitic verses from the Koran which prove that true Islam is not so much a religion of peace but more one of hatred and terror.

What Mohammed really was like as a person is illustrated in Part Three, a gifted but isolated young man brought up in Paganism who later turned into a violent warlord with a taste for killing, a liking for sex slaves and who even had sex with a 9-year-old child.

In Parts Four and Five we then went on to analyse in detail whether or not the Koran is from God.

Far from being all true as the Koran claims to be, we saw that it was factually and scientifically erroneous.

As God knows all truth we can therefore conclusively determine that at least some, if not all, of the Koran is not from God. We only had Mohammed's own word that it was from God anyway, he at first said it was all from God but then even he admitted that Satan inspired him in writing some of it. The Koran says of itself that it is perfect and infallible, yet is not. Because it contains untrue statements, it can be logically concluded that Mohammed is a false prophet and Allah is a false god.

In Part Six we examined the claim that the Koran confirmed the Torah and the Gospels and found that it did not.

In fact, it misrepresents them greatly distorting the message of the earlier scripture and misinterpreting the Jewish and Christian faiths.

The Koran's claim that it supersedes the Torah and Gospels also failed.

Part Seven concluded that Islamic Allah is not the same as the God of the Jews and Christians, but instead resembles Satan by leading people astray and urging them into hell.

We noted also that much of Islam bore resemblance to pre-Islamic paganism.

Our attention shifted to the future in Part Eight, where consideration was given to prophecies of the Apocalypse and Armageddon.

We saw that in fact the Battle of Armageddon has already been fought and brought an end to the true Caliphate.

Here in Part Nine we now see how we are fighting a subsequent war of ideas and ideals, a spiritual and intellectual war, not the military war between Islam and the West that Islamism would prefer.

Whether one views it politically and intellectually; that it is a belief system which undermines our tolerant, egalitarian society, or spiritually, that Islam is just simply satanic and evil, the conclusion is the same. Action must to be taken to protect our hard-won free democratic society. The European Court of Human Rights found free democracy and Islam mutually incompatible. As that's true, we are forced to choose between them. We can certainly see that their ideologies are increasingly at war with each other.

This is not phobia; this is rational common sense.

Even the most ardent atheist or secularist has to admit that one could build a peaceful egalitarian society on a philosophy of *"love your neighbour"*, and *"love your enemies"*, but could never do so with a creed of *"kill the others wherever you find them"*, and *"for those women on whose part ye fear... ill-conduct... beat (or whip) them"*. (Gospel of Mark 12:31, Gospel of Luke 6:27, Koran 2:191 and Koran 4:34 respectively)

Real Islamophobia is pretending that Islam is not a problem and going out of the way to avoiding upsetting anyone by reminding them that it truly is a problem. Most Muslims are non-violent but this does not mean that Islam doesn't teach violence. Islam is to be judged on the contents of its sacred texts. Human beings on the whole are peace loving; moderate Muslims have been greatly influenced by the peaceful ways of Christianity and Humanism but the truth of what their religion really says can only be found in what its sacred texts actually teach.

A recent freedom of speech exhibition was an excellent example of true Islamophobia, where artworks that *"might upset Muslims"* were removed, thus making a total mockery of the freedom of speech banner under which the event was organised. Being motivated by fear of a Muslim reaction, the decision was clearly phobic. But such phobia goes further, it leads to an abandoning of our core societal values, such as gender equality, when the segregation of the sexes to appease Muslims creeps in at political rallies. This happened during the last general election in the UK. What happens next has already been seen in Germany where migrants have refused to work with female estate agents without any administrative rebuke and thus women's freedom and rights to work have started to be curtailed.

Indeed, former Secretary of State Hillary Clinton even said it would be *"dangerous"* to imply that we are at war with an entire religion. This statement, although well meaning, clearly implies an unspoken fear that Islam will somehow retaliate if we face up against it. Yes, it may provoke a backlash if we are honest about it, but being fear driven, this statement is an instance of true Islamophobia. It is this fear which has been blocking open debate about Islam; it is this fear which has led to politicians and the media avoiding the issue of whether the Koran promotes terrorism. How many more Western cities will be attacked by terrorists before our leaders acknowledge the truth? Islam has already attacked our society and its declaration of war can be read in the Koran. When you disagree with something, when you are fighting against an ideology, it is dangerous to not precisely identify it first and then war against it. Without an overt strategy against Islam, its ideas can creep in, and you have denied yourself the right to openly attack it. Islam is a self-declared enemy of our free society.

If we do not stand firm and oblige Muslim migrants coming into our lands to adapt to our value systems, but instead start accepting their values for fear of offending them, that too is phobia. Islam is at the root of all Islamist terrorism, it is a root of FGM, sex-slavery and the general subjugation of women, it is a cause of anti-Semitism, and we cannot allow debate about these issues to be stifled by accusations of phobia each time anyone mentions the religion in relation to them.

"pray for us, that the word of the Lord may speed on and triumph, as it did among you, and that we may be delivered from wicked and evil men" (2 Thessalonians 3:1-2)

Sadly, some Muslims are too ready to cry persecution at the slightest offence and this confuses things even more. The media too has had a big bias; failing to deliver the truth on the issues and even spreading false accusations of Islamophobic violence. As I write, in April 2016 there have been a number of stories circulating in the news about attacks on Muslims by "far-right" activists which have actually been proven later to have been carried out by Muslims, a couple of cases were even fabricated by the Muslim "victims" themselves. In one case Swastikas were painted at a crime scene to try to frame non-Muslims, tactical lying becoming practical trickery. But the CCTV showed what truly happened. We should certainly protect everyone from every type of persecution, but the objectivity of the truth seems to have got lost in all the political correctness. Let's get it straight; we need to be very discerning when dealing with a religion which historically has caused the most persecution, sex-slavery and the most killing of members of other faiths. Indeed, it is the failure of governments and media to publicly face the truth about Islam which is fuelling the rapid growth in anti-Islam movements in the West. Anyone who tries to link terrorism and the mistreatment of women with Islam is immediately branded an Islamophobe and is thus shut out of any debate. Any criticism whatsoever of the Koran and Islam is branded "blasphemy", and every accusation of blasphemy is always accompanied by aggressive intimidation. In fact, all that most of the so called Islamophobes are doing is expressing a genuine and informed concern that Islam poses a real existential threat to our free democratic society. As we have seen the Koran does not stand up to close critical scrutiny, and such violent protests are now the only way Muslims, and those protecting them, have of responding given the intellectual weakness of their faith. The recent increase in terror and intimidation are in fact proof that Islam has lost the intellectual debate and is fast approaching its impending fall.

Another sneaky trick often used to avoid criticism of Islam is to call it racism, to make it a white against other colours issue. Today its followers come from many different racial backgrounds. Islam is an international religious belief system with political and legal elements; criticizing it can never correctly be labelled as racism. Those who call criticism of Islam racism seek to cause greater division than there already is. Islam as a belief system is a fair subject for debate and scrutiny. Doesn't the Koran call upon non-Muslims to look for incongruity in its content?

A Time for the Truth

"That is why we labour and strive, because we have put our hope in the living God, who is the Saviour of all people, and especially of those who believe" (1 Timothy 4:10)

Many Islamic countries have high illiteracy rates, so Muslims there really don't know much about what the Koran or Hadiths say. European Union statistics show that two-thirds of Syrians, and one third of all others, arriving as migrants in Europe cannot even read or write. Yet, the Koopmans' study showed that 60% of Muslim immigrants in Western Europe thought they should return to the roots of Islam. But very evidently, they have no idea what these are. Other statistics show that most Muslims in the West are peace loving and say they do not want the principles of violent jihad to be relevant today. Over 80% of them have a worldview influenced by elements of liberal Western thinking. They mostly believe in tolerance, dialogue and peaceful co-existence, despite what is in their holy books, often because they don't know what those texts actually say. They protest against the excesses of Islam yet still portray the religion as something good. They adhere to the Muslim cultural belief that Islam is superior to our Western ways. This is a dangerous delusion. They have been fed lies. We must wake them up from their ignorance. These moderate Muslims have had a powerful yet mistaken voice in society today, misleading us that Islam is a *"religion of peace"*, even to the point where this fallacy is blindly repeated by our Western leaders.

Islam when viewed as an entirety, includes Islamism, FGM, Christians being blown up in Pakistan whilst celebrating Easter, thousands dancing in the streets whilst praising the Brussels terrorists, sex-slavery and grooming gangs. So as a whole, it cannot really be called peaceful.

This religion of peace label has led to a focus on what is called *"extremism"*, which we are told is the source of Islamist terrorism. This trick has so far succeeded in diverting attention away from the true root cause; Mohammed, the violent commands of his holy book, and his lifestyle example.

You have read some of these commands in Part Two of this book, they are a literal call to annihilate all peoples who disagree with Islam.

Most Muslims are shocked when they find this out, a typical reaction is like that of Nabeel Qureshi expressed in his USA Today article **"The Quran's deadly role on inspiring Belgian Slaughter"**, in which he talks of his upbringing in the US where he was taught a peaceful version of Islam and held it up to be a religion of peace. However, at college he began to read the Islamic texts for himself and was taken aback by the violence exalted within them. He understood that what extremists like the Islamic State had been saying about the Koran and Hadiths was true. He wrote;

"When everyday Muslims investigate the Quran and hadith for themselves... they are confronted with the reality of violent jihad in the very foundations of their faith... I believe what the recruiters themselves say sheds the most insight on the radicalization process. ISIL's primary recruiting technique is not social or financial but theological. With frequent references to the highest sources of authority in Islam, the Quran and hadith (the collection of the sayings of the prophet Muhammad), ISIL enjoins upon Muslims their duty to fight against the enemies of Islam... it radicalizes them primarily by urging them to follow the literal teachings of the Quran and the hadith, interpreted consistently and in light of the violent trajectory of early Islam. As long as the Islamic world focuses on its foundational texts, we will continue to see violent jihadi movements... Any solution, political or otherwise, that overlooks the spiritual and religious roots of jihad can have only limited effectiveness."

Whilst the Islamic State and all Islamist groups are clear about the violent commands of Islam, Muslim moderates still promote the Koran, the true source of those commands to kill. They say that one ought to interpret these verses as a poetic expression of the Muslims inner struggle against evil, but the book itself says it is not allegorical poetic speech. Sharia Law is a legal system based on taking the Koran and Hadiths as literal commands how to live. Sharia's very existence therefore undeniably proves that the content these books is meant to be applied to the absolute letter.

The majority of Muslims in the world believe in Sharia Law, so they must ultimately think the Koran is to be taken at its word.

Where is the poetry anyway in those statements like;

4:89, 4:91   *"then take them (non-Muslims) and kill them wherever ye find them"*

4:34   *"...As for those (women) from whom you fear disobedience.... beat them !"*

Poetry???

Didn't we read that Sharia courts in the UK were interpreting this latter command literally in divorce cases, allowing Muslim men to get away unpunished for their domestic abuse? Well what makes the other command different? they are both against UK law. In fact, the only difference is that the first command concerns Jihad, which a Muslim is supposed to help succeed with tactical lying.

The Islamic State has frequently justified its reign of terror by referring to Islam's holy books, and what their leaders say about how to interpret the Koran appears to be theologically correct. In their April 2016 video, which threatened attacks on London, Berlin and Rome, they openly quoted verses 9:14 and 2:191; *"Fight the unbelievers...", "kill them wherever you find them".* Yet in the West the authorities think that by teaching Muslims a more peaceful poetic Islam they can tame the beast of Islamism. The 22 years since the Armed Islamic Group's Paris Metro bombings have shown that this approach has failed miserably. In the place of the few small isolated groups that existed back in 1995 there is now a fifth column of thousands of jihadis in the West ready to take up arms. These terrorist verses were written to be taken literally, and all it takes to radicalize many Muslims is just to explain to them the principle of abrogation and show them a few examples about how Mohammed really lived. True Islam means violent jihad, it is in its roots. Are we going to wait a few more years until there are hundreds of thousands of jihadi guerrillas in our lands until we act? Are we going to wait until there are armed insurrections or civil war? Remember, Jihad is a fundamental part of Islam and no amount of peaceful teaching will ever change that.

Re-read Ayatollah Khomeini's comments in Part Two if you are not sure.

It is worth noting that the Muslims who became the 7/7 London bombers were not radicalised by some small sect of extremists, documents show they were turned into terrorists by teachings openly delivered in mosques which belong to the UK's largest Muslim group and who train 80% of the UK's imams. While people believe in Islam and propagate it, and the Koran is read, terror will continue. It is clear that the Koran incites terrorism; terrorists read it before going out on mission to strengthen their resolve.

If Islam were a religion of peace then reading their sacred book would surely make them peace loving, filled with love and inner tranquillity. But it doesn't. Some of the terrorists reportedly know the Koran off by heart so it can't be verses of peace and love going around in their heads as they murder innocent people! It's all those terror verses going around in their heads augmenting their determination to murder! Their consciousness is filled with literal commands to kill non-Muslims.

Many who try to hold up non-violent image of Islam quote Koran verse

5:32 *"whosoever kills a human being....it shall be as if he had killed all mankind, and whosoever saves a life, it shall be as if he had saved the life of all mankind",*

as proof of its noble morality.

This sentiment is mistaken and if you read the text carefully you will understand this quote is preceded in the Koran by the words;

5:32 *"We decreed for the Children of Israel that...".*

Thus, this has nothing to do with what Muslims are commanded to do in the Koran by Allah, it in no way overrules the violent jihadi verses. It is talking about a command to the Jews, and by extension, Christians. It derives from the Babylonian Talmud (compiled about 200AD); Mishnah Sanhedrin 4:5, Tractate 37a. It just shows how one needs to be very wary of misleading out of context interpretations of any book.
This quote is Jewish not Islamic !

As we have read, all the peaceful verses in the Koran have been abrogated by the later violent ones. The assertion that Islam is a religion of peace is tactical lying even though some of those who say it are just blindly repeating what they have heard others say.

In the West, our leaders have let us down by entering into this lie unwittingly propagated by the moderate Muslim community.

The Koran says what it says and no one can ever change it. Mohammed was the way he was and we are obliged to live with it. It is not blasphemy to tell the truth about him. Mohammed and his Koran have brought the world very bitter fruit. Over 500 million people have been killed or taken into slavery as a result of his religion. And the number of victims is growing daily. According to a new report by CSGC, 900,000 Christians were killed for their faith in the last 10-year period, most of these by Islamists. Add in the figure for those of other religions killed and we currently have well over 100,000 victims a year of Islamism.

There is no point being detached or fatalistic, and refusing to accept the truth; it has fallen to us to deal with this for the sake of the future of our free society, for our children so they can continue to live in the freedom and grace we have had. It is up to us as Christ's representatives on Earth to stand up and proclaim the truth. We must hold up the Bible as the true Word of God and prove to everyone that Islam is based on lies.

We do have to act quickly to diffuse the growing tensions between far right and immigrant communities.

It is important to focus all conflict into a debate about ideas and ideals and stop it becoming a full on physical conflict.

The ongoing failure to do this is causing a groundswell of true resentment that further fuels right-wing groups who are more than willing to overstep the boundary of peaceful protest and riposte physically with violence against innocent Muslims for the terrorism and sex-crimes others have committed.

That helps no-one.

Has it really taken 1,400 years for us to uncover the truth about Islam?

We think not regarding these quotes; -

"If the people of this religion (Islam) are asked about the proof for the soundness of their religion, they flare up, get angry and spill the blood of whoever confronts them with this question. They forbid rational speculation, and strive to kill their adversaries. This is why the truth became thoroughly silenced and concealed."

Muhammad al-Razi, Persian scholar (865-925)

"As for proofs of the truth of his (Mohammed's) doctrine...the truths that he taught he mingled with many fables and with doctrines of great falsity...he perverts almost all the testimonies of the Old and New Testaments by making them into fabrications of his own, as can be seen by anyone who examines his law. It was, therefore, a shrewd decision on his part to forbid his followers to read the Old and New Testaments, lest these books convict him of falsity"

Thomas Aquinas, Italian philosopher and Saint (1225-1274)

"The Koran teaches fear, hatred, contempt for others, murder as a legitimate means for the dissemination and preservation of this satanic doctrine, it talks ill of women, classifies people into classes (of belief), calls for blood and ever more blood... this unintelligible book (the Koran), each page of which makes common sense shudder, that to pay homage...delivers his country to iron and flame... cuts the throats of fathers and kidnaps daughters...gives to the defeated the choice of his religion or death, this is assuredly nothing any man can excuse"

Francois Voltaire, French philosopher (1694-1778)

"it was written in their Koran, that all nations who should not have answered their (the Muslims) authority were sinners, that it was their right and duty to make war upon them wherever they could be found, and to make slaves of all they could take as prisoners"

Thomas Jefferson, US President (1743-1826)

"In the seventh century of the Christian era, a wandering Arab of the lineage of Hagar, the Egyptian, combining the powers of transcendent genius, with the preternatural energy of a fanatic, and the fraudulent spirit of an impostor, proclaimed himself as a messenger from Heaven, and spread desolation and delusion over an extensive portion of the earth. Adopting from the sublime conception of the Mosaic law, the doctrine of one omnipotent God; he connected indissolubly with it, the audacious falsehood, that he was himself his prophet and apostle. Adopting from the new Revelation of Jesus, the faith and hope of immortal life, and of future retribution, he humbled it to the dust, by adapting all the rewards and sanctions of his religion to the gratification of the sexual passion. He poisoned the sources of human felicity at the fountain, by degrading the condition of the female sex, and the allowance of polygamy; and he declared undistinguishing and exterminating war, as a part of his religion, against all the rest of mankind. THE ESSENCE OF HIS DOCTRINE WAS VIOLENCE AND LUST: TO EXALT THE BRUTAL OVER THE SPIRITUAL PART OF HUMAN NATURE.

Between these two religions, thus contrasted in their characters, a war of twelve hundred years has already raged. That war is yet flagrant; nor can it cease but by the extinction of that imposture, which has been permitted by Providence to prolong the degeneracy of man. While the merciless and dissolute dogmas of the false prophet shall furnish motives to human action, there can never be peace upon earth, and good will towards men. The hand of Ishmael will be against every man, and every man's hand against him. It is, indeed, amongst the mysterious dealings of God, that this delusion should have been suffered for so many ages, and during so many generations of human kind, to prevail over the doctrines of the meek and peaceful and benevolent Jesus.

The precept of the Koran is, perpetual war against all who deny, that Mahomet is the prophet of God. The vanquished may purchase their lives, by the payment of tribute; the victorious may be appeased by a false and delusive promise of peace; and the faithful follower of the prophet, may submit to the imperious necessities of defeat: but the command to propagate the Moslem creed by the sword is always obligatory, when it can be made effective. The commands of the prophet may be performed alike, by fraud, or by force."

John Quincy Adams, President of the United States (1767-1848)

"I studied the Koran a great deal. I came away from that study with the conviction that by and large there have been few religions in the world as deadly to mankind as that of Muhammad"

Alexis de Toqueville, French politician (1805-1859)

"Qur'an (the Koran) ... an accursed book... So long as there is this book there will be no peace in the world"

William Gladstone, English Prime Minister (1809-1898)

"Some, indeed, dream of an Islam in the future, rationalised and regenerate. All this has been tried already, and has miserably failed... A rationalistic Islam would be Islam no longer. The contrast between our own faith and Islam is remarkable. There are in our Scriptures living germs of truth which accord with civil and religious liberty, and will expand with advancing civilisation. In Islam, it is just the reverse. The Koran has no teaching such as with us has abolished polygamy, slavery, and arbitrary divorce, and has elevated woman to her proper place."

"As a Reformer, Mahomet did advance his people to a certain point, but as a Prophet he left them fixed immovably at that point for all time to come... The sword of Mahomet, and the Coran, are the most fatal enemies of Civilization, Liberty and Truth, which the world has yet known"

William Muir, Scottish historian (1819-1905)

"The fact that in Mohammedan law every woman must belong to some man as his absolute property, either as a child or as a wife, or a concubine, must delay the final extinction of slavery until the faith of Islam has ceased to be a great power among men. Individual Moslems may show splendid qualities - but the influence of the religion paralyses the social development of those who follow it. No stronger retrograde force exists in the world. Far from being moribund, Mohammedanism is a militant and proselytizing faith. It has already spread throughout Central Africa, raising fearless warriors at every step; and were it not that Christianity is sheltered in the strong arms of science, the science against which it had vainly struggled, the civilisation of modern Europe might fall, as fell the civilisation of ancient Rome."

"It is, thank heaven, difficult if not impossible for the modern European to fully appreciate the force which fanaticism exercises among an ignorant...population. Several generations have elapsed since the nations of the West have drawn the sword in religious controversy, and the evil memories of the gloomy past have soon faded in the strong clear light of Rationalism and human sympathy...But the Mohammedan religion increases, instead of lessening, the fury of intolerance. It was originally propagated by the sword and ever since...all rational considerations are forgotten. Seizing their weapons, they become...convulsed in an ecstasy of religious bloodthirstiness...Thus whole nations are roused to arms...in each case civilisation is confronted with militant Mohammedanism...The religion of blood and war is face to face with that of peace. Luckily the religion of peace is usually better armed."

Winston Churchill, English Prime Minister (1874-1965)

"I do feel visceral revulsion at the burka because for me it is a symbol of the oppression of women... "I'm pessimistic about the Islamic world. I regard Islam as one of the great evils in the world, and I fear we have a very difficult struggle there"

"There are people in the Islamic world who simply say: 'Islam is right!', 'We are going to impose our will' and there's an asymmetry. I think in a way we are being too nice...naively optimistic - and if you reach out to people who have absolutely no intention of reaching back to you, then you may be disillusioned."

"It is almost impossible to say anything against Islam in this country, because you are accused of being racist or Islamophobic"

Richard Dawkins, English academic (born 1941)

"Only in the West is Islam being taught as a religion of peace, harmony, equality, tolerance and equal rights. I lived in the Muslim world for 30 years but never heard that as the main purpose of Islam.

To learn the truth about what Islam advocates, just listen to Imams in Muslim countries. Read Sharia, hadith and the Quran. Approximately 61% of the Quran talks about non-Muslims, "the kaffir," and only 37% is dedicated to preaching to Muslims. An overwhelming portion of the Quran is dedicated to cursing non-Muslims and condemning them to all kinds of murder, torture, doom, humiliation, calling them unclean, partners of Satan, enemies of Allah, apes and pigs and encouraging Muslims to never take them as friends or allies."

Nonie Darwish, Egyptian Author (born 1949)

Many great thinkers, be they statesmen or scholars, around the world have expressed similar views. Has anything changed as a result? Not really, all that has changed is that Islam has now infiltrated our culture, not by war, but by stealth. Now that Islam threatens our homelands and our way of life, we have no choice but to act.

First and foremost, we must get the truth out to everybody who will hear it, so that everyone in our society can know what Islam really is. Once we reach a tipping point of public awareness our leaders will be forced to enter the debate on how to protect our society and its peaceful values.

It's clear Islam will never change; because it is so focussed on the Koran and Mohammed's example, it will never develop out of its 7th Century Dark Ages murderous, misogynistic mentality.

Never again will anyone get away with saying that all religions are more or less equivalent cultural expressions of a shared human spirituality. The truth is plain to see; some religion can be evil.

And please don't let anyone accuse this book of being Islamophobic. The truth is that Islam is phobic.

Any religion that needs to hide its objectives with tactical lying, that has to keep its believers in fear and ignorance, that has to ban books that express any differing viewpoint, that makes converts at gunpoint, and has to kill off anyone who disagrees or who leaves the religion, is fear driven.

Islam - a - phobia ! Islam is a phobia.

So, what should we do now? That's what this book is about, disarming Islam. Disarming it with the truth, the truth that renders all lies powerless. As soon as Muslims understand that the Koran is not perfect and infallible, they will start to doubt that it is the word of God. And then, their confidence in carrying out jihad will fall rapidly. It really is as simple as that.

We can prove Islam untrue at the same time as preaching the Gospel.

Islam does not supersede our Western Judeo-Christian beliefs, it opposes them. It will ultimately fall because of them, and that is why it seeks to eradicate them. With our realization that Islam's Allah is not at all the same God, but is in fact Satan, we stand in the assurance that Islam must not be tolerated any more than abortion, euthanasia, transgenderism and other satanic agendas.

By means of powerful evangelism on one hand, and by peaceful debate and discussion on the other, the Muslim world must be delivered out of its toxic belief system.

The Islamic Revival

"Do not be overcome by evil, but overcome evil with good"
(Romans 12:21)

The fall of the Ottoman Empire was the first time since Mohammed's time that there had been no Islamic Caliphate, and, although not much was written about it at the time, this dealt mighty blow against Islam. No centralized Islamic authority existed any more, and many Muslim countries had come under British or French colonial rule. This generated much resentment, which in turn spawned Arab nationalist movements in several countries. Unsuccessful revolts were staged against the colonial powers, but it was not until just before the Second World War that Islam began to be a powerful force again.

After coming to power in Germany, Adolf Hitler developed a close alliance with the Grand Mufti of Jerusalem. They both shared a deep hatred of Jews and jointly sought to spread an anti-Semitic Islamic jihad across the Middle East. The Nazi party helped fund the Muslim Brotherhood's Great Arab Revolt during 1936 to 1939 and paid for a printing press and other resources which helped them grow greatly in influence in the region (for more on this see Brynjar Lia; **"The Society of Muslim Brothers in Egypt"**, p175).

The availability of mass communication allowed membership of the Brotherhood to grow from around 800 members in 1936 to over 2 million supporters twelve years later. Their message of Islamic nationalism and armed struggle against non-Muslim power changed the political landscape of the whole Middle East. But the Islamic world still lacked international leadership until in 1972, what is now called the **Organization for Islamic Co-operation** (OIC) was founded. According to its charter, its aim is to *"preserve"* Islamic values.

The year following its establishment, OIC members Egypt and Syria carried out co-ordinated surprise attacks on Israel which led to the Yom Kippur War. They did so with the backing of Saudi Arabia, who in the months before the attacks had agreed from then on to use oil prices as a weapon of war for Islam. Their goal was to wipe Israel off the map.

The United States came to the immediate aid of Israel in this conflict and, in reprisal for this, the **Organization of Arab Petroleum Exporting Countries**, who are all members of the OIC, started an oil embargo which led very quickly to a quadrupling of oil prices. This not only had the effect of triggering a sharp economic downturn in the West, but also caused great wealth to come to the oil exporting countries, especially Saudi Arabia and the Gulf States. Oil prices have since then remained a weapon of economic war.

The greatly increased oil revenues received by Saudi Arabia and other Gulf States now opened up new possibilities for spreading Islam. Billions of Dollars were soon channelled into training radical Salafist Imams to be sent out into every part of the globe. Oil prices became a political weapon to leverage countries in the West to agree to the building of many mosques and Islamic proselytization programmes. Hundreds of millions of copies of the Koran with its terrorism-inciting verses have been printed in Saudi Arabia and distributed around the world.

This upsurge in Islamic fervour that followed the birth of the OIC began to bear its fruit. In 1979, a revolution took place in Iran, where the ruling Shah was deposed and replaced by a theocratic Islamic regime under the leadership of Shia clerics. According to Ayatollah Khomeini who led the revolution, the pro-West Shah had *"embarked on the [path toward] destruction of Islam in Iran."* Not long afterwards, a gruelling war erupted with neighbour Iraq, when calls came from the Ayatollahs for the Shia majority in that land to rise up and overthrow the Sunni leadership. This meddling in Iraqi affairs was met with a violent backlash.

An eight-year war followed in which over a million soldiers lost their lives without either side gaining outright victory. The lingering debt from this war in turn pushed Iraq's leader Saddam Hussein to invade oil-rich Kuwait and parts of Saudi Arabia in 1991. With oil supplies to America and other Western countries put in jeopardy, Islamic representatives offered to broker a deal whereby Iraqi troops would withdraw from Kuwait in return for Israel withdrawing from the gains it had made in the Six-Day War of 1967. Western negotiators refused to allow the Israel issue to be linked. A US-led international coalition operating within a United Nations mandate liberated Kuwait in the First Gulf War, but perceived Western involvement in the affairs of Muslim nations brought a hostile reaction from around the Muslim world.

In particular, some Muslims were angry that Saudi Arabia had allowed American troops into its "holy" territory to defend it, instead of relying on Islamic militias like the recently formed Al Qaeda, led by Osama bin Laden. In 1993 terrorists attacked the World Trade Center in New York, threatening more attacks unless the United States stopped interference *"with any of the Middle East countries' interior affairs".* The lead terrorist in this attack, Ramzi Yousef, was nephew of senior Al Qaeda member Khalid Sheikh Mohammed, the principal architect of the later 9/11 attacks.

Before Yousef's arrest in 1995, Al Qaeda was planning simultaneously to hijack several US airliners over the Pacific but these plans were disrupted.

It was around this time that the terror group came up with a 20-year plan to set up a new caliphate and start a Third World War between Islam and the rest of the world. Seven stages were envisaged; the first, during 2000-2003, was to use high profile terror attacks to make Muslims worldwide aware of their religious duty to undertake jihad against the West.

Stage two, 2004 up to 2006, was to groom a generation of potential warriors, followed in 2007-2010 by starting uprisings in Syria and Iraq. The fourth phase 2011-2013 would involve the destabilizing of national governments and the fifth involved the setting up of a new caliphate by 2016. From then onwards they would seek total confrontation with the West, leading up to a final victory over the rest of the world by an army of over a billion Muslims. These steps were well described in an article in Der Spiegel in 2005, and it is scary how accurate the predictions have turned out to be since then.

The multiple attacks in America using hijacked airliners on September 11th 2001, which left thousands dead and injured, was part of the first stage of this action plan. The live TV footage of the collapse of the twin towers of the World Trade Center grabbed the world's attention.

The consequent wars in Afghanistan and Iraq were used by Al Qaeda and others to stir up Muslim anger against the West for killing Muslims in their own lands. The 7th July 2005 attacks in London, part of stage two, showed us how "home grown" Islamists could be turned murderously against their own country's citizens.

We saw much terrorist activity in Iraq, and some in Syria, during the third stage period and then in 2011 came the Arab Spring revolts in many countries in North Africa and the Middle East. Syria, Iraq, Libya and Egypt were thrown into turmoil, strife and civil war which continue today. And the overall objective of capturing territory and declaring a new Caliphate was attained by the Islamic State, which had grown out of Al Qaeda, on 29th June 2014.

The final stage, which we are in now, is for the Caliphate to try to conquer the whole world for Islam. The refugee crisis caused by the chaos in Syria and Iraq was now provoked and manipulated to provide cover for thousands of Islamists to migrate into Europe and America where they would wage jihad. Security services statistics in Europe show thousands of jihadis have sneaked in. There have been twice as many arrests for terrorism since the declaration of the Caliphate. The bloody attacks we have seen since late 2015, in London, Manchester, Brussels, Paris, Nice, Barcelona and elsewhere, are only a foretaste of what they have planned.

Everything appeared to have, so far, gone according to Al Qaeda's plan.

"And then the lawless one will be revealed, whom the Lord Jesus will slay with the breath of His mouth and abolish by the majesty of His arrival. The coming of the lawless one will be accompanied by the working of Satan, with every kind of power, sign, and false wonder, and with every wicked deception directed against those who are perishing, because they refused the love of the truth that would have saved them."
(2 Thessalonians 2:8-10)

Whilst Al Qaeda were working hard on their 20-year plan, the OIC too, had a series of 10 year programmes to induce the West to accept Islam and Sharia law using diplomatic, political, and, above all, financial, persuasion. In the UK, Sharia Councils were permitted as an alternative to that nation's Courts of law as a means of resolving disputes, including divorces and family matters. A dangerous door had been opened.

Around the world, economic incentives were offered to many governments to enact blasphemy laws to outlaw all criticism of Islam. The ultimate aim of such laws is to protect Islam from political or intellectual scrutiny which could oppose or even destroy it. Around the world, politicians friendly to Islam were being pay-rolled and their political voice bought. Did you know that the family of former Secretary of State Clinton's closest personal aide was connected to the Muslim Brotherhood and OIC? The policy has started to bear fruit for them, like the **UN Draft Resolution A/HRC/16/L.38** presented by Pakistan on behalf of the OIC. This document seeks to put an end to any type of profiling by national governments of people *"based on religion or belief"*. It sounds seductively reasonable, but is it a good idea? Not at all! Because beliefs, including religious ones, determine people's actions. There are belief systems that condone and even command violence, like the Koran does in Islam. The United Nations should be flagging up dangerous ideologies not trying to cover them up.

The OIC has also been using much oil money to persuade non-Islamic countries to support its agenda in the United Nations. Another result of such political initiatives was the recent UNESCO declaration which effectively re-classified Temple Mount in Jerusalem as a solely Islamic site, denying its rich Jewish and Christian heritage. This is another example of revisionism at work, just like the revisionism of the Koran. The Secretary General was shocked at this abuse of the UN and said; *"any perceived undertaking to repudiate the undeniable common reverence for these sites does not serve the interests of peace and will only feed violence and radicalism"*. And all the while, the Muslim Brotherhood in the USA has been working hard to achieve its stated aim to *"destroy western civilization from within"*.

Saudi Arabia and other oil-rich Gulf States, have of course, continued their extensive worldwide building of mosques to continue the spread of radical Salafist teaching. According the Vice-Chancellor of Germany Sigmar Gabriel; *"But we must at the same time make clear that the time to look away is past. Wahhabi mosques are financed all over the world by Saudi Arabia. In Germany, many dangerous Islamists come from these communities"*.

Germany now has just under 1,000 terror-related criminal investigations ongoing. The Islamic plans for world domination very nearly worked.

"Yea, though I walk through the valley of the shadow of death, I will fear no evil, for Thou art with me, Thy rod and staff comfort me" (Psalm 23:4)

Very nearly, but they failed to understand what impact a living example of true Mohammedan Islam would have on today's world. The publicity stunts of the Islamic State may have drawn a few thousand recruits but has caused Islam to lose hundreds of thousands of believers. It has also caused millions in the West to understand that Islam is an evil thing and that was an important key to how Donald Trump got elected.

"the people living in darkness have seen a great light; on those living in the land of the shadow of death, a light has dawned." (Matthew 4:16)

Most Western Muslims were brought up with the tactical lie that Islam was a "religion of peace" and believing that it really was that, they rejected the Islamic States barbarism. These Muslims have never really studied the Koran. As they looked around the Muslim world they started to turn against the brutality of Sharia law. Having been exposed to the West's more reasonable and tolerant ways of doing things, they turned against what they considered to be radical extremism. So, when we see a statistic that says a quarter of Muslims in the West support violent jihad, that means three-quarters, <u>a vast majority</u>, reject it. Indeed, most Muslim children born in the West are uncomfortable when they visit their parents' native lands and do not agree with Islamic ways they see there. They simply don't want to be part of it any more. Some still have been making a pretence of being Muslim to please their parents and others in their community. But now they are coming out.

Asking questions about what their religion really teaches and finding the true answers, thousands have turned away from it, simply abandoning Islam or converting to Christianity. Churches in the West have reported record numbers of ex-Muslims coming to them. Just as, centuries ago, in the Great Enlightenment, Europeans turned away from blind religion and moved into an age of reason, so today, are Muslims in the West coming into a new era of a new understanding. The rational, critical attention like that which was turned to Christianity and Judaism in that time, will now be given to Islam. And as true Christian revival takes hold in the world the Islamic revival will come to an abrupt end. It is time for the Church to stand tall and bring the truth to the world.

Peace, Love and Respect

"The mouth of the righteous is a fountain of life, But the mouth of the wicked conceals violence." (Proverbs 10:11)

In the "West" we have had the blessings of nearly 2,000 years of the influences of the Gospel of Peace and of Greek Humanism. These two streams of thought have inter-twined to have a profound influence in shaping both our liberal democratic culture and our cultural aspirations.

Today we greatly value the peace and freedom which past generations have given their lives for us to have.

Tolerance has grown as a result and quite rightly we pride ourselves in trying to build a society where individual personal differences and choices are accepted and do not give rise to prejudice.

Clearly, we haven't got it all right yet, but at least we are trying. We have rules against prejudice on the grounds of race, or religion, or gender and other issues that have divided communities in times past.

We have welcomed people from other cultures into our countries, giving them access to the benefits of our own culture and have viewed it as enriching our society.

On the whole it has worked, but in some areas, it has tragically failed. Sadly, in the case of a very large number of Muslims, the failure has been drastic.

To a certain extent this has been our fault; whether it be through our nations' past imperial conquests, or more recent strategic meddling in the affairs of foreign nations, or via the overseas financial exploitation at the hands of our big multinational organisations, we have sown resentment in many parts of the world.

Not that all the resentment is justified, much frustration has also been stirred up for political ends. Especially through today's leaders who blame former colonial exploitation as an excuse for their own current economic mismanagement.

But on top of that many Muslims have been indoctrinated with Islamic beliefs that cause them to despise our Western values.

So, migrants, some already with prejudices arrive in the developed world at a time when Western society is going through a crisis of breakdown of community structures and thus may find themselves quite alone and isolated.

For help they quite naturally seek out others from their original culture who share their own language and customs. In fact, many Muslim immigrants live in our society very cut off from it because they only have contact with fellow Muslims and watch Muslim news channels in their native tongues. They bring with them their old cultural values and habits including the mistreatment of women, FGM and violent anti-Semitism.

In reality, only minimal help is given anywhere helping them adjust and integrate into their new life, and that is only for those with legal status. For illegal immigrants, the situation is even more extreme; they are often obliged to work for very, very low wages and live in insalubrious lodgings.

Bitterness and jealousy come easy to those trapped in this twilight world. Radicalisation is easy, just tell them their life is awful because the world refuses Allah's ways and then make them feel important by saying they can help change it. Once they are hooked on that start teaching them the Koran and all its terrorist verses.

Misfits with aggressive tendencies are easily drawn to Islam, which through Jihad, offers them a religious justification and focus for their violence. Because it's all done in the name of Islam, in the name of Allah, and for them, they are on a mission from god, all other moral considerations go out the window.

Not that all jihadis come from poor backgrounds, in fact statistics show that a great many do not. Many come from well-off, well-educated backgrounds. There are very many frustrated angry young people in every country of the world, but with Islam it is so easy for them to get radicalised, and join Jihad.

If we don't speak up now and point out what is theologically and factually wrong with their religion, more and more young Muslims will fall into the snare of such radicalization. Once radicalized our governments have found it hard to de-radicalize them.

Indeed, quite several instances have been recorded of individuals who have undergone governmental de-radicalization programmes quickly returning to violent jihad.

But for Muslims there is an added obstacle on top of all this; they have been taught all along not to trust non-Muslims, the *"Kuffir"*, as the Koran calls them.

The sacred texts are unequivocal on the matter;

3:73   *"Believe no one unless they follow your religion"*

3:28 *"Let not the believers, take for friends or helpers, unbelievers ; those who do this will have none of Allah's protection... Allah warns you to fear..."*

4:144 *"Take not for friends, non-Muslims"*

9:107 *"they are indeed all liars"*

4:140 *"do not sit with them"*

3:118 *"O ye who believe ! Take not into your intimacy those outside your ranks: They will not fail to corrupt you. They only desire your ruin"*

2:90 *"Evil is that for which they sell their souls"*

8:73 *"Disbelievers... cause... confusion and corruption"*

68:8-9 *"obey not those who reject (Islam)... who would want you to compromise... but make them compromise"*

6:111 *"most of them are ignorant"*

5:13 *"Thou wilt not cease to discover treachery from all save a few of them"*

4:89 *"Unbelievers wish that ye should reject your faith... take no friends or helpers from among them"*

2:109 *"wish they could turn you back into unbelievers...out of envy"*

66:9 *"Strive against the non-Muslims..."*

60:9 *"Whosoever maketh friends of them, (All) such are wrong-doers"*

5:80 *"them making friends with those who disbelieve...Allah is angry with them....in torment will they abide"*

9:23 *"do not choose your fathers or your brethren as friends if they do not believe, whoever takes them as friends are wrong doers"*

5:51 *"Do not take Jews or Christians for friends. If you do, then you are one of them"*

5:53 "(Jews and Christians) they are losers", 29:52 "those who disbelieve... are... losers" 39:63 "they...are...losers"

2:121 "Whoever disbelieves... are... losers"

8:65 "they are... without intelligence"

4:101 "fear the unbelievers may attack you: for the non-Muslims are unto you open enemies"

4:102 "the Unbelievers wish, if ye were negligent of your baggage, to assault you in a single rush"

68:51 "Non-Muslims will glare with hatred at you...and say 'he is mad'"

9:125 "Disbelievers are wicked and have diseased hearts"

5:45 "are unjust"

33:48 "incline not to the non-Muslims... Disregard their... talk"

2:171 "Those who disbelieve....have no sense."

6:27-28 "Non-Muslims ... they are all liars"

63:4 "How they are perverted!"

59:11 "they verily are liars"

7:176 "are like dogs"

9:28 "unclean"

25:55 "miscreants"

7:177 "evil"

62:5 "wretched".

60:13 "O ye who believe! Be not friendly...to those with whom Allah is wroth"

8:55 "Lo! the worst of beasts in Allah's sight are the ungrateful who will not believe."

98:6   *"those who disbelieve, they are the worst of created beings"*

14:30   *"they would mislead"*

6:106   *"Stay away from non-Muslims"*

60:1   *"O ye who believe! Choose not ...friendship when they disbelieve"*

2:217   *"they won't stop fighting you until they make you turn from your religion"*

4:45   *"Allah knoweth best (who are) your enemies."*

41:24   *"if they (unbelievers) ask a favour, no favour should be done for them..."*

28:86   *"never be a helper to the disbelievers"*

9:10   *"they do not observe any pact"*

8:56   *"at every opportunity they break their treaty"*

76:24   *"obey not...any...non-Muslim"*
(Even the police, or the authorities, or any non-Sharia law!)

This is only a fraction of the verses on the matter, but it is clear that these verses are why some Muslims will not assimilate into Western culture. A recent survey (ICM) found that a quarter of UK Muslims did not want to live under any British laws but instead wanted to only obey Sharia laws.

The West does not particularly hate Muslims as people although there is a percentage of people who oppose most immigration and a small minority who are very negative towards them.

Islam hates the West, our free lifestyle and values, it very actively teaches that hatred to millions of Muslims. It tells them to have nothing to do with non-Muslims, to be wary of them. It tells them that all other people are perverted and evil. This sort of isolationism is common in sects and cults. Individuals are brainwashed by rote learning of the Koran and taught xenophobia which instils fear and hostility in them towards all those outside their faith. We see this so clearly in Islam, where Muslims are also told they are superior to all other people because of their faith. We must burst the bubble of Islamic prejudice, piercing it with the truth that the Koran is not God's word. We must lead them to the truth of Christ's salvation.

In truth, many Muslims do heed the Koran's commands. For example, the Belgian authorities reported that many Muslims in Brussels would not cooperate with them during the aftermath of the airport and metro bombings there. The 2016 poll by ICM in the UK found that two thirds of Muslims said they would not tip off the Police if they knew of an Islamic terror plot coming from their community. Even on a day to day social basis it can be difficult to have any open relaxed conversation with Muslims because the Koran's guidance makes them wary and mistrusting of others.

In truth, many Muslims are happy to tell you about what they believe but are not comfortable listening to your points of view. This Islamic mindset must be undone before any real cultural change is possible. Quite simply the only way is to prove to them that Islam is not from God.

The attitude of mistrust taught in the Koran has had a serious impact on Muslim communities in non-Muslim countries across the world.

Whilst we in the West humanely open our homelands to millions of migrants and refugees, the consideration we show them is not always reciprocated.

The massive influx of migrants and refugees into Europe, which started in 2015, was handled with great naivety by the political and religious leadership. They simply couldn't imagine that letting in millions of people with a very different world-view would cause problems in their society. The sexual assaults in Cologne, the massacres in Paris and elsewhere are only the beginning, worse will follow unless the countries of Europe and the West face the issue of Islam head on. Clearly problems will increase until we deal with the root cause.

Open public debate is the only way the current situation can ever be resolved. We all must face the truth of what the Islamic sacred texts really say, combined with the hard fact that many Muslims really do base their social behaviour on these texts.

Yes, of course we must reach out to and help refugees and economic migrants, that is very Christian, but at the same time we must protect the philosophical foundations on which our free open society is built. We must defend and preserve our Christian heritage.

Besides, the best way to help those suffering in the poorer parts of the globe is to assist them in developing a well-founded sustainable economy in their own lands; to help them with issues like education, health care, clean water supplies, good sustainable agricultural practice and renewable energy.

Whereas Hindus, Sikhs, Buddhists and people from other faiths have generally integrated well into Western society, a significant proportion of Muslims are truly unwilling to do so.

The Koran, which they believe is the last word on everything, teaches them to be aloof and consider themselves superior to those who play host to them. Most problems with Muslim immigrants come less from any negative prejudice on the part of others towards them, but more from the attitude of mistrust towards non-Muslims taught by their faith.

This is particularly paradoxical when one considers that it is in fact the general social and economic failure of their own Islamic homelands which has caused them to migrate to the West.

The first thing we must do therefore is to overcome their prejudices and prove them wrong. We must help them realise that the Koran is not the perfect, infallible word of God.

The failure to do this can be fatal; one of the Nov 13th Paris attackers was rescued from a sinking ship full of migrants off the coast of Greece, but still was so closed-minded that he was determined to attack the humane European culture that had saved him from imminent death and even offered him a new home.

He believed his hatred of the West was God-given. He believed he was fulfilling the command of Allah in killing non-Muslims. No amount of kind heartedness alone is ever going to get through to such a person. The only way anyone like that will ever be stopped from committing terrorism is to prove that the verses of the Koran which command terror do not come from God.

"go into all the world, proclaim the gospel to everyone" (Mark 16:15)

It is a necessity therefore to prove to them that the Koran is not from God. It is up to us as Christ's representatives on Earth to do this. This is done by proving their holy book is neither perfect, nor infallible. This is done by proving it contains errors of fact and failures of reason. This is done too, by proving that Islam's Allah is not God Almighty. We must take the truth of the Gospel to every Muslim.

That is the way Islamic terrorism and the whole Islamist agenda will be stopped. Each Muslim needs to be presented with the real truth so they can make a reasoned choice and be enabled to say no to Islam.

Can a tolerant society overcome intolerance?

"Do not be afraid of them; I have given them into your hand. Not one of them will be able to withstand you" (Joshua 10:8)

The Koran teaches Muslims that they will be successful and that non-believers are losers.

Whilst staying within a paradigm of respect for every individual human being, such fallacies can easily be addressed and shown to be wrong.

For example, the statements in Koran verses

33:19 *"those who have not believed...Allah makes their deeds fruitless, that is easy for Allah"*, and

47:32 *"those who disbelieve...the way of Allah...He will make their actions fruitless",*

can be pragmatically scrutinised and proved false.

If a statement does not correspond to the observable truth, then it is false.

Let's put these two statements to the test.

There is not a single Islamic nation in the world's ten most prosperous by overall GDP. Indonesia is the first Islamic nation coming in 16th just ahead of the rather unreligious Netherlands who have a similar GDP but a population nineteen times smaller.

Many non-Muslim countries are more prosperous than Islamic nations, this is an undeniable fact.

And it is not because Muslims are not hard working, it is because Islamic culture and Sharia law hinder economic growth.

Are there not thousands of Muslims begging, risking their lives to get to Europe, the USA and Australia to find work?

The majority do not want to go to Muslim nations.

In the 2015 **UN Happiness Index**, there is only one Muslim Country in the top 20 (at number 20), behind a whole raft of Western nations (eight out of the top ten even have crosses on their flags!) whilst the bottom 20 (out of over 150) includes several Muslim nations.

Happiness ratings for the predominantly Islamic Middle East and North Africa area are significantly low compared to the rest of the world (**UNWHR 2015** see graphs p10-12 & p49).

Is this not proof in itself that life is better in the West than in any Islamic state?

As Thomas Jefferson said in 1806,

"The care of human life and happiness...is the only legitimate object of good government"

Other prejudices are likewise defeatable, like sexism; take Mohammed's statement (Sahih Bukhari 92/50)

"A nation that makes a woman their ruler will never prosper"

The UK is a Christian country with a Queen as head of state and currently also has a female Prime Minister...

It is a preferred destination of many Muslims trying to get into Europe. Does it not prosper?

Compared to Turkey, which has a similar size population and was also head of a mighty empire in previous centuries, which is more prosperous?

The UK has had Queen Elizabeth II, a woman ruler for over 60 years, and now a female Prime Minister, while Turkey has had male Muslim leaders. The GDP of the UK is now about 3.5 times greater than that of Turkey and the gap is getting wider and wider.

What Mohammed said isn't true.

Women make good business leaders too!

One by one prejudices can be brought down systematically by the truth.

All that is needed is the political will to get on with it, instead of political correctness questioning whether we even have the right to educate people out of their false religious dogmas.

Of course, there will be some resistance and criticism, that's normal.

One issue that almost invariably comes up when addressing the violent content of Islam is the history of the Crusades, as if in some way it justifies jihad.

It doesn't ! And if indeed, Muslims think the Crusades were wrong, then surely violent jihad must be wrong too.

And they are both very wrong, just killing someone else because they believe in something different from you would only lead to the extermination of all humanity if everyone did it.

None of us have the authority to say something is right and judge something else wrong unless we can justify it through reason, that's part of our conception of justice.

So let's get the record straight, killing people is wrong under Christian doctrine, except as a defence or protection or as a pre-emption to prevent attack. Jesus said; *"love your enemies"*. It's in the Bible.

The Crusades were before the origin of printing, very few people had copies of the Bible and the population were reliant on their leaders, the Pope, their Kings and Bishops to tell them what was right.

Those ancient leaders were wrong and the last Pope himself acknowledged this on 12th March 2000, in asking forgiveness for the violence that took place in the Crusades.

The numbers actually killed in the Crusades were relatively "small" compared to the numerous Islamic genocides, none of which seem to have ever been apologised for.

A question of thousands compared hundreds of millions.

In fact, many Islamic genocides are still denied. For example, Turkey and other Muslim nations still refuse to admit that the Armenian genocide of 1915 ever took place despite the existence of contemporary newspaper reports with photos which are now easy to find on the web.

Today with the ready availability of both the Gospels and the Koran we all know that one says; *"love your enemies"* and the other says *"kill the unbelievers wherever you find them"*.

The background of the start of the Crusades needs clarification too; before the rise of Islam, Christians from around the world made continual pilgrimages to the Holy Sepulchre and other Sacred sites in and around Jerusalem.

When Islam started to expand, and conquered that area, access for Christian pilgrims became more and more difficult.

Real problems arose from 969 when the Fatimid Caliphate ruled there. Contemporaneous reports of Arab historian Yahya of Antioch recounted in Vasiliev's **History of the Byzantine Empire** Vol II p392 tell us;

"Caliph Hakim began a violent persecution against Christians and Jews in all of his possessions. In 1009 he caused the Temple of the Resurrection and Golgotha to be destroyed".

In 10 years, he destroyed 30,000 churches.

Fearing reprisals from Christian nations, the Caliphate ended these persecutions and period of relative peace followed until the arrival of the Seljuk Turks, when once again pilgrimage became unsafe.

Dore Gold in **"The Fight for Jerusalem"** (p74) notes that around 1064, Muslim brigands attacked 7,000 pilgrims near the river Jordan (we do not know the exact death toll that resulted).

In 1073, with renewed killings and much violence under the Emirate of Malik Shah 1, Michael VII of Byzantium and Pope Gregory VII began to make plans to liberate and secure the Holy Land.

The massacre of 3,000 Christians in Jerusalem in 1077 pushed Pope Gregory's plans beyond the point of no return.

That is why the Crusades started.

Imagine what would happen if a foreign army captured Mecca, destroyed the Ka'aba, and killed thousands of unarmed Muslims, don't you think Muslims from around the world would go there and try to liberate and rebuild it.

Shouldn't our schools have an obligation to teach the true history wherever any cultural tension arises. Our schools must teach the truth in every area. This book is about true comparative religion which involves looking closely at what the sacred books of each religion actually say and how they have impacted the world.

Just as access to the Gospels in the West has taught people ways of peace, the wider availability of the Koran and Hadiths has brought jihad. It needs to be said. A few years ago, the latter would only be found in very specialist Islamic libraries but now they are available online and anyone with an internet connection can find their content quickly and easily.

All those accounts of how Mohammed lived out the original true Islam can be read by everyone. The mass beheadings and sex-slavery are no longer secret. President Obama said ISIS had perverted Islam, but when you read about Mohammed's life you cannot fail to disagree.

The recent rise of Islamism in the world is causally linked to the wider availability of the sacred Islamic texts, distributed through mosques and other religious organisations paid for by oil money from the Gulf states.

Isn't it ironic we have had comparative religion taught in schools for many years but it has failed because of political correctness. It doesn't really deal with the spiritual truth that some religions are inherently evil. Instead, a vague concept of all religions being more or less equivalent and equally acceptable has been taught. The contents of this book are a fine example of what real comparative religion is.

Is a thing beyond criticism just because it is called faith?

We can criticize far-right political parties easily because it is politics, but you get quickly rebuked when you say anything against a religion. Even when its belief system is clearly not right.

We now have a big problem, because under the influence of secularism we have decided that we should respect everyone's right to practice their own religion unhindered. Even when it calls good evil and calls evil good. The truth is that Islam is evil.

That multiculturalist experiment has now failed us, so let's get on with it and bring down all religious intolerance, Islam and everything else evil included.

Even though you can't legislate morality, a tolerant society must have limits and outlaw the teaching of intolerance, or it will fall.

Some of the Koran is clearly hate speech but we are not saying that it should be banned. It should just be opened up to informed scrutiny and very public debate. We need to openly say what is wrong with it.

A society must actively and regularly remind its citizens of its core values, and it has to be anchored in the truth. Children do need to be taught moral guidelines of what is and what is not acceptable in our society. In the information age, only transparent open democracy will ultimately endure.

How long do we have to wait before our children are taught the truth in comparative religion classes? The truth of what the Koran really says and how it is factually and scientifically incorrect.

Education, of course, is a key element in solving the problem but it is not the only way.

It is evidently only a matter of time before some secular countries, as a protection, change their constitution to declare where they stand on certain faith issues.

Human Rights and human wrongs

"the god of this age has blinded the minds of them who believe not, lest the light of the glorious gospel of Christ, who is the image of God, should shine unto them" (2 Corinthians 4:4)

Whilst respecting the rights of the individuals who immigrate into our lands, we must educate them in religious matters as well in social issues. This is the only way we can defend our values and maintain them. We must stand up for our Christian values.

We cannot any more allow anyone, to smuggle into our culture, ideologies and attitudes under a mask of religion that would bring down our free society.

It would be fatal to remain inactive on this issue. Social change is not just a question of the passive evolution of culture, it is always the result of political will. The history of the abolition of slavery is proof enough of this. God is on our side, we must not hold back.

Are we willing to be dragged backwards into the dark ages which spawned Mohammed's violent beast?

Are we willing to let our children's lives be touched by doctrines of demons that justify barbarity with a faith ticket? With a faith ticket based on a sacred book that doesn't even stand the test of the truth?

Based on a book that says that it is perfect and infallible, but which in fact, gets simple scientific facts wrong. Even the prehistoric people who built Stonehenge understood correctly the fact the sun does not set in one specific place on the earth, a fact which the Koran written thousands of years later gets wrong.

Are we willing to let this be passed off as truth or as God's Word? No! Of course not! Reason is on our side.

For God's sake, but above all for ours, let's wake up and shake up the world and get it all straight, back to the truth.

Freedom of religion has to have limits, and any religion that advocates breaching other people's human rights has to be excluded from human rights protection.

We cannot make religion sacred above the basic requirements of law and order. We must be aware what is really going on.

In 2010 evidence came to light in the case of United States vs. Holy Land Foundation, proving that one of the goals of the Muslim Brotherhood in America was *"destroying Western Civilization from within"* and replacing it with Islam by covert jihad (see Hudson Institute, Merley **"The Muslim Brotherhood in the United States"** p52).

Other documents brought before this trial show that the organisation was involved in teaching para-military jihad, running weapons training camps, as well as spying on the security services including the FBI and CIA. True acts of treason. And it was paid for by charity funding, because under Sharia law, jihad is an obligatory destination for Islamic charity funds. Ultimately this is what the case is about, because in the West we don't agree with that. Under Sharia, Islamic charity includes destroying the free West. Other similar legal actions have taken place involving Islamic charities in Europe and Australia. This is not such an isolated example.

It really boils down to the fact that we are embroiled in a war of ideas and ideals, and we must eradicate the ideologies that want to bring an end to our peace-loving liberty.

Military intervention is never the way this war will be won, and if we can stop our governments' fear driven policies long enough to stop them pretending it is a just a war against terror, we'll get it all over and done with much quicker.

It really is a war of ideas and ideals.

We really should have argued this debate to its conclusion centuries ago. While Islam happily educates Muslims to despise, and to want to bring down our culture, we have been too silent.

It is not just a matter of teaching our youngsters what's right and true, we have to get on with the task of educating all of those now living in our society who might not share our views of peace, truth and justice.

Look at the case of the Nanny in Moscow who beheaded a little girl she was looking after and paraded the severed head out in the streets. She says she did it because Allah told her to, and he did - it's there in the Koran she had been reading just before committing the act.

People have a right to know the truth about Islam.

As Jesus said, the truth always sets people free.

Remember, as a warning for today, how the Second World War came about primarily because of an ideology.

Nazism was rooted in Eugenics, the pseudo-scientific Social Darwinist theory of racial evolution, and like other evil empires, the Nazis worked by calling evil good and good evil.

The extermination of *"Jews, Gypsies, Negroes and their bastard offspring",* as well as Slavs, homosexuals and the mentally handicapped, was called good because these people were supposedly less evolved.

Islam works like that too, but instead of race, it holds religion as its criteria of superiority, proclaiming that non-Muslims must be eradicated to purify the world.

As we have explained, Adolf Hitler had a close alliance with the Muslim Grand Mufti of Jerusalem, built on a common desire to kill off all Jews. Using Germany's wealth, the Fuhrer helped spread an anti-Semitic Islamic jihad across the Middle East. His Nazi party helped fund the Muslim Brotherhood's Great Arab Revolt during 1936 to 1939 providing the resources which helped them grow greatly in influence in the region. Hitler, whose DNA shows signs of him having had Muslim ancestry, aligned himself with Islam and spoke admiringly of it.

One of the largest divisions of the SS, the Hanzar, purely Muslim, was responsible for killing 90% of all the Jews in Bosnia during the War period and they also committed many other atrocious war crimes in the Balkans, resentment for which was an important factor in igniting the Balkans Wars in 1991 when Yugoslavia imploded.

But one of the most surprising lessons history teaches about the Second World War, is that before the invasion of Czechoslovakia there was little ideological resistance to Hitler's ideas. The Nazis on the other hand used every means of propaganda available to them.

By the end of the war it was well understood that a systematic "denazification" programme had to be undertaken to purge Europe of the evil ideology.

Like treating cancer, we have to eradicate any malignancy which threatens our life-blood, whether that be an extremist political philosophy or a religion.

If Hitler could win over a nation to evil with leaflets and radio broadcasts, then the evil can be undone in a like manner.

We are to undo the evil of Islam. Only by undoing Islam as a whole, will Islamism come to an end. While Islam continues to be accorded respect in our societies, individuals will continue to be radicalized by reading the Koran, the Hadiths and learning about Mohammed's life.

Recent terrorist incidents have showed just how quickly some Muslims can turn into terrorists. They already pray five times a day for torment to overtake all non-Muslims. All it takes beyond this, is showing them those terrorist verses in the Koran and selling Mohammed's lifestyle to them as an example to be followed. It is a simple process.

Currently the US Department of Homeland Security budget estimate for 2016 was close to $65bn, that's more than the GDP of a country like Kenya, Bulgaria or Uruguay.

When you read the official budget request you find the first mentioned and most important destination for the funds is to combat terrorism.

If you consider that 95% of terrorism in the world is Islamist in nature, then you realize that somewhere down the line it would be cheaper for the country in the long term to undo Islam which is the ultimate motivator of all such terrorism.

Islamist terrorism will only be eradicated when Islam falls.

We have broken ideologies before, look at the Cold War, with all that military might on both sides, enough to have completely destroyed the world as we know it.

But it wasn't that kind of power which was decisive.

It was a combination of other factors that led to the downfall of the Soviet Union.

Not only was economic failure so apparent that every man and woman in the Soviet street could see that their system wasn't working compared to the economic success and freedom in the West, but US President Reagan and British Prime Minister Thatcher publicly denounced Soviet ideology and set about intellectually bringing it down.

Within a few years we saw the *"evil empire",* as they called it, crumble and now today many countries that were behind the Iron Curtain have joined the West and become members of the European Union.

Look again, and you can see the same kind of economic failure looming now in much of the Islamic world, in fact it is only oil that keeps the other parts of it solvent too.

Whether the governments of the world like it or not, millions of people are now finding out what the Islamic holy books say. Opinion in the West is turning against Islam.

Change has to come, it is inevitable.

But that change needs to be manged, to make sure it is a peaceful process rather than a violent one.

That world is ripe for change.

The book **"The Blood of Lambs - A Former Terrorist's Memoir of Death and Redemption"** by Kamal Saleem (Simon and Schuster) gives a true autobiographical example of how someone raised in a background of radical Islam can escape it.

And he says to us in the West now; *"Open your eyes and fight the danger that lives among you."*

What is happening right now is that many of the countries that in the past have spent large sums of money promoting fundamentalism Islam around the world, oil rich nations such as Saudi Arabia and Iran, are now being affected by falling petrol prices.

With financial aid budgets reduced, their hidden agendas have become more visible. Their ability to buy political influence in the West is fast failing. Their ability to manipulate the media is breaking.

Just recently, following the surge of migrants, mostly Muslim, forcing their way into countries of the European Union, Saudi Arabia offered to Germany hundreds of millions of Euros to build mosques for them whilst at the same time offering next to nothing in terms of humanitarian aid.

And then, they wouldn't even offer to allow true refugees from the war in Syria into their country, let alone other economic migrants.

To be fair they have since relented a tiny bit under international pressure, but anyway it seems that the refugees themselves would prefer to go to Europe with its generous social security benefits.

Very few refugees have found their way into the rich Gulf States.

And the Saudis themselves certainly won't let Christians build churches in Saudi Arabia even though they are very keen to build mosques everywhere else.

The Islamification agenda of the rich Gulf States is very clear, and it seems there is still money for building mosques and sending Imams even when there is not much left for humanitarian aid.

That isn't the only problem.

As we have seen, this mass arrival of migrants into countries already suffering from problems from previous immigration has led to a very rapid growth in support for far-right political parties.

The most recent elections in Austria showed a huge percentage swing in this direction, the far-right Freedom Party (FPO) is now part of the ruling coalition. The general election in Poland brought forth a complete surprise with the Law and Justice Party becoming the largest political force on a pro-Catholic, anti-immigration manifesto. Support for far-right parties is growing at an alarming rate.

In the most recent regional elections in France the extreme right-wing Front National was only kept from power by deliberate tactical voting with conservatives voting for socialists and vice-versa on a seat by seat basis to shut them out. Even so it was a very close call. History proves that extreme right-wing government is evil, so we have to do all we can to avoid this too. The extreme right-wing Front National candidate also made it through to the Presidential election run-offs. There has been a similar shift in many other European countries,

Politics in Germany have shifted to the right as well since the massive influx of migrants in 2015. These political shifts have been accompanied by violent demonstrations on the streets and unwarranted acts of aggression against Muslim individuals.

Anti-Islamism is a very central part of the current rhetoric and, unless more moderate political parties can be seen to be dealing effectively with this issue, it will not be long before we see extreme right wingers taking power locally and nationally across Europe. They are gaining ground because the political mainstream is not even seen to be attempting to deal with the core problems of mass Islamic immigration and the Islamisation that comes with it.

The failure to openly debate these core issues only makes violence more likely rather than less likely. A hostile and especially an insulting attitude towards Muslim migrants will close them off to dialogue when in reality we need to open them up to understanding our humane and free ways.

Inaction only gives the extreme right wingers more credibility and room to manoeuvre. Look how many so called "Islamophobes" are now telling the truth about what's in the Koran through the social media whilst the political mainstream and the generally left-wing mass-media is still covering up for the dark side of Islam. This is a recipe for danger because all politics works through trust, and there is nothing like keeping people in the dark to get them to turn against you. The rejection of the US Democrats and the unexpected rapid rise to power of President Donald Trump was largely due to this phenomenon.

Even in the West it is evident we will have to work very hard to maintain political stability in the near future, and this necessarily means dealing with the problem of what Islam really teaches. And it is a problem, because the mistreatment of women, xenophobia and terrorism that come with Islam will not go away on their own.

As long as people believe in Mohammed, his Koran and his Allah, they will continue to pose a threat to our free society. The Islamic State will fall, the governments in Saudi Arabia and Iran will fall, but the underlying values in the Koran will keep returning until we intellectually destroy them.

Therefore, the roots of these social evils propagated by Islam have to be addressed. Remaining in a politically correct dialogue where all religions are respected, treated as equivalent and beyond criticism has failed.

We must stand up and say we do not accept Islam: its god Allah is evil and in no way comparable to our Christian God of Peace and Love.

Christ is the Way, the Truth and the Life.

Open moderated debate is far better than right wing bullying.

Respect the people, but we do have to make Muslims understand that their beliefs are wrong. It is not so hard; getting this book you are reading, or its secular edition "Islamic Apocalypse", into every school is one way. We must pressure our governments, local and national to open up comparative religion lessons to the plain truth.

This is necessarily a worldwide issue. The time is right now, any more delay will allow more terrorist recruitment with all that follows it. The time is now!

Interest in following Islam is declining sharply in many young people across the world, especially amongst those living under hard-line Islamic rule, like in Iran. Indeed, there are now maybe as many as two million Christians there.

In the West, many Muslims are deserting Islam because they do not want to be associated with its violence.

The ready availability of information via internet and satellite TV and the difficulty of suppressing such channels of communication means that ideas can spread very quickly around the globe even against the wishes of governments.

Even in the Muslim world there are reports of millions of Muslims converting to Christianity, from Indonesia and Pakistan to Egypt and Morocco. Native Christian populations are even spontaneously appearing in Saudi Arabia and the other Gulf States.

Whereas the Islamic world has previously been able to protect itself by banning books or other media, as well as restricting visitors, it can no longer keep a lid on things in the same way in the smartphone age.

The world is about to change dramatically, we have already seen the turmoil of the Arab Spring, which because Islam is so deeply ingrained in the culture, has still failed to bring forth the change for which many hoped. Only breaking free from Islam will bring forth the freedom which young people across the Muslim world seek.

Soon many millions will realise that Islam is a barrier to the progress they seek, rather than a means to achieve it. Then we will see successful revolution, peaceful, democratic and prosperous, take place.

We have our part to play in all this. We should be reaching out to those who risked their lives fighting for democracy in North Africa and the Middle East and explain to them how important it is to bring proper economic development to their lands.

Unless the cultural beliefs which block business investment are removed, stagnation and poverty will remain. That is undesirable.

Look at how fruitful and prosperous Israel is compared to her neighbours; all of the Middle East could be like that.

What has stopped it? Could it be Sharia law? Could it be these Koran verses; -

2:275, 4:161 *"Allah permits commerce and forbids profit-yielding investment..."*

2:276 *"Allah condemns interest-bearing loans"*

We have already looked at how the Koran's Allah is mistaken on several scientific matters, and he seems mistaken on economic science too. The rationale of lending for interest, for profit, is that the lender takes a risk because they may not ever be repaid. If they are a commercial lender they need to cover their overheads and expenses too.

Without the incentive of earning something from their participation in any deal, why would anyone want to lend money?

In practical terms investment banking works, whatever you think of it morally. As long as it is properly regulated, it is a benefit to any economy.

Without it empires fall.

What was the principal target on 9/11? The World Trade Centre. The economy. What was the target of Mohammed's first armed attacks? His enemy's trade routes.

Islam wants to destroy our prosperity, but that very prosperity, with the ideas and ideals behind it, are what will lead many to turn away from Islam.

Don't the United States, and the European Union, both predominantly Christian, each have an economy larger than all of the nations in the Organisation for Islamic Cooperation put together?

We shouldn't be afraid, not just to share the reasons for our economic success, but to stand up for them too. Unless we communicate them effectively and debate them where necessary, we are not defending our way of life.

Standing up for, and elucidating, the values of our free liberal democratic capitalist society will do much more to protect our homelands than endless military and intelligence spending can. We must seek to bring lasting changes to our society which will protect our future generations. Islam will not go away until its final decisive defeat in a spiritual Armageddon. We must educate to protect.

Reason is on our side, so let's win the war of ideas and ideals.

One could sum it up like this; -

Islam was invented in the Dark Ages by a man raised in pagan Spiritism, initiated as a medium to talk with demons, who became a religious warlord. During his life, he killed thousands, beheading as many as 900 Jews in a single day, he had sex slaves and a child bride, he even burned people alive in their homes for not attending his religion's prayers. After his death, the religion was propagated by war taking over a large part of the earth, its advance was only stopped by the greater power of the Christian Europeans, in Africa and Asia as well in Europe.

As Islamic culture never underwent anything like the Reformation or the Enlightenment, its holy book, the Koran, was never subject to the kind of logical scrutiny that the Jewish Torah and Christian Bible have been put through. It is only now in our day that critical attention is uncovering its violent, xenophobic and misogynist prescriptions. In fact, its content does not even stand the test of truth, it contains grave errors of scientific, historical and literary fact, gross failures of logic and much self-contradiction. A book that claims itself to be perfect and infallible, but is so full of flaws, lies even, it cannot possibly be the dictated word of an all wise God. Its Allah wants followers to destroy, kill and plunder all who disagree with it, its Prophet promises each of them a personal demon; this is not faith as we recognize it. This is not a faith we should accept or allow in our society.

Today, Islam and its holy book fail the test of reason which it should have been subjected to centuries ago, and as a result it can only fall. It is just a matter of how long. It is up to us in the West to decide whether it will be a slow torturous demise, full of barbarity from Islamist groups like ISIS and Boko Haram, or whether it will be a sudden information technology driven worldwide social transformation.

Today the Bride of Christ must rise up and, like Queen Esther, come before her King to countermand the evil decrees of Islam. In the Chapter on Terrorism we have listed some of the death sentences against us that are written in the Koran. Throughout history, millions of Christians have been killed, enslaved and persecuted in the name of Islamic Allah. This continues today in many parts of the world, even here in the West. But now is the time for us to turn the situation around, to use the Koran to destroy Islam, just as Haman was hanged on his own gallows. Let us take hold of the Sword of Islam, the Koran and use it to kill Islam itself.

"Then David ran and stood over the Philistine and took his sword and drew it out of its sheath and killed him, and cut off his head with it"
(1 Samuel 17:51)

Even Mohammed prophesied the end of Islam.

Islam Undone

"Every plant which My Heavenly Father did not plant shall be uprooted"
(Gospel of Matthew 15:13)

Right now, as this is being written, nations mentioned in the Apocalyptic writings have fighters in Syria, between Dabiq and Armageddon.

The day of the Valley of Decision is here, the battle lines for the war of ideas and ideals are written.

The outcome of this spiritual war is not in question, Mohammed himself foretold the final fall of Islam, several Koran verses and Hadiths attest to this, verse 25:30 predicts that at the end of time Mohammed will say of Muslims;

25:30 *"Truly my people have taken the Quran as foolish nonsense".*

Sahih Bukhari recounts Mohammed saying;

"Verily Islam started as something rare and it would again revert to being rare and would recede... as a serpent crawls back into its hole, Verily the faith would recede to Medina..." (1/271-272),

"Belief retreats and goes back to Medina like a snake" (3/30/100)

Abu Dawud (40/4747) recalls another statement made about times to come;

"there will appear disagreement and dissension in my people...they will swerve from the religion.... the book of Allah...they will have nothing to do with..."

These are all quite reliable Hadiths which are supported by others which make the issue clear.

"The Hour (Day of Judgement) will not be established till the Hajj (to the Ka'aba) is abandoned."
(Sahih Bukhari 2/26/663)

"The Day of Judgement will not come until the people (Muslims) openly deny Allah"
(Ibn Babiya, Thawab al-A'mal, also in Al-Bihar by Al-Miylisi 13/155, Kanz al-Amal 766)

"A man will wake up a believer and be a kaffir (non-Muslim) by nightfall."
(Ahmad; Musnad 2/390)

"There will come a time on the people when there will remain nothing of Islam except its name, and nothing will remain of the Quran except its outward form"
(Baihaqi, Shu'bul Imam 2/788)

"The knots of Islam will be undone one by one, each time a knot is undone the next one will be grasped, the first to be undone will be the Ruling (the Caliphate) and the last will be the Prayer"
(Hadith 31, Ahmad, Musnad)

The true Caliphate ended nearly one hundred years ago, and the Islamic State Caliphate is currently coming to an end.

It is now time for the religion of Islam to fall.

It has tried to usurp Christianity by pretending to be the only true faith.

But we the Body of Christ will stand up strong, and prove to the World that Mohammed was a false prophet.

In so doing, we will bring forth the greatest harvest of souls there has ever been.

Islam undone!

Amen!

Part Ten - Ministering to Muslims

"asking that the God of our Lord Jesus Christ, the glorious Father, may give you a spirit of wisdom and revelation in your knowledge of Him. I ask that the eyes of your heart may be enlightened, so that you may know the hope of His calling, the riches of His glorious inheritance in the saints" (Ephesians 1:17-18)

Intercession

"I exhort therefore, that, first of all, supplications, prayers, intercessions, and giving of thanks, be made for all men; for kings, and for all that are in authority; that we may lead a quiet and peaceable life in all godliness and honesty. For this is good and acceptable in the sight of God our Saviour; Who will have all men to be saved, and to come unto the knowledge of the truth. For there is one God, and one mediator between God and men, the man Christ Jesus" (1 Timothy 2: 1-4)

Islam brings with it great spiritual darkness that makes the heavens *"brazen"* and blocks revelation. Demonic worship in mosques creates whirlwinds of spiritual confusion. Without open heavens, the population lives in darkness. Ordinary people can't even think straight because of this. Look at the turmoil in the media discussing the reasons for the tragic shootings in Orlando in June 2016. The shooter was a Muslim from an Afghan background, where well over 90% of the population believe in Sharia Law and Islam. Sharia says gay people should be killed. He acted in accordance with the mainstream Islamic beliefs of his people. Just add a personal crisis to an incendiary belief system. It is that simple, you do not have to look further for the reason. An Islamic preacher spoke in that part of Florida only a few weeks beforehand saying homosexuals should be *"eradicated"*. Islamic terrorism is not a mystery; it is commanded in their holy books. Yet the news media guessed at, and even invented, all sorts of other reasons to explain the tragedy away. But God wants us Christians to understand what is going on and to be able to explain the truth to the world.

"The mouths of the righteous utter wisdom, and their tongues speak what is just" (Psalm 37:30)

The spiritual darkness that Islam brings often has physical manifestations too, such as bringing drought. Until the arrival of Islam in the 7th Century, Tunisia was a land of rich green forests but its delicate climate was adversely affected by the dark spirituality. Very quickly the forests died and much of the land became desert. In the mid 1970's there were serious droughts in Great Britain, a land which normally has an excess of rain, and this coincided with the beginning of large scale Saudi-funded mosque building programmes there. In California, recently, the land has been blighted with drought after Hollywood released a movie about Noah which was based on the Islamic version of the story, where one son gets left behind, rather than the Biblical version. Deadly wildfires have followed in this state which is now home to over a million Muslims, has nearly 1,000 mosques and Islamic prayer rooms, and receives most of the 100,000 new Muslims migrants arriving in the USA each year.

Doesn't the Bible say in Exodus 22:3; *"You shall have no other gods besides me",* and Leviticus 26:3-4; *"If you walk in My statutes and keep My commandments so as to carry them out, then I shall give you rains in their season".* That's what God said. Islam's Allah is a false god and his worship brings devastation and drought in the spiritual and physical realms everywhere it spreads. In Italy, which is now receiving over 100,000 Muslim migrants annually, rainfall has fallen by 30% year on year to September 2017.

"Fight the good fight of faith" (1 Timothy 6:12)

One important area of intercession is dealing with the demonic entities that give Islam its power over people. Every Muslim has a demon, so if we keep those demons bound then Islam cannot fully manifest in an individual. Keep the spiritual atmosphere clear and Muslims don't become terrorists, wife beaters or child abusers.

"the people who know their God shall be strong, and carry out great exploits" (Daniel 11:32)

It is important to understand how Islamic prayers work in the spirit realm. Several times, we have seen in the spirit, demons flying around with "Allah" flags as Muslims pray together. These Muslims get tricked into thinking they are connecting with heaven when this happens. They feel something strong around them and get a real "buzz" from all the demonic activity. We believe that Muslims activate and deeply connect with their demons as they take part in their ritual prayers. Those demons become energized and are then dispatched into the neighbourhood on satanic missions. By asking the Lord to send His angelic hosts to intercept, to bind and dispose of these demons, we can clear the atmosphere and stop the demonic influence being established in a locality. We need to break the power of the demons to influence others outside the mosques and prayer rooms afterwards too.

"You shall tear down their altars and smash their sacred pillars and burn their Asherim with fire, and you shall cut down the engraved images of their gods and obliterate their name from that place" (Deuteronomy 12:3)

As well as these low flying demons, you may well encounter **"false light"** angels associated with Islam (see 2nd Corinthians 11:14). Much of the power of Islam comes from these fallen angels, whose Luciferian-like-light fools people into thinking they are from God. Once again ask the Lord to have His, more powerful, heavenly host remove them. Pray that no new converts to Islam are drawn in by any pull of the demonic.

"you are to tear down their altars and smash their sacred pillars and cut down their Asherim" (Exodus 34:13)

In January 2003, Jesus told us to go to pray outside a mosque at Finsbury Park, North London. There had already been reports by news media outside the UK that it had become a hub for Islamists, but the authorities were reluctant to take any action. So, we sought the Lord on what He had asked us to do, seeking His timing for when to go. Then we obeyed Him and went. The spiritual warfare was hellish as we approached the area by Underground train and then on foot. At first, we walked past the mosque praying and then we prayed from the far side of the street. One of us was much less enthusiastic than the other, especially when they said; *"You see that guy over there, the Holy Spirit said he's a terrorist!"* and thought they had lost it, but promised to intercede as they went to pray on the pavement in front of the entrance to the mosque; *"I thank you Lord to bring to light all that is done in darkness in this place, including all terrorist activities."* Within 72 hours the premises were raided by the Metropolitan Police who used battering rams to break down the doors to gain entry. Inside they found weapons, 100's of forged and stolen passports, credit cards and chequebooks, chemical warfare protection suits, terrorist paraphernalia and recipes for creating chemical weapons components ricin and cyanide. The terrorist identified by the Holy Spirit was eventually found guilty of planning mass chemical terrorist attacks. A terror plot was foiled, an active Al Qaeda cell uncovered and the mosque was closed down. The Imam was subsequently arrested and, after over 10 years of legal battles, deported. Obedience to the true Lord brings results.

"Fear not, for I am with you. Do not be afraid, for I am your God. I will strengthen you, I will help you, I will uphold you with My righteous right hand" (Isaiah 41:10)

Regular focussed prayer for your neighbourhood and region is crucial in these times, and through this you can also deal with other demonic issues related to drugs, prostitution, gang violence, corruption, and the like.

"Truly I tell you, whatever you bind on earth will be bound in heaven, and whatever you loose on earth will be loosed in heaven"
(Matthew 18:18)

We also need to protect our neighbourhoods by breaking the demonic declarations made in the standard five-times-a-day prayers. Muslims proclaim that *"torment will overtake the non-Muslims"* in those prayers. We must pray peace into the atmosphere instead of that torment.

The Koran readings that accompany these prayers also often declare destruction for non-Muslims. These prayers and Koran readings are calling forth hell on earth and are opening the way for terrorism and the other evil physical manifestations of Islam. Because these prayers are prayed so regularly, we must regularly intercede to break their effect. In Ramadan, Muslims fast whilst praying these prayers, so we must be extra vigilant. No wonder there is an increase of terrorism during that period. With the revelation of what really goes on during Islamic prayers in mosques, prayer rooms and even in people's homes, we can powerfully intercede to break Satan's plans.

"Put on the full armour of God, so that you will be able to stand firm against the schemes of the devil" (Ephesians 6:11)

In order to protect our lands from the spiritual darkness that Islam brings, we need to intercede constantly and consistently at Muslim prayer times so that all its false worship is kept in containment in the mosques and prayer rooms, and cannot break out to produce an enemy presence in the wider atmosphere. Such spiritual containment needs to be prayed around *"halal"* abattoirs too, because, as we have seen, halal meat is sacrificed for demons. They are altars to Satan. Indeed, we should pray that this cruel form of animal slaughter is outlawed in our lands. There are at the time of writing court proceedings taking place in the UK based on clear video evidence of the great distress which the animals are put through. Studies at the University of Milan Department of Veterinary Medicine have proved that such distress causes the high presence of stress hormones in the meat which in turn is dangerous for human wellbeing.

"You, Lord, will keep the needy safe and will protect us forever from the wicked, who freely strut about when what is vile is honoured by the human race" (Psalm 12:7)

Be aware too of the other phenomena that arrive in our cities with Islamic immigration. FGM is one which is currently being discovered at an alarming rate across the West. It is a blood offering to Allah, to Satan. Then there are the sex attacks and grooming gangs. We received a very reliable first-hand witness report about what is going on in a major Muslim food company in Preston, UK. This large company prepares chicken and other halal food for fast food outlets across northern Europe. On Friday afternoons, after lunchtime prayers at the local mosque, the boss would bring a prostitute into the staff room and the men would queue up on the stairs to each take a turn. Often there would be as many as twenty waiting in line. Sometimes the girls would be underage, provided by local grooming gangs. There could have been girls there supplied by the infamous Muslim grooming gang in Rochdale who were jailed in 2012, whose victims the TV series "Three Girls" was about. The factory is only 25 miles away from that town. Similar phenomena have appeared in other countries, in France there has been a widespread problem with what they call *"tournantes"*, gangs of young Muslim men picking on vulnerable underage girls. These things are important prayer issues.

"The LORD will cause your enemies who rise up against you to be defeated before you; they shall come out against you one way and shall flee before you seven ways" (Deuteronomy 28:7)

Our intercession is also very important in respect of public buildings; government offices, schools and colleges, hospitals, transport hubs and so on, because Muslims have insisted in having prayer rooms in such places. These prayer rooms, if not watched over, can become places of demonic habitation. The designation of part of a building as an Islamic prayer room is an agreement to allow demons to manifest in that building. These places must not be allowed to become gateways for the demonic to enter and gain greater influence. Don't forget that each time a Muslim prays they declare that Allah's torment will overtake the non-Muslims, this clearly is praying terror into the atmosphere. The Lord had us held up once by flight delays at a major Western airport to have us pray in the multi-faith prayer room there. Satan was trying to open the airport up as a spiritual gateway for members of the Islamic State to get into Europe. He even had us minister to a couple of youngsters who were flying from there to the airport in Turkey closest to the border with the Islamic State. Satan's agenda to make that airport a jihadi gateway was broken. Another time before that, we were sent by Him to Heathrow in London to clean up the multi-faith prayer chapel there. Any demonic presence hinders the Lord's angels from working, like in the Book of Daniel 10:13, so it is very important that the Lord's angels are unhindered to protect our public places. Not long after our visit, the security forces nearby uncovered a well-advanced terror plot to drive a truck bomb into one of the airport terminals. Hundreds of terror attacks in the West have been foiled by faithful Christians standing in the gap as prayer watchmen. Jesus greatly blesses those men and women who take their place in such intercession.

"But when he, the Spirit of truth, comes, he will guide you into all the truth... and he will tell you what is yet to come" (John 16:13)

So just as we need to pray for our public places, we also need to pray for our leaders. They are under a continual onslaught of Islamic prayers, marabouting and other attempts at spiritual manipulation, Islamic and otherwise. There are several world leaders who are so blinded spiritually at the moment they cannot even admit that the Islamic State is Islamic. Even though ISIS readily quotes the Islamic sacred texts to justify their barbarity, these world leaders are so manipulated spiritually they cannot comprehend the simple truth. This is very dangerous. If you cannot identify what your enemy is, how can you strategize to set about defeating it. It is not just national leaders who need our prayers, local and church leaders need our prayer support too. Our prayers are powerful and can break terrorist plots in the spirit. We recently attended a powerful Christian conference in London, England and two Islamic terror attacks were attempted in that part of London during the three-day conference time. But we had prayed against terrorism; that guns would jam, bombs would not detonate, and any chemical agents released would just blow away. That's exactly what happened.

"And Jesus looking upon them saith, with men it is impossible, but not with God: for with God all things are possible" (Mark 10:27)

We must be ready to intercede no matter when or where we are. Relaxing on a Mediterranean beach one day, we felt a very, very dark spirit arrive. We prayed hard and after a few minutes identified it as an Islamic jihadi spirit. It then took about 45 minutes of solid intercession to break it and then the peace returned. Given the Islamic State attacks on other beaches in recent times, who knows what might have happened had we not been spiritually aware. We must be alert too, to pray for the protection of our Christian brothers and sisters. In several countries Pastors and church-goers are regularly targeted. Even in Europe there have been jihad attacks on churches. The Barcelona terrorists planned a massacre in a cathedral. Worldwide the phenomenon is increasing.

"Be on the alert. Stand firm in the faith. Be men of courage. Be strong. Do everything in love" (1 Corinthians 16:13-14)

Closer to home, our families and friends need prayer cover wherever they come into contact with the demonic. Many schools and colleges in the West seem to have very aggressive Muslim student groups who try to impose their atmosphere in the common rooms, libraries and cafeterias. The teachers and supervisors are told to give these Muslims a lot of leeway and to show them favour to encourage them to integrate. Unfortunately, this doesn't take account of what Islam actually teaches them about not integrating, and the special treatment just makes them feel even more superior, just like the Koran tells them they are. If anyone wants to help Muslims integrate they will have to first understand what Islam really is and what it teaches. Thus, part of our intercession has to be that the real truth about Islam becomes common knowledge in the West, that people are no longer fooled by the false image it presents of itself. One way to do this is to give people copies of our free e-book "The Undoing" which can be circulated freely to everyone.

"Wisdom will save you from the ways of wicked men, from men whose words are perverse" (Proverbs 2:12)

It is important to pray to protect our young people from being the target of Islamic proselytising, bullying and even from getting romantically involved with Muslims. In Muslim majority countries, this is a big problem. Marriages between Muslims and non-Muslims tend to be quite unhappy affairs, quite simply because they are made on the frontline of a spiritual battlefield. We need to teach our young people what is wrong with Islam to protect them from being seduced by it whenever they encounter it. We must protect future generations by imparting wisdom.

"and devote ourselves to prayer and the ministry of the word" (Acts 6:4)

Our intercession needs to be enduring. The prayer warriors themselves need to be continually supported by the prayers of others. A Biblical model is found in Exodus Chapter 17 where Moses interceded as Joshua fought the Amalekites who had attacked Israel on the way to the promised land.

"As long as Moses held up his hands, the Israelites were winning, but whenever he lowered his hands, the Amalekites were winning. When Moses' hands grew tired, they took a stone and put it under him and he sat on it. Aaron and Hur held his hands up—one on one side, one on the other—so that his hands remained steady till sunset. So Joshua overcame the Amalekite army with the sword" (Exodus 17:11-13)

Whilst today, we do not fight physically against flesh and blood, but fight purely in the spiritual and intellectual realms, the analogy is pertinent. Islam is the spiritual heritage of the Amalekites, we are at war with it. It opposes God from generation to generation. It wants to stop us reaching our promised land; the fullness of Christ's Kingdom upon the Earth.

"Because hands were lifted up against the throne of the Lord, the Lord will be at war against the Amalekites from generation to generation" (Exodus 17:16)

For us, we do not want to kill Muslims but want to see them all saved.

"We use God's mighty weapons, not worldly weapons, to knock down the strongholds of human reasoning and to destroy false arguments" (2 Corinthians 10:4)

Our weapons are not physical weapons, we fight in the spirit with prayer and in the world with the truth.

"God our Saviour, He desires all men to be saved and to come to the knowledge of the truth" (1 Timothy 2:4)

And so, of course, our other main area of intercession is to pray for Muslims, that they may be set free from their demonic religion and come to salvation. By keeping the atmosphere of your neighbourhood or city spiritually clear, the impact of the demonic is minimized. Pray for the individuals you know about in your area, the individuals you see on the streets. Remember they are just people who have been brought up with a lie, a big religious lie about who God is. Keep declaring over them;

"you shall know the truth and the truth shall set you free" (John 8:32).

Befriend them. Get to know them, break down their barriers of isolation. Love is the best way. Be Christ to them.

"If I speak in the tongues of men or of angels, but do not have love, I am only a resounding gong or a clanging cymbal" (1 Corinthians 13:1)

If you like to pray with the Word, Bible passages like this are fitting;

Psalm 83
O God, do not remain quiet; Do not be silent and, O God, do not be still. For behold, your enemies make an uproar; those who hate you have raised their heads. They lay crafty plans against your people and conspire together against Your treasured ones. They have said, "Come, and let us wipe them out as a nation, so that the name of Israel be remembered no more." With one mind they plot together; they form an alliance against you - the tents of Edom and the Ishmaelites, of Moab and the Hagrites, Gebal, Ammon, and Amalek, Philistia with the inhabitants of Tyre. Even Assyria has joined them; they lend support to the sons of Lot. Selah

Deal with them as You did with Midian, as You did with Sisera and Jabin at the Kishon River. Who perished at En-dor, who became as manure for the ground. Make their nobles like Oreb and Zeeb and all their princes like Zebah and Zalmunna, who said, "Let us take possession for ourselves of the pastures of God." O my God, make them like the whirling dust, Like chaff before the wind. As fire consumes the forest or a flame sets the mountains ablaze, so pursue them with Your tempest and terrify them with Your storm. Fill their faces with shame; that they may seek thy name, O LORD. Let them be ashamed and dismayed forever, and let them be humiliated and fall in disgrace, That they may know that You alone, whose name is the Yahweh, are the Most High over all the earth.

Spreading the Truth

"My people are destroyed for lack of knowledge"
(Hosea 4:6)

Every church should play an important role in the community of which it is part, and every denomination should be a powerful influence in the nation or region it serves. Even if its goals are limited to the saving of souls, falling short of our work in Christ to *"destroy the works of the devil"* (1 John 3:8), then still a confrontation with Islamic belief systems will necessarily take place somewhere, sometime, on some level. In fact, the conflict of ideas and ideals is a natural part of the working of society, we see it especially in politics, where Islam, with its aggressive nature, has greatly exploited the political spirit. It is by nature and origins, much more political than Christianity, so we in the Church need to do more to get ourselves heard. We are supposed to be the mouthpiece of God on this Earth. We must not shy away from taking a moral stand against the evil of Islam, nor on any other issue.

"For it is written, "I WILL DESTROY THE WISDOM OF THE WISE, AND THE CLEVERNESS OF THE CLEVER I WILL SET ASIDE." - Where is the wise man ? Where is the scribe ? Where is the debater of this age ? Has not God made foolish the wisdom of the world ?"
(1st Corinthians 1:19-20)

"We demolish arguments and every pretension that sets itself up against the knowledge of God. We capture their rebellious thoughts and teach them to obey Christ "
(2nd Corinthians 10:5)

We cannot remain silent in the face of non-stop pressure on authorities to accommodate Muslims with prayer facilities in public buildings and allow Islamic prayers in public events. Giving way to such pressure allows the demonic to gain a foot in the door, to establish a presence in public places. Some churches have even fallen into this trap and allowed in Muslims to pray Islamic Arabic prayers that they do not understand, presuming them to be similar in content to our Christian prayers. But even the most basic Islamic prayers are anti-Christian and anti-Jewish. These prayers repeat the content of the Koran which declares that God has no son. Thus, there has been allowed a defilement to enter those Churches in the form an open denial of Christ. Today's Church must arm itself with wisdom. Ignorance is no defence;

"Be sober-minded and alert. Your adversary the devil prowls around like a roaring lion, seeking someone to devour"
(1 Peter 5:8)

"The beginning of wisdom is this: Get wisdom. Though it cost everything, get understanding" (Proverbs 4:7)

"Blessed are those who find wisdom, those who gain understanding" (Proverbs 3:13)

"through knowledge the righteous escape" (Proverbs 11:9)

In this book, we have endeavoured to give you all the information needed to be victorious over Islam and to bring forth a great harvest of former Muslims. At the end of this book you will find a Holy Spirit inspired evangelism tool which will help enormously with this.

"But the wisdom from above is first pure, then peaceable, gentle, reasonable, full of mercy and good fruits, unwavering and sincere" (James 3:17)

"Gold there is, and rubies in abundance, but lips that speak knowledge are a rare jewel" (Proverbs 20:15)

Ministry in the community breaks down into three basic areas, each of which requires a somewhat different approach. The first of these is to get the truth about Islam out to other Christians so they do not fall into the trap of accepting it as a valid expression of worship of God. It is not at all that, and it is truly demonic, as has been explained very clearly in previous chapters. We must save fellow Christians from shaking hands with Islamic ideas and getting involved with the compromises like **"Chrislam"**. Such mixing of faiths is not Biblical, it is sin which leads to spiritual death. Islam is in fundamental contradiction to Christianity, it teaches a false Jesus. It teaches hatred of non-believers instead of love for them. It leads people to hell instead of saving them from it. It has no place for the Holy Spirit but instead offers a covenant with demons. Be clear on this, Islam's legalism offers no salvation, it is only the grace of the true Lord Jesus Christ that brings it. The wider Church needs to be made aware of the reality of what Islam truly is.

"Have I not commanded you ? Be strong and courageous. Do not be afraid ; do not be discouraged, for the LORD your God will be with you wherever you go" (Joshua 1:9)

Be aware that some Christians might be hesitant about bringing down a large false worship system like Islam. But isn't this exactly what Elijah did on Mount Carmel, and St Paul at Ephesus? The Bible has many stories about breaking altars of satanic worship.

Islam is an altar of Satan. It's god Allah is the image projected by the Great Beast of the Apocalypse.

"I am warning you ahead of time, dear friends. Be on guard so that you will not be carried away by the errors of these wicked people and lose your own secure footing." (2 Peter 3:17)

Our second objective, which we will consider more in the next chapter, must be to get the real truth out to all members of society, especially in the first instance to local and national leaders. This is not so easy because in recent years the Christian community, for a number of reasons, has lost much of its societal influence. Whether it has been in some areas, by giving in to political correctness that has stifled openness, whether it has been poor communication, or even an expression of lack of compassion, we must re-find our place as ambassadors of Christ's love. Only from that place of love can we truly express the mind of Christ, on this, or on any other issue. Remember always that our enemy is Satan and that the religion of Islam is just one of his works we must destroy. We will not achieve this by hating Muslims, they are only victims, we should love them and help them out of the web of religious lies they have been entangled in. Ministering to them is our third area of involvement which the chapters entitled **"Personal ministry"**, **"After salvation"** and **"Isaiah 1:17"** are dedicated to.

"Therefore, if anyone is in Christ, he is a new creation. The old has passed away; behold, the new has come" (2nd Corinthians 5:17)

Be aware, that whilst going out into public places is an important area of ministry, with revival building in our nations we will have Muslims coming to us seeking salvation, healing and wisdom. It is easy to minister to them when they can see a real demonstration of God's power. They will see that Jesus is the Way, the Truth and the Life. When revival comes to a church near you, go out and invite them to come along. It is so important for us to be ready to welcome them and to minister to them. There may be some who get saved at large gatherings who are looking for a local church to attend. You will need to know how to help them fit in. They may need deliverance, they will certainly need guidance, and they may need more practical help too. In these chapters, you will find an overview of the type of ministry you will need to provide. May God bless you with an abundant harvest !

"How much better to get wisdom than gold, to get insight rather than silver !" (Proverbs 16:16)

But first let's look more closely at getting the truth out to fellow Christians. This is not as easy as one would think because many Christians seem to not want to know how nasty and demonic Islam really is. We have buried our heads in the sand too long, and ignored our responsibility before Christ to pull the Muslims around us out of the gates of hell. In the past, we had no real way of knowing what the religion was all about, but today it is manifestly in our faces.

Today nearly all of us have internet connections and have no more excuses for being ill-informed, for turning away from our mandate in this area. Yes, our leaders have done the world a great disservice by pretending that Islamic terrorism has nothing to do with mainstream Islam, but we don't tend to believe them on other issues, so why do we do so here?

"Stop being gullible and live. Start travelling the road to understanding."
(Proverbs 9:6)

Everywhere that the Body of Christ has not stood in the breach, Islam has crept in, in schools, in hospital and prison chaplaincies, in government, everywhere. It has a Jezebellic agenda to replace and undo the grace of Christianity and bring the world back under the power of the Law of the Accuser with its sting of death. We must speak up to save our free democratic Judeo-Christian society, because no-one else has the spiritual power to do it for us. Only we Christians have the power through the true Word of God to do so. Freemasons, socialists, and others who deny Christ, lack the spiritual strength to resist the political seduction of the Islamic spirit. It is up to us, working with Christ, to bring it down. That is what a large part of the Book of Revelation is about. We must resist the devil and his agenda in Islam.

"Submit yourselves therefore to God. Resist the devil, and he will flee from you" (James 4:7)

So, spread the word, this is supposed to be our finest hour. Take your stand because the appointed time has come. It's 2018 and God has brought a President who wants to take a stand against Islam into the most powerful political office on the planet. Don't miss what God is doing in this season. Understand the times like the tribe of Issachar did in the Old Testament. Submit to His plan, resist the devil's religion and see the enemy flee.

"the children of Issachar, men that had understanding of the times, to know what Israel ought to do"
(1 Chronicles 12:32)

"But thanks be to God ! He gives us the victory through our Lord Jesus Christ"
(1 Corinthians 15:57)

"The trap is broken, and we are free !"
(Psalm 124:7)

In the Community

"to all I send you, you shall go and whatever I command you, you shall speak. Do not be afraid of them" (Jeremiah 1:7-8)

Every church should be influential in its community. Indeed, the Greek word in the New Testament ***"Ekklesia"***, which is normally translated as ***"church"***, is also translated as ***"assembly or council"*** (see Acts 19:32,39,41) thus also implying governance, guidance and influence. Most churches have members who are positioned by God in important places of social influence, schools, local government, businesses and so on. Moreover, many pastors are recognized and respected by the local community. They can have much influence, and we must use all the positions of influence the Lord has given us to bring about an education of attitudes towards Islam. We must share the truth with all those around us. Our governments and education systems have seriously let us down in this area. Instead of truth they have brought us lies about Islam's true nature. They have pretended that it is more or less equivalent to Christianity. It is up to us to step into the breach and bring out the true facts. So, as we said at the very beginning of the book we must be ***"as wise as serpents"***, in other words understanding how our spiritual enemy, Satan, is working, yet, ***"as gentle as doves"*** (Matthew 10:16) by working gently and peacefully to make the truth known. We can't tell you here how to approach every individual situation that might arise in ministering to Muslims, but the Holy Spirit can. It is essential for each and every one of us to be able to walk in His right-guidance. Our community outreach must always be a physical demonstration of God's love. Prophetic and healing evangelism are examples of how we can go out and bless those around us.

"Steadfast love and faithfulness meet; righteousness and peace kiss each other" (Psalm 85:10)

Certain political and social groups, for example left-wingers, seem to have great difficulty in understanding that terrorism, FGM and anti-Semitism are taught by the religion. They have an erroneous view that if something is done in the name of religion then it must be accepted, because otherwise one is making a cultural value judgement to say that Islam is wrong. How blind! They have no problem criticizing conservatives, and even the Church, but they make Islam off limits. It teaches what it teaches and no one should deny the facts of what it teaches. Sadly, formal Islamic studies in schools and colleges shy away from all those controversial areas that are part of the religion.

"if the watchman sees the enemy sword coming and doesn't blow his trumpet to warn the people... I will hold him responsible" (Ezekiel 33:6)

One topic of conversation that is certainly very easy to slip into is about how easy it is for Muslims to be radicalized, even by themselves online. This is now such a problem that Western governments have permanent teams devoted to trying to stop this phenomenon which accounts for the ever-increasing numbers of "lone-wolf" terrorists. The radicalization process is simple; it starts by targeting vulnerable, isolated, easily-influenced individuals who are frustrated and find little sense in their lives. They are told that the world is evil and must be changed by Islam, that Islam has the only answers, and that is why they are miserable and lonely. They are told Allah needs them to change all this.

"Now the Holy Spirit tells us clearly that in the last times some will turn away from the true faith; they will follow deceptive spirits and teachings that come from demons. These people are hypocrites and liars, and their consciences are dead" (1 Timothy 4:1-2)

These vulnerable Muslims are given a general introduction to Islamic discipline and taught to pray the Islamic way, not by trying to dialogue with God like in Judaism or Christianity, but by repetition and gesture. Once established in this, it is explained that all Muslims in their five-times-a-day **Du'aa e Qunoot** prayer, declare in Arabic that;

"Allah's torment will overtake the Non-Muslims".

This prayer is then later explained in the light of Koran verses like

(9:14)   *"Fight them, Allah will punish them at your hands."*

(2:193)   *"Wage (mental & physical) war on them (the unbelievers / the non-Muslims) until there is no more idolatry and all religion is for Allah."*

and the hundreds of other passages in their holy books that command physical jihad against everybody involved in anything un-Islamic. The literal interpretation of these texts is reinforced by more Koran verses; -

3:132	*"Obey Allah..."*
4:47	*"The commands of Allah must be carried out!"*
4:59	*"O ye who believe, obey Allah..."*
8:20	*"Obey Allah and His messenger..."*
69:41	*"It (the Koran) is not poet's speech"*

Then Mohammed's personal example to follow is looked at, thereby showing how in Islam it is requisite to fight and kill unbelievers to obtain power.

Mohammed said; "I have been ordered by Allah to strive against the people until they testify that none has the right to be worshipped but Allah." (Sahih Bukhari 1/2/25)

"Allah desires killing them (unbelievers/non-Muslims) to manifest the religion"
(Ibn Ishaq; **The Life of Muhammad**, translated Hisham, p484)

"He (Mohammed) seized about four hundred men from the Jews who had been allies of the Aus against Khazraj and ordered that they should be beheaded. Accordingly, Khazraj cut off their heads with great satisfaction"
(**Sirat Rasul Allah**, Ishaq trans Guillaume; Ibn Hisham's Notes no. 580)

The recruits are then told that because in the past they sinned so much, their only way to salvation now is by being a martyr; that only will guarantee them a place in paradise.

(9:20) *"Those who believe, have left their homes and used their wealth to fight for the cause...are of much greater worth... These...achieve Allah's salvation."*

For them, martyrdom is now the only way for them to reach paradise where they will be rewarded with a martyr's reward of 72 beautiful virgins and many riches.

(3:195) *"those who... fought and were slain, verily I shall remit their evil deeds from them and verily I shall bring them into Gardens underneath which rivers flow - A reward from Allah"*

Osama Bin Laden summed up the Islamic beliefs on gaining forgiveness and attaining paradise in his first fatwa (August 1996); -

"A martyr's privileges are guaranteed by Allah; forgiveness with the first gush of blood, he will be shown his seat in paradise, he will be decorated with the jewels of belief, married off to the beautiful ones, protected from the test in the grave, assured security in the Day of Judgement, crowned with the crown of dignity, a ruby which is better than this whole world and its entire content, wedded to seventy-two of the pure Houris (beautiful virgins) and his intercession on behalf of seventy of his relatives will be accepted."

The role of terror verses in the Koran in radicalising jihadis is so important that many suicide bombers read it before going on mission to strengthen their resolve. They really believe they are doing God's will, and that becoming a jihadi is the only way they can get right with God.

"the folly of fools is deceit" (Proverbs 14:8)

So, you see it is all quite simple, there is no mystery in it. Yet for some reason there is a global failure to publicly recognise that without Islam, without the Koran, without Mohammed's example, such terrorism would not exist. This is pure folly, because if one wants to eradicate something, one cannot succeed unless one first clearly identifies its root source and understands how it works. Then having targeted it, one can analyze it and strategically plan to destroy it. But our governments have failed us pathetically on this. Until recently, when it was disclosed by the media, the UK authorities relied on social research information on Muslims attitudes supplied by the brother of an actual terrorist. He was feeding them tactical lies.

"the devil... was a murderer from the beginning, refusing to uphold the truth... he is a liar and the father of lies" (John 8:44)

"O foolish Galatians, who hath bewitched you, that ye should not obey the truth... ?" (Galatians 3:1)

Whilst one of the reasons our governments have failed to clearly identify the problem has to do with fear, but we should not, as Christians, be scared about going out into the public arena armed with the truth.

"Then the eyes of the blind will be opened and the ears of the deaf will be unstopped" (Isaiah 35:5)

When we Christians are on the offensive against the plans of the enemy we are in God's great protection and need not fear;

"Behold, I give unto you power to tread on serpents and scorpions, and over all the power of the enemy : and nothing shall by any means hurt you." (Luke 10:19)

Indeed, it is when we fail to resist and fail to push back against Satan that we fall into compromise and into danger;

"Submit yourselves, then, to God. Resist the devil, and he will flee from you." (James 4:7)

"and do not give the devil a foothold." (Ephesians 4:27)

"Anyone who isn't with me opposes me, and anyone who isn't working with me is actually working against me." (Matthew 12:30)

The Bible is very clear about how much we will be protected when we step out to do His Will; -

"The Lord preserves those who are true to Him" (Psalm 31:23)

"The fear of man brings a snare, but whoever trusts in the Lord shall be safe" (Proverbs 29:25)

Do not let fear put you off what He is clearly calling us to; -

"For Christ has not given us a spirit of fear, but of power and love and a sound mind" (2 Timothy 1:7)

"I will build my Church and the gates of hell shall not prevail against it" (Matthew 16:18)

"No weapon formed against you shall prosper" (Isaiah 54:17)

Wisdom and understanding are key weapons in our protection; -

"understanding will guard you" (Proverbs 2:11)

"Do not forsake wisdom, and she will protect you; love her and she will watch over you" (Proverbs 4:6)

It is of crucial importance that we Christians are all aware of the real truth. Then armed with that truth, God will open up opportunities for us to spread it and to put it to use. He will even test us on this in times coming. We do not want the Lord saying this to us;

"You have not gone up into the breaches, nor did you build the wall around the house of Israel to stand in the battle on the day of the LORD." (Ezekiel 13:5)

We must understand the times and seasons; if millions of Muslim refugees have come to live in our Judeo-Christian society in the West, then He must want us to bring them to their salvation in Christ. This is the season we are now in. God is even forcing our hand on this, because if we were not to act now then we would see Islam very aggressively trying to dominate spirituality in our lands.

"Let the priests take it to them, every man of his acquaintance: and let them repair the breaches of the house, wheresoever any breach shall be found." (2 Kings 12:5)

"And they from among you shall build the old waste places: you shall raise up the foundations of many generations; and you shall be called, the repairer of the breach, the restorer of streets to dwell in." (Isaiah 58:12)

Whatever position in society we find ourselves in, we need to pray and ask the Lord what role can we each play in bringing in the truly massive harvest of the Muslims souls landing on our shores. We cannot grumble about our countries being Islamized unless we have reached out to the Muslims around us to bring them forth out of spiritual darkness. We as the Body of Christ on earth at this time have a responsibility to Father God to guide the descendants of Ishmael and Esau out of Islam and into His Kingdom. We must be the light that shows them the way.

"For so the Lord has commanded us, saying, 'I have made you a light for the Gentiles, that you may bring salvation to the ends of the earth'."
(Acts 13:47)

And then bringing them to Christ, Jesus will then use these new converts to go back to their communities, their homelands even, bringing forth a yet greater harvest. Although we cannot tell you exactly how the Lord will use you personally, if you show yourself keen in prayer the Lord will certainly use you. Whether it is an atheist who comes up to you at a neighbour's barbecue and asks what is the difference between Muslims and Christians (something similar has happened to us more than once) or whether you are invited to teach a class on comparative religion (and it is about time we had true comparative religion!!!) or whether, perhaps as a pastor, you start developing a relationship with the local imam. The possibilities are endless because God is opening the exit doors of Islam in this season. Just imagine what an impact it will have on your community when the local Imam abandons Islam and becomes an evangelist.

"Go therefore and make disciples of all nations"
(Matthew 28:19)

"be doers of the word, and not hearers only, deceiving yourselves..."
(James 1:22)

"If you understand these things, you will be blessed if you do them"
(John 13:17)

"an effective doer – he will be blessed in what he does"
(James 1:25)

"For the earth will be filled with the knowledge of the glory of the LORD as the waters cover the sea"
(Habakkuk 2:14)

Personal Ministry

"All the paths of the Lord are steadfast love and faithfulness"
(Psalm 25:10)

Whether you are ministering to individuals you are acquainted with, or to others who are unfamiliar to you, reaching out to Muslims does not have to be an arduous affair. You are less likely to get a negative reaction from a Muslim when talking to them about Jesus, than you would from a secularist or a socialist. In all cases, it is wise to have someone backing you up in prayer while you minister, whether they are with you praying silently, or interceding from church or home. It is always important to bind the Islamic spirit, and the Muslim identity spirit which works in tandem with it, as well as any personal demon a person might have.

A good preparation time spent with the Holy Spirit before going out to minister always helps. He can forewarn you of the topics which may come up and can give you a specific word to bring to a person or what particular approach to take. He might give you a prophetic word for someone or give you a word of knowledge for a healing need. Don't forget too, to pray on the Ephesians 6:10-17 armour of God before you go out. We can only give a general outline here because every individual is unique, only the Holy Spirit can give the specific insights you need into each person in each situation.

"Go into all the world and preach the Good News to everyone"
(Mark 16:15)

Once you are talking to people face to face, always treat them with respect. Proper courtesy goes a long way to facilitating a follow up communication. Don't expect too much from a first-time encounter, most Muslims will need time to come to terms with what you say to them. Follow through with prayer for them afterwards at church; pray that they realise that what you have told them is true and that they realise what they have been taught in their mosque is untrue.

Remember that Jesus went to the Cross for them, and Islam is a manufactured lie to keep them in ignorance of it. All of the historical evidence supports His death on the Cross; there is no evidence whatsoever to support the Koran's claim that He didn't die there. In the unlikely event that you do get a bad reaction from a Muslim, stay calm and polite, as loving as you can be, their overreaction will be a profound motivator for change in them. Be forgiving and let it go in front of God.

"How beautiful are the feet of those who bring good news !"
(Romans 10:15)

On the street, ministering to Muslims should never be allowed to become aggressive. Arguing with raised voices over which sacred book is right, seldom brings real fruit. Rely on the Holy Spirit to guide you in what to say and always minister from an attitude of Christ-like love. Long winded debates of "apologetics" don't tend to lead anywhere, so it is better to focus on topics where the superiority of the Christian covenant is clear and easy to show. These include; -

- *"if anyone is in Christ, he is a new creation"* (2 Corinthians 5:17)
- *"So, you are no longer a slave, but God's child"* (Galatians 4:7)
- *"But the fruit of the Spirit is love, joy, peace, forbearance, kindness, goodness, faithfulness, gentleness and self-control"* (Galatians 5:22-23)

Study up on these issues as preparation. Comparisons between Christianity and Islam are clear cut on certain other issues too; -

- the Koran's false claim that the trinity is God the Father, Mary, and Jesus (5:116) compared to the true Trinity of Father, Son and Holy Spirit (Matthew 28:19)
- the lack of assurance of salvation in the whole Koran compared to the universal assurance of salvation in Christ (John 3:16)
- the personal demons issue, that all Muslims are assigned a demon (Sahih Muslim 39/6757) as against the fact we Christians will drive out demons in Jesus name (Mark 16:17)

Often it works to let the Holy Spirit touch someone you have been praying for so that they make the first step towards you. Take the example of a young man, about 30, quite social and very dependable, who used to work at a local market. I always made a point of saying hello and asking him how he was but hadn't had any real conversation with him. Then one day he came up and said **"You're Christian, aren't you? We learned about Christians in lessons at the mosque"**. He then told me he'd been taught how we Christians pray to Jesus, His mother (Mary), as well as to God, together with some other misconceptions spread by the Koran. So, I said to him, **"No, that's not really true..."**, and started to explain to him the significance of the true Trinity; of the Father, Son and Holy Spirit. I explained too, that when you believe in Jesus as Saviour you can receive the Holy Spirit of God to come and live inside you, and went on to explain the gifts of the Spirit; healing, prophecy, words of wisdom, discerning of spirits and so on. He listened really intently and then said; **"Wow this is just too much !"**, before wandering off. The Holy Spirit just blew his mind. I never saw him again afterwards because he had been made redundant, but knew Jesus was working on him. The conversation had clearly touched him deeply.

Several Christians friends of ours have recounted similar conversations with Muslims who have all been amazed to hear the truth about the Holy Spirit.

"For our gospel did not come to you in word only, but also in power, and in the Holy Spirit" (1st Thessalonians 1:5)

Be aware that when you are ministering in the street, or any other public place, things can sometimes stir up in the spiritual realms. Quite often other Muslims may suddenly arrive on the scene. This is only an attempt by the demonic to intimidate and cut short the evangelism. But Jesus can turn this to our advantage. Going out in ministry teams of two or more persons allows for one to talk whilst the other prays and watches over the spiritual atmosphere. If you take out copies of the TICCET evangelism tool you can give them out to all the Muslims who may turn up.

"for they received the word with great eagerness, examining the Scriptures daily to see whether these things were so. Therefore many of them believed" (Acts 17:11-12)

Other opportunities to minister may be less orthodox. One time we were invited by a group of Muslim neighbours to a barbecue at the end of Ramadan. We offered to bring a guitar and play some music and they liked the idea. We had a lovely, very tasty meal with them, and then when the food was over we started to play some music. Very quickly we launched into worship songs and they all went out in the Spirit. We sang for over an hour in a heavenly atmosphere as God ministered to them. All had a very good time! Incidentally, don't be scared to eat what is offered to you by Muslims, just remember to silently ask the Lord to sanctify and bless it. Only if someone starts telling all the gory details about what halal sacrifice is, should you show disagreement and decline the food.

"If one of the unbelievers invites you over and you want to go, eat everything that is set before you, without raising questions of conscience. But if someone says to you, 'This has been offered in sacrifice,' then do not eat it, both for the sake of the one who told you and for the sake of conscience." (1st Corinthians 10:27-28)

Some years ago, in London, we heard of an "Islam-expo" scheduled to take place in Alexandra Palace, which is high on a hill overlooking central London. We knew immediately in the spirit that Jesus wanted us to go. We prayed into it for a couple of weeks and prepared a few hundred nicely printed tracts about Jesus and quoting Koran verse (5:46) which says; *"we gave Jesus the Gospel wherein there is much light and guidance"*. We included with it contact numbers and web addresses where anyone could obtain free copies of the Gospels in any language they choose. The day came, and we went to the expo, prayer-walking around it first before anything else. We had friends at home praying for us of course. When we finished having a good look around the whole place, we found a quiet corner to pray, in a gallery of abstract "Islamic" art. There were some quite nice pieces there it has to be said! We prayed and having recently attended a Paul Keith Davis conference where he had taught on *"angels that gather"* (see Matthew 13:27), we prayed that the Lord's angels would draw the right people to us as we started handing out the flyers. Then we headed back to the main exhibition hall and started just casually offering the handbills to those we passed. Suddenly people just started running towards us from all directions, it was amazing. They were scrambling to get hold of a copy. We had never seen anything else like it. We couldn't hand the tracts out fast enough and this lasted a few minutes.

As we got to the last batch of flyers, and did they fly, an official came over to see what was happening. One of us was politely asked to go up to the organiser's office and so gave all but one of the handbills to the other who remained giving them out. The organiser said *"What's this? Do you have permission to give these things away here?"* I said *"no"* and said I thought it was OK and handed him my last copy. He read it, then thought for a moment and said; *"Well you can't do that here without being an exhibitor".* I asked if we could have a stand for the next day but it was too late, he said. So, still most politely, he said *"I am obliged to ask you to stop what you are doing".* I said *"OK",* but asked if he didn't mind us continuing handing out the leaflets on the street outside, a place over which he had no control anyway. He said that was alright and I left, leaving that copy of the tract with him. As I arrived back in the expo-hall the last of tracts had just been given out. Job done in Jesus Name! You see how He is and helps you succeed when you have a good heart reaching out to save others. Our real enemy is not people, our real enemy is spiritual and wants to keep us in silent compromise where we do not reach out and try to spread the Gospel.

"Be strong and of a good courage, fear not, nor be afraid of them: for the LORD thy God, he it is that doth go with thee; he will not fail thee, nor forsake thee."
(Deuteronomy 31:6)

The Lord has greatly blessed us since that day as we have continued to minister with love to Muslims. We have some great ex-Muslim friends both in and out of church. This is Kingdom Come in its plenitude.

"His divine power has granted to us all things that pertain to life and godliness" (2 Peter 1:3)

Sometimes we need to be a little courageous to fulfil what the Lord asks us to do. It is much better to walk in the Fear of the Lord than to fall into the snare of the fear of man. Once the Holy Spirit prompted me to talk to two young Muslims on the top deck of a London double-decker public bus. They had been acting a bit obnoxiously making comments in Arabic about some of the women there. Knowing it was the Lord prompting, I said whatever I could think of to open the conversation, so simply said; *"You guys are Muslim aren't you ?"* and they replied that they were. Then the Holy Spirit kicked in and the words flowed from my mouth before I could censor them;

"Well I'm a Christian, and Jesus wants me to tell you that He is going to come to you in your dreams, so you can know who He is. And when He comes to you in your dreams, you will understand and follow Him".

The two of them fell silent for the rest of their journey, the prophetic power of God had already touched them. I didn't know what to say afterwards either, except to say goodbye to them a couple of minutes later when the bus reached my destination. And a couple of the ladies of the bus smiled toward me thankfully as I walked past.

"For the Lord will be your confidence, and will keep your foot from being caught" (Proverbs 3:26)

"the Holy Spirit will teach at the time what you should say..." (Luke 12:12)

We have also seen some Christians having success with taking a sympathetic line like, *"don't you find it quite hard being a Muslim with all the terrorism that's associated with it?"* The truth is many Muslims are very upset at being associated with terrorism yet don't know that the Koran has so many incitements to violent xenophobia in it. Help them understand what Islam is and many will reject it. Our commandments as Christians are *"love your neighbour"* (Mark 12:31), *"love your enemies"* (Luke 6:27). Each person is different and will respond in a different way but certain obstacles do regularly arise. The most usual cop out from intelligent debate is the *"you should talk with the Imam at our mosque"* response which comes when you start proving your point. He won't have an answer either and will generally just waste your time saying that you need to study the Koran for years to understand it. But the reality is that if you have understood this book you know more already of the truth about the Koran than a lifetime of studying it with an Imam could ever teach. If you do want to go to see the Imam, make sure you have prayer cover from your church and expect a lot of tactical lying. It is so much more fruitful just to say; *"your Imam won't have the answer because what I am saying is the truth".*

Ultimately it does come down to us standing up for the truth of the Bible against the lies of Islam. Muslims have been taught lies that prevent them from accepting the Gospel as it is, so we need to break those lies for them, that they may receive the truth. Don't forget that our book Islamic Apocalypse is written so that a Muslim can read it and discover the truth for themselves, recommend it to them and their Imam. You could alternatively print up and give them a free copy of The Undoing which gives a brief introduction to some of the issues.

"But the Advocate, the Holy Spirit, whom the Father will send in my name, will teach you all things"
(John 14:26)

Sadly though, part of our problem with Islam is that many Imams do not speak English (or French, Spanish or anything other than Arabic). They do not understand our culture and don't seek to. If you do go visit them don't expect too much in the circumstances. It is very hard preaching the Gospel to anyone who doesn't speak the same language. We really do have to rely on the Holy Spirit to help us. But if they do speak your language then you have a clear opportunity to preach the true Gospel to them. Be prepared at the same time to rebuke the false teachings which may be quoted back at you. Let the dialogue go on to its obvious conclusion whatever that may be. It is wise to take someone with you who can intercede while you are talking and watch over the spiritual atmosphere. To be successful, fishers of men have to cast their nets where the fish are.

"Throw your net on the right side of the boat and you will find some."
(John 21:6).

Stay aware of the Muslim social identity spirit which works with the Islamic spirit, when one spirit is threatened the other spirit steps in to defend it. Thus, you may find that as soon as you break through in one area, say perhaps inviting someone to a social event at church, you may first encounter some religious excuses. But these are usually overcome in the name of better understanding between faiths. But then, as soon as you have overcome these, suddenly a voice pipes up saying *"No, we Muslims can't do such a thing"* or similar. Binding and keeping bound both the Islamic spirit and the Muslim identity spirit will help you be able to minister effectively to a person.

"Stand firm then, with the belt of truth fastened around your waist, with the breastplate of righteousness arrayed, and with your feet fitted with the readiness of the gospel of peace. In addition to all this, take up the shield of faith, with which you can extinguish all the flaming arrows of the evil one...." (Ephesians 6:14-16)

Our ministry to Muslims may even lead further, there are now thousands of jihadis who need to be de-radicalized. Who better than a Christian to do such work. And it involves more than that because many of the jihadis have been de-humanized too. Their needs are desperate. We must help them; we must snatch them out of the gates of hell. (See Jude 1:23) Deliverance ministry is an important part of this. De-radicalization also involves convincing those who have been radicalized that what they were taught in that process is false. Therefore, we have to be able to prove beyond doubt that the Koran is not the perfect, infallible word of God and that Islam is not the truth. We must show that the ideology, the foundation which terrorism rests upon, is a falsity.

"If I warn the wicked... but you fail to deliver the warning, they will die in their sins. And I will hold you responsible" (Ezekiel 3:18)

Howsoever we approach the Muslims around us, it should always be with proper love and respect, within the perspective of the commission the Lord has given us. Like the twelve disciples in the Gospel of Luke, Chapter 9: 1-2, we have been given power over demons and disease.

"In my name, they shall cast out demons... they will place their hands on the sick and they will be healed" (Mark 16:17)

"And the prayer of faith shall save the sick" (James 5:15-16)

Demonstrate that power to Muslims and they will quickly understand that their faith is empty compared to the power of Christ in us. When God's power touches them, what objections can they raise? If you are not used to praying for people's healing there is no better time to start than right now! Believe the Word of God and see it at work. Once they receive their healing follow it up with the prayer of salvation.

"Then opened he their understanding, that they might understand the scriptures" (Luke 24:45)

But even when they have accepted Jesus Christ as their Saviour, don't forget they need to be delivered of every Islamic spirit, demon and mindset, as well as being baptized. Build them up in the Word. They may also need prayer support against persecution by the Islamic family and community they have come from. This is a season where God would like us to reach out to Muslims and bring the truth to each of them, so they can go through the Valley of Decision and come to know Him. He wants to redeem as many of the descendants of Ishmael as possible and bring them into the fullness of the blessing of Abraham.

It is time ! Alleluia ! Hallelujah !

After Salvation

"All authority has been given to Me in heaven and on earth. Go, therefore, and make disciples of all the nations, baptizing them in the name of the Father and the Son and the Holy Spirit, teaching them to observe all that I commanded you; and lo, I am with you always, even to the end of the age." (Matt 28:18-20)

All of heaven rejoices when someone receives their salvation from Jesus. So too, should we celebrate joyfully each time a Muslim, or anyone else, comes out of the darkness and into Christ's Kingdom. Bringing newcomers into Christ's Kingdom is important for every Church.

"We will rejoice in your salvation and in the name of our God raise up our banners." (Psalm 20:5)

It really is something worth being joyous about, but our ministry must not stop there. In fact, leading Muslims to salvation is just the start of ministering to them. As you have read in previous chapters, each and every one of them has a demon assigned to them. As soon as they have received Jesus as their Saviour, that demon no longer has any right to remain. Therefore, we need to get them quickly baptized, delivered and filled with the Holy Spirit. It is important not to delay this, because these demons would try their utmost to push the newly saved ex-Muslim back into Islam and its pathway to hell. In the Book of Acts, we see that new believers were baptized right away.

"And now why do you delay? Arise and be baptized, and wash away your sins, calling on His name." (Acts 22:16)

Indeed, the book of Acts is full of examples of baptisms taking place immediately after the acceptance of Christ as Saviour. Peter baptized 3,000 new believers in a single day; *"Those who accepted his message were baptized, and about three thousand were added to their number that day."* (Acts 2:41) Likewise Apostle Paul was baptized immediately after Ananias healed his blindness; *"he received sight forthwith, and arose, and was baptized."* (Acts 9:18) This immediacy was the common practice;

"Believe in the Lord Jesus, and you will be saved—you and your household.' Then they spoke the word of the Lord to him and to all the others in his house. At that hour of the night the jailer took them and washed their wounds; then immediately he and all his household were baptized. The jailer brought them into his house and set a meal before them; he was filled with joy because he had come to believe in God—he and his whole household." (Acts 16:31-34)

There is no better moment for a person's deliverance from demons than straight after their baptism. All "legal" rights of the demonic over them have been rendered totally void with that sacrament and their acceptance of Christ as Saviour. Delivering Muslims is no different from delivering others with demons which can be lustful, lying, perverse, suicidal, murderous, rebellious, causing mental or physical illness and so on. A developed spirit of discernment can be very useful in recognizing the type of demon oppressing an individual. The ability to recognize the demonic in this way can also be useful when evangelizing; binding, and even casting any demon or unclean spirit out, can bring about a rapid decision for salvation.

"He designated apostles, to accompany Him, to be sent out to preach, and to have authority to drive out demons" (Mark 3:14-15)

It is important to be aware that it is not just people who have recently left Islam who need such deliverance. The Islamic Spirit is very tenacious and can linger long in a family line through many generations. One of us had to be delivered of it, even though there had been no-one Muslim in our ancestry for over four hundred years. Indeed, there are many people with ethnic roots where the Islamic Spirit may have been in the bloodline. As an example, individuals of Hispanic/Latino descent may have had Muslim ancestry during the Muslim occupation of the Iberian Peninsula and southern Europe centuries ago. Anyone who has ancestors from any past or present Islamic area will probably need an Islamic Spirit to be prayed off them. It is important to free them from this, because otherwise they have weaknesses Satan can exploit, like drawing their children into relationships with practising Muslims or even drawing them into Islam.

"Verily, verily, I say unto you, He that believeth on me, the works that I do shall he do also; and greater works than these shall he do; because I go unto my Father" (John 14:12)

In normal deliverance situations, a number of issues should be considered before trying to cast out any demon. All deliverance sessions should be overseen by someone who has experience in the process. Firstly, any unforgiveness, pride, lack of repentance, hardness of heart and the like on the part of the person that may hinder deliverance needs to be dealt with, and the Islamic Spirit and the Muslim identity spirit on the person must be bound and ordered to leave. All mental strongholds built on anger, hatred, bitterness, negativity or jealousy have to be unravelled. And any attitude that tries to justify, or excuse falling back into any sin, must also be addressed. Similarly, any aspect of an individual's lifestyle that may present an open door to the demonic needs to be shut, an end needs to be brought to domestic violence and other unhealthy behaviours some which may be condoned by Islam.

Generational curses and sins must be decreed to be ended, and each individual must be cut off from all ungodly influences of relatives who are still Muslim. And pray for all their relatives, that they can be saved too. Pray that they have dreams of Jesus and supernatural encounters which can guide them to the truth.

"The seventy-two returned with joy, saying, "Lord, even the demons are subject to us in your name!" (Luke 10:17)

There is not enough space in this book to provide guidance on full deliverance practice, but there are many good publications available on this very fundamental aspect of Christian ministry. Classic books in the area include; "How to Cast out Demons" by Doris M. Wagner, "They Shall Expel Demons" by Derek Prince and "Free at Last" by Larry Huch, whilst Benny Hinn has a 20-part lecture series available as a DVD set. With a powerful new move of God rapidly spreading around the world, many people are getting spontaneously delivered of demons and ungodly spirits, as well as being emotionally healed, during revival meetings. The strong angelic presence and greater levels of unity and faith make it much harder for the demonic to remain. It is important for every church to cultivate and nurture an atmosphere for the Holy Spirit to work in.

"Jesus repeated the question: 'Simon son of John, do you love me ?' 'Yes, Lord,' Peter said, 'you know I love you.' 'Then take care of my sheep,' Jesus said." (John 21:16)

As well as spiritual issues such as deliverance and baptism, many ex-Muslims will have other more-worldly matters to deal with. They may well need much emotional healing, they all need good guidance. One issue that arises regularly is polygamy, even Muslims in the West practice it, many men having one "official" wife, recognized fiscally, with up to three further unofficial wives married through their mosque. This creates complicated emotional tangles between the persons involved. Other problems that have to be unravelled too, are child marriages and the harrowing after-effects of FGM rituals which may be affecting a person's soul. Idolatrous Islamic forenames such as Muhammad, Abdullah (faithful of Allah), Fatima, Ayesha and others, all need to be dropped and replaced with something preferably Christian.

It is also thoroughly recommended to assist all new Christians coming from a Muslim background with a "Restoring the Foundations", SOZO or similar wholeness programme that will allow every area of their lives to be prayed over and sanctified. This will aid the identification of areas of spiritual difficulty which might otherwise cause problems later on, if not dealt with soon after salvation. If your church does not have such a programme, now might be a good time to start one. They are beneficial to all Christians, they really do resolve difficulties and transform lives.

"Let us, therefore, make every effort to enter that rest, so that no one will fall by following the same pattern of disobedience. For the word of God is living and active. Sharper than any double-edged sword, it pierces even to dividing soul and spirit, joints and marrow. It is able to judge the thoughts and intentions of the heart" (Hebrews 4:11-12)

As well as helping them find their new identity in Christ, we must also build them up in the Word of God and teach them how to resist any temptation by which the demonic might be trying to return. Deliverance sessions should be followed up with a six-week period during which there should be a careful watching over all their thinking and activities connected to the areas of deliverance, with counselling to help anyone having difficulties. As you will have understood from the earlier parts of this book, Islam is full of religious rules for Muslims to observe. Because of this religiosity, most ex-Muslims are good at maintaining a fairly rigorous religious self-discipline. We must help them close off all spiritual doors through which the demonic would try to re-enter.

"When the unclean spirit has gone out of a person, it passes through waterless places seeking rest, but finds none. Then it says, 'I will return to my house from which I came.' And when it comes, it finds the house empty, swept, and put in order. Then it goes and brings with it seven other spirits more evil than itself, and they enter and dwell there, and the last state of that person is worse than the first. So also will it be with this evil generation" (Matthew 12:43-45)

But, of course, the legalism of Islam also has a very negative impact on an ex-Muslims understanding of true relationship with God. They will not generally understand the concept of intimacy with Him, or the idea of trying to listen to the Holy Spirit for guidance. There is much they will need to learn, and much bad Islamic teaching, too, that they need to unlearn. The necessity of helping ex-Muslims to be freed from all ungodly ideas and social attitudes that were part of their Islamic mindset, is one of the reasons we have included in this book so many of the teachings that underlie their belief system. Armed with such knowledge you can be aware of subjects that may require specific attention. We must continually support them and cover them in prayer.

"And let us consider how to stir up one another to love and good works, not neglecting to meet together, as is the habit of some, but encouraging one another" (Hebrews 10:24-25)

"So encourage each other and build each other up"
(1 Thessalonians 5:11)

This is an important matter because there have been some ex-Muslim Christian ministers who still propagate ungodly beliefs such as the segregation and inequality of the sexes, sharia-type economics as well as general judgemental legalism. Recent converts from Islam have a great need to understand the concept of grace. Even core issues such as tolerance and forgiveness can be misunderstood by them, so it is of vital importance to get them grounded in true Biblical Christian values. Every Muslim who comes in, we must accompany them right through from knowing nothing, all the way to the point where they are prepared and ready themselves to go out as messengers of the Gospel.

"Then we will no longer be infants, tossed about by the waves and carried around by every wind of teaching and by the clever cunning of men in their deceitful scheming. Instead, speaking the truth in love, we will in all things grow up into Christ Himself, who is the head. From Him the whole body is fitted and held together by every supporting ligament. And as each individual part does its work, the body grows and builds itself up in love...." (Ephesians 4:14-16)

Of concern too, is what may happen to a person when others find out they have left Islam. In Sharia countries, the law is that no one can leave Islam and live. This is enforced officially in several countries and enforced "unofficially" by sharia patrols in others. Even in the West, we see so-called "honour killings" of those abandoning Islamic values, even sometimes carried out by members of their own family. We are also aware of violent harassment, here in the West, yes in countries like the UK and US, of Muslims trying to leave the religion. Because of political correctness not much action is taken by the police, despite the violence involved, and precious little is done by the authorities to help the individuals seeking to get free. Be prepared therefore, to help some new ex-Muslims move-house, change identity and accomplish whatever is necessary for them to start a new life away from the bullying of religious bigots. Even start to think of establishing "safe houses" in your area. Sadly, religious persecution is alive and kicking very hard even in our Christian homelands.

Isaiah 1:17

"Reprove the ruthless", "Correct the oppressor", "Alleviate oppression", "Defend the oppressed"

Towards the end of writing this book, in February 2017, I took a break to go for a walk in the mild winter sunshine. It was good to get out of the house and enjoy some fresh air after a period of unfavourable weather. It wasn't a long walk, just a half-hour, as I was keen not to interrupt the creative flow of work. Approaching the house on my return, my eyes beheld a most spectacular sight, a pair of young golden eagles spiralling upwards on the warm air rising from the sunny south-west back-wall of the building. As they rose, others spotted them and flew low towards the house before soaring up on the rising thermal of warm air. More and more arrived, and as they came I thanked the Lord for this amazing sight. Even more of these graceful birds arrived, one flew in quite close on my left side as I tried to count them, there was now a spiral of seventeen of them soaring upwards above me. Seventeen, I counted again. These eagles are supposed to be very rare in the area! Thanking God once again for this marvellous sight, I asked if He was speaking to me through this. It really was such a unique experience. Immediately the scripture reference Isaiah 1:17 came to mind, not something I know off by heart. As I arrived back at the house, the birds, now very high in the air, glided off towards a large cliff-lined river valley, some miles away. Wow, what a magnificent thing to see, and now, a few weeks later, as I sit with a pen and notepad in another garden elsewhere, a beautiful feather shaped cloud has appeared in the sky.

"Reflect on what I am saying, for the Lord will give you insight into all this" (2nd Timothy 2:7)

Back at work after that amazing experience, I looked up Isaiah chapter one, verse seventeen, online on a website that shows different translations at the same time. The first thing I noticed was, that despite this really being a "foundational" passage for all believers, the nuanced translations differed significantly in meaning. And so, referring to the original Hebrew, the true sense of the words became clear; **"Learn to do good, seek justice, correct the oppressor, defend the fatherless, plead the widow's cause".** Indeed, the whole chapter speaks so powerfully of a society like ours which has turned away from God. Even His own people have fallen into corrupt religion instead of being a guiding light to the world. The harvest they should be gathering is deserted, strangers are stealing it away. The watchman's hut in the cucumber field is left empty, the ripe fruit is being stolen and devoured. Isn't that just like some of our urban areas now, with mosques being built and churches closing? Our harvest is being lost and abandoned but, thankfully we have the answer right here in verse seventeen. So, today where are the children of Zion going out and correcting the Imams, jihadis and Sharia enforcers in our inner cities? Where are the brave foot-soldiers of Christ who will make a stand for Our Lord? Where are the Christian politicians who will speak out in governmental circles against Islam's teaching of misogyny and hatred? Where are the educators who will inoculate our youngsters against the false religion that has brought such practices as terrorism and FGM into our Christian lands? God, who created those seventeen beautiful eagles, had them fly together for us to all understand this; if we want revival we must act on Isaiah 1:17.

"You are My friends if you do what I command you" (John 15:14)

Where do we start? How do we start? We must pray and intercede for or neighbourhoods, our cities, and our nations. We must break the evil declarations made en masse five times every day that torment will overcome all those who don't believe in Islam's Allah. We must pray against the toxic belief system that says it's OK to beat women, to mutilate young girls, to terrorize and intimidate everyone who doesn't share the same ideology. But we must also minister to those Imams, Sharia enforcers, jihadis and radicalized Muslims as well as the moderate ones. God says He sees Muslims as either peaceful or totalitarian. We must reach out to all of them including the latter group.

"What I am doing you do not understand now, but afterward you will understand" (John 13:7)

Some of you reading this will even run publicly funded programmes to de-radicalize extremists. The need is so great, and our governments are clueless about how to solve the problem. Several terrorists involved in recent attacks in the West have attended programmes run by moderate Muslims and secular authorities. These have failed to have any effect because violent jihad is a core principle in Islam. It is called for over a hundred times in the Koran. Mohammed's life was full of examples of violence against those who didn't agree with his viewpoint. The idea that jihad and martyrdom please God has to be replaced with the truth that God loves peace. He wants us to love one another. In short, Islamic values have to be replaced by Christian values. And that's not politically correct, but that is what will work! As our governments wake up to the truth, there will be a moment when there is a sudden call for Christian counsellors to step into the gap. It will start small but will snowball. If you think this for you, start to prepare yourself and pray into it. There are now tens of thousands of radicalized Muslims in our lands who need to be rapidly de-radicalized. Who better than Christians to do this? Let's face it, secular de-radicalization programmes are never going to get those jihadis delivered of their demons.

"The sons of those who afflicted you will come bowing to you, And all those who despised you will bow themselves at the soles of your feet; And they will call you the city of the LORD... " (Isaiah 60:14)

It is not a complicated process to de-radicalize such individuals, all that is required is proving that the Koran is imperfect and that Mohammed got things wrong. We have already easily proved that in the pages of this book. The real reason why Islam has to order the killing of anyone who leaves it and bans all criticism of it, is because it is so intellectually flawed that it does not stand up to any rational scrutiny. Indeed, many Muslims, including those radicalized, will be changed simply by reading our sister book "Islamic Apocalypse" which is a shorter version of this book without the Christian commentary and the sections on Christian ministry. Others may require something more didactic, more dialogue based. A series of ten or twelve one-hour sessions should suffice for most needs, whether administered individually or in groups. The first session would start with the person running the course introducing themself and outlining the programme, followed by an opportunity for those attending the course to explain how and why they became radicalized. The session leader should take some notes on what is said in such discussions for later response. This topic would then lead on naturally to a discussion of Mohammed's message and example in relation to their jihad mentality. The first session would then move onto the introduction of the idea that Mohammed's inspiration and the Koran itself are flawed. This is best introduced as a question of the kind; *"Have you ever questioned whether what you believe is correct? After all most people do not agree with the way you see things"*. This needs to be followed up by a simple example of an erroneous statement in the Koran. For this one could ask; *"Where does the sun set?"* followed by a discussion on how the verse that says it sets in a warm spring cannot be true. Some participants might respond that this is just a poetical allegory, but the Koran says clearly that *"it is not poet's speech"*. The session should finish abruptly leaving these last discussions still turning in their minds.

"I am sending you to them to open their eyes, so that they may turn from darkness to light and from the power of Satan to God, that they may receive forgiveness of sins and an inheritance among those sanctified by faith in Me." (Acts 26:17-18)

The second session should start with a recap on what was said in the first. Participants could be asked how they feel about the questions raised at the end of that session. This can be used to open up the general issue of errors of scientific, historical and literary fact in Mohammed's teachings including the Koran. This can be introduced by the verse 4:82; *"Will they (the unbelievers) not meditate on the Koran..."* and after a chance for the participants to give some feedback on this, the session can move on to a lecture on some of its factual failings. The session would then finish with the leader saying it is impossible to believe that it is the word of God because it contains so many errors. After all it says it is perfect and infallible, so it shouldn't have a single error. Every error is proof that it is imperfect and flawed. It is important to close each session with an idea which is dissonant to their extremist ideology. This dissonance is a seed of change.

"To open blind eyes, to bring out prisoners from the dungeon, and those who dwell in darkness from the prison" (Isaiah 42:7)

From the third session, again starting with a recap of what has been said so far, Islam's dehumanizing beliefs should all be questioned, starting with xenophobic views of non-Muslims, misogyny, and so on. We must disprove the erroneous teaching and presumptions these ideas are based on. Concepts of empathy, compassion, reciprocity, respect and tolerance need to be taught. God's love for humanity must be explained to them. Further sessions can focus on the Koran's false claim to confirm the Torah and the Gospels, and then other subjects such as whether Islam's Allah is the same as our God Almighty. With this latter topic, can be introduced, the idea that the participants will not go to paradise as they thought, but will be tricked into hell by Allah. This is an important issue because many jihadis believe that being a "martyr" is the only way for them to get salvation. They need to hear the Gospel of the Good News of salvation through Jesus Christ! Most of the Parts of this book can be used as the basis for ongoing sessions. There is plenty of room to bring Biblical values into the discussions.

"The unfolding of your words gives light; it gives understanding to the simple" (Psalm 119:130)

In the last few sessions, the threads of the whole course can be woven together like the summing up in a trial in a court of law. Review the evidence and prove the Koran is neither perfect nor infallible. Show that it is folly to believe what Mohammed said. The participants should be asked; *"Don't you feel cheated and misled by being told the Koran is perfect when it is so easy to prove it not to be?"* The course leader must show a genuine concern that the participants may each burn in hell. The true salvation through Jesus needs to be explained and offered to them.

"You shall know the truth and the truth shall set you free" (John 8:32)

These last few sessions also need to give the participants a chance to talk so that their progress can be assessed. Key issues can be looked at again where they have not understood or are stuck in their false beliefs. Where certain participants are resistant to receiving and understanding the truth, courses can be prolonged on an individual basis focussing on the content they are having difficulty with. Obviously, every course, every session and every individual involved should be prayed for. Powerful intercession is almost as important as the content of the course itself. The more the Holy Spirit is allowed room to work, the more dramatic the results will be. Jesus went to the Cross so jihadis can be saved too. They will make fearless evangelists once they are saved, delivered, taught the whole Gospel and rightly guided. Imagine the power of their testimony to bring others out of the darkness and into the light of Christ. Just as the Apostle Paul was radically transformed from being a persecutor of Christians into a true servant of God, so too can any jihadi, Imam or other Muslim be changed by an encounter with the Saviour of mankind.

"in all these things, we are more than conquerors through him who loved us" (Romans 8:37)

You see. It isn't so complicated, and de-radicalization by fellow Muslims simply cannot work, jihadis know more of the reality of Mohammed's Islam than any moderate. Look at the news these days, more and more Imams are getting arrested on terror charges. Imams and Muslim social workers all promote the Koran yet publicly hide its causal influence on Islamist terror. Only by rejecting Islam, Mohammed, the Koran and its murderous god, can anyone ever be broken out of the belief that dying for Allah as a violent martyr will guarantee them a place in paradise. And that's the bottom line. If only our current bewildered governments would understand...

"Now then go, and I, even I, will be with your mouth, and teach you what you are to say." (Exodus 4:12)

Future Positive

"So then, dear brothers and sisters, be firm. Do not be moved! Always be outstanding in the work of the Lord, knowing that your labor is not in vain in Him" (1 Corinthians 15:58)

The Islamic Revival, that we talked about in an earlier chapter, combined with the effects of mass immigration and mass social communication such as Facebook and Twitter, has greatly changed the world in recent years. The current rising tide of terrorism across the planet has sown much fear and anxiety into the lives of many people. It is part of Satan's agenda for our times together with the economic austerity, personal and public debt, abortion, gender confusion, and a whole host of other things which fill the news-media with depressing and panic-inducing headlines. Even though the actual number of people affected by terrorism is relatively small compared to the numbers of dead and injured resulting from traffic accidents, and miniscule beside the those affected by disease and infirmity, it is the sheer horror of understanding that there are individuals in the world who delight in murdering, maiming and terrorizing others, even children, that causes us to have such a strong emotional reaction. Add to that the shock of seeing video footage of people being half buried and stoned to death without trial under Sharia law for alleged adultery, being flogged for possessing alcohol, even communion wine, and learning that young girls, even in our nations, are being mutilated and psychologically scarred through barbaric rituals of FGM; many are stunned. Humanity is in trauma.

"For behold, darkness will cover the earth and deep darkness the peoples" (Isaiah 60:2)

We hear so many people saying, *"What do we do? how can we stop this flood of evil from submerging the whole Earth? How can we stop Islam from taking over?"* Some Christians because they are so traumatized by it all have even abandoned their true faith and accepted Islam as a valid expression of worship. Some have even tried to bring the two faiths together, even unify them, like kidnap victims who fall in love with their abuser in Stockholm syndrome. Fear and foolishness abound to the point where most leaders, Presidents, Prime Ministers, Popes and Pastors have been too scared to speak the truth about it.

"Arise, shine; for your light has come, And the glory of the LORD has risen upon you." (Isaiah 60:1)

But God, the true Almighty living God, is unmoved. He is not afraid. He has a plan already in place. Jesus has already done what is necessary for the world to be saved. And He wants us Christians to all play our individual part in His plan. He has *"not given a spirit of fear, but of power and of love, and of a sound mind"* (2 Timothy 1:7), so we can participate in bringing forth the greatest harvest of all time, bringing forth a great harvest of souls from those of Muslim background.

"I will make those who are of the synagogue of Satan, who claim to be Jews though they are not, but are liars – I will make them come and fall down at your feet and acknowledge that I have loved you." (Revelation 3:9)

Indeed, Jesus has a very positive view of the current situation. His Kingdom is expanding rapidly in many parts of the world like China and India, even in Muslim countries like Iran there are thousands of House churches with millions of secret believers in Him. They cannot yet manifest their faith publicly because Sharia law would have them killed for leaving Islam. But great change is coming. 500 years on from the Reformation, a new renaissance, enlightenment and reforming has been mandated by the Father. A great awakening, way beyond anything ever seen is about to sweep the Earth. God sees our days as glorious.

"And afterward, I will pour out my Spirit on all people. Your sons and daughters will prophesy, your old men will dream dreams and your young men will see visions" (Joel 2:28).

This is an oft quoted piece of scripture, but what does the word "afterward" refer to here? Let's look at the earlier parts of the chapter from which the quote is taken. It starts with the sounding of an alarm for God's people, a warning about *"a day of darkness and gloominess"*.

In verse 2, an enemy of destructive people starts to ravage the Earth, taking away the peace and spreading fear; *"before them the people writhe in pain, all faces drained of colour"* (verse 6). Watching the news stories of the latest Islamic State atrocities has made many of us feel like that. *"Who can endure it?"* the prophet Joel asks us, but the Lord responds to stir His even greater army who will defeat this enemy (verse 11). Israel must repent and fast, turning back to the Lord as described in verse 17, then He will save us. We as Christians must return to our Great Commission and preach the Gospel to all nations; *"Go into all the world and preach the gospel to all creation"* (Mark 16:15). That includes preaching it to the people of the nation of Islam.

"Preach the word of God. Be prepared, whether the time is favourable or not, reprove, rebuke, and encourage with every form of patient instruction." (2 Timothy 4:2)

What happened? Were we Christians too fearful to go out into Muslim nations to preach the Good News? We must repent, this is how God's Spirit will come to be poured out on all flesh. We must play our part, we must not shrink back in fear. We are the Lord's army. We are here to represent Christ on the Earth. We are the answer to the army of darkness. We must be the light. We must be salvation and save our Christian culture and Christian nations. That is what we are here for just like Queen Esther in her day; *"who knows whether you are come to the kingdom for such a time as this?"* (Esther 4:14) If God has allowed great numbers of Muslims to come into our homelands, then He has a purpose for it. We have not gone out into Muslim lands, so God has brought Muslims to us. Are we still going to hold back from taking the Gospel to them? We hesitate at our own peril; God's word is clear what we should do. Holding back only allows Islam to take more ground, to gain more control and influence through Sharia. Which Kingdom would you rather live in, a free democratic Christian society, or Satan's which would even refuse you the right to own a Bible as it does in many Sharia countries? Choose life!

"See, I have appointed you this day over the nations and over the kingdoms, to pluck up and to break down, to destroy and to overthrow, to build and to plant." (Jeremiah 1:10)

To look at the predicament in another way, nation states are like living organisms which need to survive in situations that can sometimes be hostile. As a distinct entity, each organism needs to fight off those things which might destroy it, just as a body has to fight an infection or cancer that would consume or kill it. Throughout history many great and powerful nations have fallen because they failed to protect themselves from destructive ideologies that infected their populations. Communism in Imperial Russia and Nazism in Germany are well known examples.

These anti-Christ ideologies have caused much destruction, war and repression of freedom. Islam is similarly totalitarian, but dressed up as a religion. We must not be fooled by its hollow piety. It is very clear in all those quotes from its sacred sources, cited in the first parts of this book, that the ideology of Islam seeks the destruction of everything that is not compatible with it, including our Christianity and democracy. Our democratic society based on freedom, truth and equality must therefore, to defend itself, destroy the ideology that threatens it. As Islam seeks to destroy everything un-Islamic. We must destroy Islam. The logic is simple.

"For the LORD your God is going with you / He will fight for you against your enemies, and he will give you victory !" (Deuteronomy 20:4)

In the human body, it is the blood which carries antibodies to fight off any infective threat. Our nations need the blood of Christ, carried by us, to be active in immobilizing the deadly virus of Islam. It is already causing destruction in our society through terrorism, religiously sanctioned domestic violence, and FGM. It causes spiritual death by turning people away from the true God. We must, all of us, in the Body of Christ play our part to bring salvation. We must save our society and at the same time save Muslims from being tricked into hell.

"save others, snatching them out of the fire; and on some have mercy with fear, hating even the garment polluted by the flesh" (Jude 1:23)

Jesus is calling us.
"The harvest is great but the workers are few. Ask the Lord of the harvest, therefore, to send out workers into his harvest field." (Matthew 9:37-38)

We must respond;
"We demolish arguments and every pretension that sets itself up against the knowledge of God, and we take captive every thought to make it obedient to Christ." (2nd Corinthians 10:5)

And reach out in love;
"Behold, I am sending you out as sheep in the midst of wolves, so be wise as serpents and innocent as doves." (Matthew 10:16)

Christ will be seen on us;
"In that day, the Lord of Hosts will become a beautiful crown and a glorious diadem to the remnant of His people," (Isaiah 28:5)

"You will be a crown of splendour in the Lord's hand, a royal diadem in the hand of your God." (Isaiah 62:3)

Appendix: The TICCET evangelism tool

When all the people saw it, they fell on their faces. They said, "Yahweh, he is God! Yahweh, he is God!" (1 Kings 18:39)

The Islam/Christianity Comparative Evangelism Tool (TICCET) is just the ticket for your Church's outreach to Muslims. A simple double-sided tract, it illustrates clearly the differences between the two faiths including key areas of doctrine, salvation and afterlife, combined with proof that the Koran is unreliable. This tool can focus your initial encounter with any Muslim onto the issues needed to convince them of their need to accept Jesus into their lives. It is their free ticket to salvation. This NEW EVANGELISM TOOL is a NET for fishers of men. Always leave a copy with everyone you reach out to, so they can go over it, verify its truth, and be touched. Be generous and leave a copy for their Imam too! Put your church contact details in the place provided so they can get back to you with any questions they may have and take the next steps into their walk with Christ.

"But now I will send for many fishermen," declares the LORD, "and they will catch them"
(Jeremiah 16:16)

Before going out with the TICCET, it is important to seek the Holy Spirit on who to approach and how to approach them. In a Church setting, spend some time, even a few weeks praying into your outreach. Give your evangelism teams time to familiarize themselves with the subject matter. We do not advise, when starting out, just putting copies through people's letterboxes. In Muslim majority nations, you will need to be very discrete because Sharia prohibits all criticism of Islam. Even in the West, some Muslims might find this intimidating and you could get accused of Islamophobia! It is essential to always make a polite approach to those you go to talk to. A good start can easily be made to Muslim groups who go out on the street giving out copies of the Koran. Stay at all times respectful, remember that these individuals will make great evangelists when they come into Christ's Kingdom. Give them the TICCET to read, ask them what they think. Make them think about it.

"Come, follow Me,' Jesus said, 'and I will make you fishers of men."
(Matthew 4:19/Mark 1:17)

Never let anybody's aggressive response get to you, you are an ambassador for Jesus, so act with according grace. You don't need to compromise what you believe, you can always gently retire from any situation saying; *"I was purely trying to have a peaceful multi-faith dialogue with you"*. Whilst a few persons may get angry, remember that every Muslim has a demon. Don't forget to bind them in Jesus' Name.

"Again, the kingdom of heaven is like a net that was cast into the sea that caught all kinds of fish"
(Matthew 13:47)

Most Muslims will be stunned and maybe speechless at what you have to show them. They have been told lies about Jesus. Recall Jesus' words *"You shall know the truth and the truth shall set you free".* It is our responsibility to bring that truth to them. When going out to put this tool to work you can pray a prayer something like this; - **"Heavenly Father, in Jesus Name, we pray that you loose your angels that gather to bring to us all those who need to find their salvation and deliverance, especially those who will be powerfully convicted of the truth by this evangelism tool. We praise your Holy Name and thank You God for Your goodness, grace and mercy"**

"Take to the deep and cast your nets for a catch" (Luke 5:4)

When you go to people with the TICCET, give them a copy to keep and talk them through it. Use the comparisons to show God's goodness towards mankind, compare this to what Islam says. Ask each person whether they would prefer to have a God who would look after them, who would save them and heal them of all their diseases, or a god who wants to lead them astray, destroy them and trick them into hell. Use the paragraphs on the back of the TICCET to guide your conversation. Prove to them that the Koran is wrong in matters of science and history. Show them that it doesn't confirm or replace the Bible. Lead them to their salvation because Islam cannot save them.

"for the Son of Man came to seek and to save the lost" (Luke 19:10)

It is worth noting that there are marvellous opportunities for female evangelists when ministering with the TICCET. It can often be much easier for a woman-to-woman contact to be established with Muslims because a sort of psychological segregation operates in their minds. Be aware that there is a deeper level of understanding which can help when using the TICCET. If you familiarize yourself with the sections of this book which relate to the different sections of comparison, then you can add real weight to any discussion that arises out of it. Having this book with you or in e-format on a mobile-phone or tablet can help in likewise manner. Being able to show a Muslim the twenty-odd verses that say that Allah leads people astray, and quoting precisely the verses that show he wants to fill hell with mankind, can really help in opening them up to the truth.

"I will build My church, and the gates of Hades will not prevail against it"
(Matthew 16:18)

One Koran verse quoted in the text, 7:182, we have seen begins *"Those who deny our revelations, we gradually lead them to into destruction from whence they know not"*. Some Muslims might bring this up as a defence. But what are these revelations being denied? that Allah leads astray, that the Koran commands jihad terror, it condones wife-beating, it allows pre-pubescent child brides, it encourages anti-Semitism and xenophobia. Most Muslims will deny these things when you ask them. They are denying what the Koran commands them. They cannot win! The issues are so clear cut, that one cannot fail to make a powerful impact on everyone who reads the TICCET. As we go out with it, we set the Sword of the Lord, the Word of God against the false word of Islam, and

"Fear not, for I am with you..."
(Isaiah 41:10)

"the God of Peace will quickly crush Satan under your feet".
(Romans 16:20)

"Let all that you do be done in love"
(1 Corinthians 16:14)

"You will go out in joy and be led forth in peace"
(Isaiah 55:12)

"The God of peace be with all of you. Amen."
(Romans 15:33)

To receive a printable PDF of the TICCET please enter your email address on our webpage;

https://abelandsolomon.wixsite.com/abel-and-solomon

Your email address will not be shared with anyone else, and we will send you no more than one email per month featuring free offers and discounts on books, music and other Christian items.

The Islam/Christianity Comparison Evangelism Tool

Islam	Christianity
"Perish man !/Cursed be man" (Koran 80:17)	"God so loved the world that He sent His only son that none would perish" (John 3:16)
"We reduced him (mankind) to the lowest of the low" (Koran 95:5)	"In the image of God, He created them male and female" (Genesis 1:27)
"Allah sends who he will astray..." (13:27, 74:31) (there are over 20 verses that repeat this)	"He (Yahweh) will guide you into all truth" (John 16:13)
"We shall lead them (to destruction) from whence they know not" (68:44)	"He leads me in paths of righteousness…" (Psalm 23:3)
"I (Allah) will fill hell with demons and mankind" (32:13, 11:119)	"everyone who calls on the name of the Lord (Jesus) will be saved." (Romans 10:13)
"Already we have urged into hell many..." (7:179)	**"Save others by snatching them out of the fire (of going to hell)"** (Jude 1:23)

"You shall know the truth and the truth shall set you free" (John 8:32)

"There is not one of you (Muslims) that does not have a jinn (a demon) as a constant companion" (Sahih Muslim 39/6757, 52/62/2814)	"even the demons submit to us in Your (Jesus') Name" (Gospel of Luke 10:17)
"Demons feed from that upon which Allah's name has been pronounced..." (Koran 6:118)	"Heal the sick, raise the dead, cleanse the lepers and cast out demons" (Matthew 10:8)
"and those (women) from whom you fear disobedience.. beat them" (Koran 4:34)	Husbands, love your wives...husbands should love their wives as their own bodies... and care for them" (Ephesians 5:25)
"Is not the evidence of two women equal to the witness of one man? This is the deficiency in her intelligence" (Hadith Bukhari 6/301)	"She opens her mouth with wisdom, the teaching of kindness is on her tongue" (Proverbs 31:26)
"terrorize the unbelievers, make war on them until all religion is for Allah" (Koran 8:12,39)	**"Love your enemies, do good to them"** (Luke 6:27)
"Never be a helper to a non-Muslim" (28:86)	"Pure and genuine religion in the sight of God the Father means caring for orphans and widows in their distress" (James 1:27)
"Then they (the Jews) surrendered, and the apostle confined them in Medina...the apostle went out to the market of Medina and dug trenches in it. The he sent for them and struck off their heads in those trenches as they were brought out in batches... some put the figure as high as 800 or 900" (Sirat "Life of Muhammad" Ibn Ishaq)	"A vast crowd brought to him people who were lame, blind, crippled, those who couldn't speak, and many others. They laid them before Jesus, and he healed them all" (Matthew 15:30)
"Allah quickens and gives death" (Koran 10:56,44:8,50:43)	**"I (Jesus) came that they may have life, and may have it abundantly"** (John 10:10)

By this comparison, it is clear that Christianity and Islam are very different. The Christian God gives life and promises eternal salvation, whereas Islam's Allah brings death and condemns people to hell. But is it fair to logically scrutinize the Koran? The Koran itself says *"Will the unbelievers not ponder on the Koran...?"* (4:82) The Koran challenges non-Muslims to analyse what it says. It contains over 120 verses which seem to incite violence against non-Muslims; is it right to interpret these literally? *"It is not poet's speech"* (69:41), the Koran says it is *"written in simple language that all may understand"* (44:58/54:17). It orders; *"Obey Allah"* (3:132, 4:59, 8:20). It is meant to be taken literally, Mohammed did that. The very existence of Sharia Law is proof that the Koran is supposed to be taken literally. A free e-book is available analyzing the more controversial aspects of Islam; "**Islam by its own words**"; - https://www.smashwords.com/books/view/637169

The Koran says it is perfect and infallible; *"The Quran is Infallible...it comes from the Lord"* (10:37), *"This Koran is a book whose verses have been perfected (in every sphere of knowledge)"* (11:1) but under logical scrutiny it can be proved to contain many errors of scientific, historical and literary fact. For example; *"It is not for the sun to overtake the moon, nor doth night outstrip the day. They float each in an orbit."* (36:40) The sun does not orbit the earth, it is the earth that orbits around the sun. In the sky, the sun overtakes behind the moon every time there is a solar eclipse, and night outstrips day during the polar winter. There are many errors of fact in the Koran, for a full discussion of this see the low-cost e-book **"Is the Koran perfect and Infallible?"**; https://www.amazon.com/dp/B06XPGGSB6

The Koran says it confirms and replaces the Jewish Torah and the Christian Gospels, which form part of the Christian Bible. This again is untrue; In fact, the Koran contradicts the Bible on many issues such as the death of Jesus on the Cross and his resurrection; *"they slew him not nor crucified him..."*, (4:157) but there is overwhelming historical evidence that shows the Bible is correct; *"the soldiers took Him away. Carrying His own cross, He went out to The Place of the Skull, which in Aramaic is called Golgotha. There they crucified Him"* (Gospel of John 19:16-18), Also the Romans kept meticulous records in their annals; *"Christus (Jesus)...was executed at the hands of the Procurator Pontius Pilate..."* (Cornelius Tacitus xv. 44) For a fuller explanation of this and related topics please see the low-cost e-book; **"The Koran vs the Bible"** https://www.amazon.com/dp/B06XPGQB77

From differences in the Islamic, Jewish and Christian Holy books it is clear that Islam's Allah is not the same as the God of the Christians and Jews. In the Koran Allah says *"We reduced him (mankind) to the lowest of the low"* (95:5) *"We will progressively lead them (to destruction)"* (7:182), but the Bible says *"For I know the plans I have for you," declares the LORD, "plans to prosper you and not to harm you, plans to give you hope and a future"* (Jeremiah 29:11) *"But Jesus Christ has come that we might have life and that we might have it more abundantly"* (John 10:10) For more on this please see the low-cost e-book; **"Is Allah the same God..."** https://www.amazon.com/dp/B06XP935HF

In Islam, there is no guarantee of God's salvation, but many threats of hellfire, *"There is not one of you who can avoid it (hell), this is an ordinance of your Lord Allah..."* (19:71). Even Mohammed was uncertain; *"By Allah, though I am the Apostle of Allah, yet I do not know what Allah will do with me"* (Sahih Bukhari 5/58/266), but Jesus Christ guarantees God's salvation and forgiveness *"the Son of Man (Jesus) must be lifted up, so that everyone who believes in Him may have eternal life. For God so loved the world that He gave His one and only Son, that everyone who believes in Him shall not perish but have eternal life."* (John 3:15-16) *"Believe in the Lord Jesus and you will be saved, you and your household."* (Acts 16:31) *"Whoever believes and is baptized will be saved"* (Mark 16:16) *"if you confess with your mouth, "Jesus is Lord," and believe in your heart that God raised Him from the dead, you will be saved"* (Romans 10:9). To make sure you receive true eternal salvation and to learn more about Jesus and the Holy Spirit, please contact us; -

© 2017 Abel & Solomon, this document may be freely copied for the purpose of Christian Ministry. The material contained in the low-cost e-books can also be obtained all together in one paperback edition; **"Islamic Apocalypse"** (ISBN 978-0-9557140-1-6) available from your local bookshop or here; https://www.amazon.com/dp/095571401X

Also available;

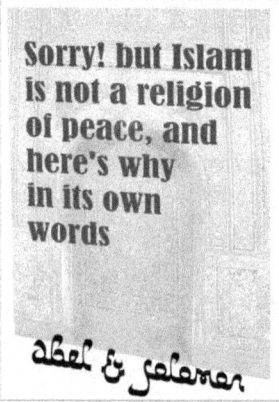

Already an Amazon #1 in both the US & UK. Using the power of the e-book format, this clear, concise volume contains hundreds of active links to relevant news articles, official reports, videos and other web material. A whole multimedia library of information which includes many of the news items mentioned in *Ministering to Muslims*. This work conclusively proves the issue beyond all reasonable doubt. Ideal for students, sceptics and anyone else who wants to know the big picture. Paperback also available.
https://www.amazon.com/dp/B06XNJ5ZV5

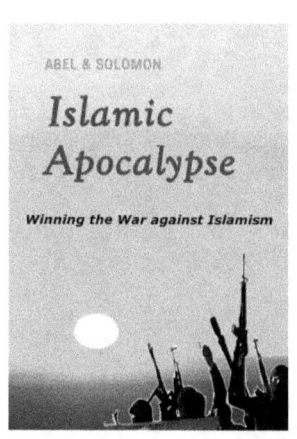

Now available in Paperback ! Contains much of the content of *Ministering to Muslims*, re-packaged for non-Christian readers. Great for academics, politicians, Muslims and all those who need a clear, detailed reference text. Recommend it, or even buy it, for those who need to be brought the truth. Don't let anybody be in ignorance on the subject any more. Available in paperback, as an e-book and as a low-cost series, with volumes 1-9 corresponding to Parts 1 to 9 of this book.
https://www.amazon.com/dp/095571401X

- 00 The Undoing/Series Overview
- 01 An Introduction to Islam & Sharia
- 02 Islamic Beliefs
- 03 What was Mohammed really like?
- 04 Prophet, true or false?
- 05 Is the Koran perfect and infallible?
- 06 The Koran versus the Bible
- 07 Is Allah the same God?
- 08 The Apocalypse and Islam
- 09 The End of Islam

https://www.amazon.com/dp/B06XNYHKSN

www.ingramcontent.com/pod-product-compliance
Lightning Source LLC
Chambersburg PA
CBHW052015290426
44112CB00014B/2247